GUIDE TO THE

Connecticut Shore

"This volume contains a wealth of information for the Connecticut-bound."

—*The Village Times* (Setauket, N.Y.)

"Gives the insider's touch to the state's 120-mile stretch of coast."

—*Soundings* magazine

D1416990

Help Us Keep This Guide Up to Date

Every effort has been made by the author and editors to make this guide as accurate and useful as possible. However, many things can change after a guide is published—establishments close, phone numbers change, facilities come under new management, etc.

We would love to hear from you concerning your experiences with this guide and how you feel it could be improved and kept up to date. While we may not be able to respond to all comments and suggestions, we'll take them to heart and we'll also make certain to share them with the author. Please send your comments and suggestions to the following address:

The Globe Pequot Press
Reader Response/Editorial Department
P.O. Box 480
Guilford, CT 06437

Or you may e-mail us at:

editorial@globe-pequot.com

Thanks for your input, and happy travels!

GUIDE TO THE

Connecticut Shore

Third Edition

by Doe Boyle

The Globe Pequot Press

GUILFORD, CONNECTICUT

DEDICATION

In loving memory of my father

Text design: Nancy Freeborn
Map design: Lisa Reneson

ISSN 1541-8014
ISBN 0-7627-2500-1

Manufactured in the United States of America
Third Edition/First Printing

ACKNOWLEDGMENTS

The third edition of this book was born with the help of countless curators, chambers of commerce, librarians, park rangers, publicity directors, innkeepers, restaurateurs, and the staffs of Connecticut Department of Environmental Protection, and the Tourism Division of the Connecticut Department of Economic Development.

In the process, I had some extra-special assistance I must acknowledge. Thanks are owed to: Jon Nathanson of the Coastal Fairfield County Convention and Visitors Bureau and to Linda Kavanagh, for the generous arrangements they made on my behalf and for enormously useful lessons on the tools of the trade; Laura Charron of Connecticut's Mystic & More Convention and Visitors Bureau for similar contributions she made to this project; Mimi Egan and Hrissi Haldezos, Globe Pequot project editors, and Patricia Nelson copyeditor, for their cheerful and skillful assistance on the manuscript; and lastly, my cherished family, whose companionship ensures that all my days on the shore are sunny ones.

CONTENTS

The prices and rates listed in this guidebook were confirmed at press time. We recommend, however, that you call establishments before traveling to obtain current information.

THE CONNECTICUT SHORELINE

Rhode Island

New York

Hartford

Pawcatuck
Stonington
Mystic
Noank
Groton
New London
Waterford
East Lyme/Niantic
Old Lyme
Old Saybrook
Westbrook
Clinton
Madison
Guilford
Branford
East Haven
New Haven
West Haven
Milford
Stratford
Bridgeport
Fairfield
Westport
Norwalk
Darien
Stamford
Greenwich

N E S W

INTRODUCTION

I was born by the sea, and I have noticed that all great events of my life have taken place by the sea.

—Isadora Duncan

Among my earliest memories are many closely linked to the sea—in particular, the pretty expanse of Long Island Sound just steps from the wide front porch of my grandparents' cottage in Fairfield County. I remember salt-stiffened hair and shell-stubbed toes, sandy bathing suits and outdoor showers, green wicker rockers and moonlit bonfires, Coca-Cola straight up from frosty sea-green bottles and pretzel rods taken outside to savor while nestled in the cool sand underneath the cottage itself. The rhythms of the tides and the winds predicted the movement of our days, and the sounds and aromas of the sea and the sand and the salt marshes aroused our appetites and our imaginations and finally, over time, our passion for life near the shore. A connection with the sea is one not easily denied or forgotten—perhaps then, if evolutionists are correct about humankind's origins in the seas, it is no surprise to learn that most of the world's population is crowded at the shores of nearly every continent. A love for the sea is in the blood, and there is no forsaking it.

The Connecticut shore is a unique and busy place—a far cry from isolation and wilderness but no less beautiful in parts than the edges of Maine or Cape Cod or Maryland. Long Island Sound is a mere 110 miles long, but the meanderings of its margins into coves and inlets results in a Connecticut coastline triple the length of the estuary. Its shape, its unusual east-west orientation, and its shallowness—an average of 65 feet in the center—contribute to the relatively gentle nature of its waters and thus its extreme popularity as a recreational resource. Sheltered from the high waves and winds of the ocean, it attracts an enormous fleet of pleasure boats, and the Connecticut shoreline is peppered with marinas, boatyards, launch ramps, sportfishing centers, ferry docks, and other sites specifically dedicated to marine recreation.

A mixture of salt water from the Atlantic and freshwater from the Housatonic, Thames, and Connecticut Rivers, the Sound is also a unique and fragile habitat. Its temperate waters and its barrier beaches, dunes, salt marshes, and tidal pools teem with life, collectively creating a diverse and valuable ecosystem that warrants protection. Programs and organizations such as the Long Island Sound Study, Connecticut Sea Grant, Save the Sound, and the Connecticut Department of Environmental Protection have ensured that the ecosystem is as well protected as possible from catastrophic misuse or overuse.

Tourism at the shore accounts for a significant portion of the state's economy, so the Connecticut coast is jam-packed with establishments that serve the visiting public. On the Connecticut shore, no shortage exists of parks, nature centers, amusement areas, boardwalks, campgrounds, museums, outdoor recreation sites, and other attractions catering to the pleasures of daytrippers and long-term vacationers alike. Likewise, hotels, motels, inns, and cottage rentals. Eateries ranging from ramshackle seafood shacks and charming tearooms to glamorous waterfront inns and urban rooftop restaurants keep the touring crowd well fed, and transportation systems of all kinds help keep the traffic moving (usually).

Guide to the Connecticut Shore will lead you to the best places to visit, to eat, and to stay at the northern fringe of Long Island Sound. I have spent the better part of a lifetime wandering the shoreline towns and cities, and this guide reveals the gems I have discovered. The crowded nature of this stretch of coastline prevents the inclusion of *every* minor attraction, performing arts venue, eatery and hotel, and so on, but the best are here and the rest you'll uncover as you explore. Don't be reluctant to wander farther afield than the towns and cities covered in this book. If space had allowed, I would also have included information on towns located as little as 10 miles from the sand. The towns along the Connecticut River, for instance, are also closely linked to the Sound and the maritime history of Connecticut, and the town of Ledyard, once a barely known rural community north of Groton and Stonington, is one of the most talked-about and visited tourist destinations in the Northeast. Its incredible Foxwoods casino and its fabulous new Mashantucket Pequot Museum and Research Center on the Mashantucket Reservation are bringing in tourists by the busload and ferryload. Revenues from the casino in Ledyard and the Mohegan Sun casino just a bit farther inland in Montville have led to the development and improvement of all kinds of tourist-oriented facilities, from highways to hotels, at many points along the eastern shore.

Heavily urbanized and industrialized in some parts and still pristinely serene and rural in other parts, the Connecticut shore includes world-famous universities and state-of-the-art museums, as well as fishing villages and lighthouses. You might tour a microbrewery that lies only yards from oyster beds and salt marshes, or go parasailing over a beautiful bay that has a nuclear power plant right at waterside. The fascinating inconsistencies you will encounter along the Connecticut seaside add to its vitality in all seasons. Put a good map on the car seat along with this guide, and enjoy the adventure of exploring both city hotspots and country niches. May the salt breezes draw you seaward, and the sounds of the waves and the gulls help you navigate.

Using This Book

This book includes twenty-six chapters devoted to the state's shoreline cities, towns, and villages. I explore each town in order geographically from west to east. Each chapter includes entries on major as well as little-known attractions and sidebars on everything from local lore to annual events. Each entry includes basic information such as addresses, telephone numbers, Web sites, admission fees, and hours, plus a review of what you might expect to see or experience at each site or event.

Following this detailed information are suggestions for places to eat and places to stay. Information on public launch sites for cartop or trailered boats is also listed after the main attractions entries. Ideas for obtaining further information are added last.

The Connecticut shore is one of the most densely populated sections of the entire eastern seaboard, and Long Island Sound attracts more recreational boaters than any other body of water in North America. Space restraints prevented the author from compiling a comprehensive list of *all* charters, *all* seafood shacks, and so on. The selection was based on personal visits, recommendations, amenities, and services. For more information on topics of special interest to you, consider contacting the following agencies or consulting the following specialty publications:

Connecticut Department of Economic Development, Tourism Division, 865 Brook Street, Rocky Hill CT 06067 (800-CT-BOUND or 860-258-4355). Ask for a free copy of the *Connecticut Vacation Guide* or ask for information on specific areas or sites along the coast.

Connecticut Department of Environmental Protection, 79 Elm Street, Hartford CT 06106 (860-424-3200). Ask for a free copy of their guide to state parks and forests, the *Connecticut Angler's Guide,* or the *Connecticut Boater's Guide,* or ask for a list of other publications that may be useful to shoreline travelers. Call the DEP Fisheries Division (860-424-3474) for information on obtaining freshwater fishing licenses. (Saltwater anglers need no license.)

Embassy's *Complete Boating Guide and Chartbook to Long Island Sound,* published by Embassy Marine Publishing. Comprehensive listing of marinas, boat repair yards, and so on, with navigational directions and charts.

Rates

In the sections in each chapter that list *Places to Eat* and *Places to Stay*, dollar signs provide a sense of the price range at those establishments. For meals, the prices are per individual dinner entrees; for lodging, the rates are for a double room, European plan (no meals), unless otherwise noted. Keep in mind that meal prices generally do not change seasonally, but lunch may be less expensive than dinner. Lodging rates usually *are* seasonal, with higher rates prevailing during the warm months or on and near major holidays. In Connecticut's coastal towns, the mild weather of spring and the foliage of fall can stretch the in-season from late April through Columbus Day, but rates are usually at their peak from mid-June through Labor Day. You may discover that weekend rates are higher in resort and top tourist destinations like Mystic and lower in cities where hotels usually cater to business travelers on weekdays. In any case, be sure to inquire about special packages and discounts.

Rates for Lodging		Rates for Restaurants	
$	up to $50	$	most entrees under $10
$$	$51 to $75	$$	most $10 to $15
$$$	$76 to $99	$$$	most $15 to $20
$$$$	$100 and up	$$$$	most over $20

If you would like to arrange lodging in an inn or bed-and-breakfast, call well in advance of your visit; relative to the total number of lodgings on the Connecticut shore, these types of hostelries are the rarest—and often the most popular. Be sure to ask about the number and size of the beds in each guest room; one double or queen-size bed is the norm. Roll-away cots and cribs (usually $10 to $15 extra) can be added to some inn or B&B rooms, but not all rooms are large enough to accommodate families. Some inns and B&Bs do not, in fact, cater to children and may indeed turn families away in deference to an older or "romantic getaway" clientele. Others are small enough to welcome families one at a time and offer special amenities for their needs. These differences are not necessarily noted in this book, so be sure to inquire.

Greenwich

Plush with green lawns and magnificent hardwood shade trees in the summertime, Greenwich presents one of the state's prettiest pictures of life along the Connecticut shore. One of the largest groups of islands on the Sound hugs closely to the town's coves and harbors, and sailboats and yachts cruising offshore add to the aura of wealth and leisure that is firmly anchored to this affluent suburb.

Located just 29 miles from Times Square with views of the New York City skyline from its beaches, Greenwich provides posh shelter for about 60,000 residents who take great pride in the rarefied ambiance of their coastal enclave. The varied interests and talents of its residents have enriched the prestigious town, which offers travelers perhaps the best dining options in the state, the most upscale shopping, and a state-of-the art natural history and art museum.

Best known for these features and for its multimillion-dollar homes, Greenwich also offers much more than glitz. Adding to Greenwich's riches are its most beautiful assets: More than 1,500 acres of the town's 50 square miles are rolling hills and verdant woodlands preserved as parkland. In addition, counting the perimeters of its islands, the quirky twists of its coves, and the banks of its estuaries, the town claims 32 miles of shoreline. Although nearly all the coastal area and much of the woods is privately owned or reserved for the use of Greenwich residents, there is still much that visitors can share in this top-drawer community.

Originally home to the Siwanoy and Petuquapaen, subgroups of the Algonkians who came to the shore 10,000 years ago, Greenwich was "discovered" by Adriaen Block shortly after the turn of the seventeenth century. Although Dutch settlers were in the area because of its proximity to their colony at New Netherlands, the English seem to have laid out the first permanent European settlement in Greenwich in 1640.

The details of the next few years are not entirely clear, but before long, tensions arising from the culture clash between the natives and the newcomers resulted in the 1644 massacre of the entire native population by the combined forces of the Dutch and the English. A famed account of the incident recorded that "Nor was any outcry whatsoever heard"—a fact hardly surprising considering that every single native man, woman, and child was brutally murdered by the self-declared "saints" of the colony, who believed they were fulfilling the Lord's wish

THE BEACHES OF GREENWICH

Summertime shore access in Greenwich is limited by fees charged for nonresident use of beaches and shoreline parks. Town officials fear that an open-door policy would bring in so many visitors that parking facilities would be inadequate and the ecology of the fragile shorelands would be compromised by overuse. They are probably correct, but the policy has been judged in violation of the state's public trust doctrine. The town, determined to protect the beauty and ecology of the beaches, is in the process of determining seasonal and/or day-use fees for nonresidents. Be sure to call ahead to inquire about those fees, which are charged only in-season (April 1 to December 1). The beaches and parks of Greenwich are open to all visitors at no charge December through March.

Travelers who want to enjoy the beauty of the Greenwich shore can visit Byram Park and Greenwich Point Park (also known as Tod's Point) as well as the beaches at **Great Captain's Island** and **Little Captain's Island.** The ferry service ($2.00; mid-June to September) at the **Arch Street Dock** takes visitors to **Island Beach** on the three-acre island or to the more primitive seventeen-acre island, where you may enjoy swimming, picnicking, and walking the trail to the nineteenth-century lighthouse. A concession operates on Little Captain's Island, but pack a picnic and beverages for a day on Great Captain's Island. For information on beach passes, call the Beach Card Office at (203) 622-7817. For Ferry Service information, call (203) 661-5957.

The beach at 149-acre Greenwich Point is a true gem. Connected to the mainland by a tiny strip of land called Tod's Driftway, Greenwich Point features ponds, a seaside garden, an arboretum, a swimming beach, and jogging and bicycling paths. Concessions and rest rooms are here, and a family play and learning area called the **Seaside Center** offers programs run by naturalists working for the Bruce Museum. Anglers may enjoy the opportunity to fish here. Also a great bird-watching spot, the park offers beautiful views of the Sound and of Long Island's Oyster Bay area, only 7 miles across the water. The park is generally open from dawn to sunset. Take Sound Beach Avenue south 1.8 miles from Route 1 to a right turn on Shore Road, and onward to the park entrance.

that the saints inhabit his earth. Conveniently, this concept also left the English plenty of room to build their houses and lay out their extensive fields of potatoes and grain.

By the nineteenth century, gristmills, a woolen mill, a stone quarry, and other industries established Greenwich as a place where jobs could be found, and along with the railroad and trolleys came immigrant workers and their families. Soon Greenwich farms were subdivided into residential lots for a great variety of homeowners, both rich and working class. Come to Greenwich to discover how its history has affected the growth of the town into one of the world's wealthiest suburbs—and one of the most sparkling communities on the Sound.

The Best of Greenwich

Downtown Greenwich

The commercial district of Greenwich centers largely on Greenwich Avenue between Railroad Avenue and Route 1, which in Greenwich is called West or East Putnam Avenue. Scores of shops ranging from the hometown jeweler to upscale chain stores to one-of-a-kind custom shops offering everything from couture evening wear to hand-painted tiles and French textiles can keep even the most energetic shopper busy for days on end. Restaurants of every description ensure that no one faints from hunger in the process of consuming other goods. It is not unfair to exaggerate that there is not a bargain in sight anywhere, unless you consider 50 percent off a $600 duvet (or dress or place setting) a good deal. Come with a large credit line on your plastic or wads of cash in your pocket, or just window-shop until you drop. Parking is mostly metered street parking; bring plenty of quarters.

Exit 3 off I–95 (Arch Street) to Greenwich Avenue and surrounding streets.

Bruce Museum of Arts and Science

One of the most sophisticated and definitively state-of-the-art museums in the region, the magnificently expanded and renovated Bruce houses more than 25,000 objects in three major categories: fine and decorative arts, cultural history, and environmental sciences. Pre-Columbian and Native American artifacts, nineteenth-century American paintings, prints, and sculpture, costumes, pottery, and more are on view in the art galleries. The environmental science galleries focus on the past 500 years of local New

England history and ecology, taking visitors from ancient to modern times with an environmental perspective. Within this wing, the cavelike minerals gallery preserves an extensive collection of ores, crystals, precious stones, and fluorescent minerals. An archaeological dig tucked in the Formation of Our Coast exhibit depicts the discovery of the Manakaway site on Greenwich Point and includes Native American artifacts unearthed during the excavation. Interactive exhibits allow visitors to experience the evolution and ecology of Long Island Sound. The environmental galleries also include a precisely re-created cross section of a tidal marsh ecosystem, a 2,400-gallon marine touch tank, an Ecological Awareness gallery focusing on tree and water communities, and an interactive wall narrating the natural and human history of Long Island Sound.

If you'd like to learn in a more interactive way, in the summertime you can visit the Bruce's small nature center at the beach at Greenwich Point. Perfect for families with young children, the **Seaside Center** offers free educational activities about the environment for all ages of visitors. A touch tank is maintained at the site along with other modest displays on marine life, but the best parts of a visit here are the guided beach and marsh walks, sensory hikes, nature crafts, beach seining activities, and environmental games. Seaside Center is open July 1 to September 5 on Wednesday through Sunday from 10:00 A.M. to 4:00 P.M. Nonresidents should contact Anne Burns at (203) 869-6786, extension 338 for information on access to Greenwich Point and the schedule of programs.

The Bruce also offers a museum store and a continuous schedule of festivals, workshops, concerts, and lectures. Visitors with an interest in functional and decorative arts will appreciate the outdoor crafts festival in mid- to late May and the fine arts festival on Columbus Day weekend; both juried shows feature entertainment, activities for children, and free admission to the museum.

Adjacent to the museum is the **Bruce Memorial Park and Playground,** a great place to rest, run, or picnic. A playground and picnic tables make the park perfect for families, and views of a real tidal marsh and Long Island Sound provide the backdrop. Look for the herons that inhabit the area—they are beautiful. Leave your car at the museum or park on Museum Drive.

1 Museum Drive; follow signs from I-95 exit 3 or the Merritt exit 31 (203–869–

0376). Web site: www.bruce.museum.org. The museum is open year-round, Tuesday through Saturday 10:00 A.M. to 5:00 P.M.; Sunday 1:00 to 5:00 P.M. Closed Monday and major holidays. $4.00 adults, $3.00 seniors and children 5 through 12; under 5 are free. Free to all on Tuesday.

Audubon Center

Up in Greenwich's northern reaches, 15 miles of trails lead through 686 acres of open woodlands, meadows, ponds, and streams in three separate parcels. The center's Interpretive Building houses an exhibit gallery, a demonstration beehive, a bird observation window, a model backyard wildlife habitat, and the excellent Environmental Book and Gift Shop. Free trail guides, maps, plant and bird lists, and a history of the area can be obtained at the shop.

Several loop trail options are available to fit schedules and hiking abilities. None of the trails are strenuous, but some are moderately demanding. The Discovery Trail leads past a great little pond, replete in summer with bullfrogs, duckweed, and dragonflies. Stay on the trail long enough and you'll be able to walk right across the top of a very pretty waterfall at the edge of Mead Lake. The landscape here is extraordinarily restful. The trees are among the most awesome specimens in Connecticut. Return in the fall for the spectacular foliage and for the annual migration of hawks that can be observed from the Quaker Ridge Hawk Watch Site.

The Audubon Center offers outdoor walks, camps, and naturalist workshops for children, adults, and environmental science teachers. Every Saturday at 10:00 A.M. from June through August and on Sundays at 2:00 P.M. during the remainder of the year, you can join a guided trail walk at no extra charge, either here on this property or on other nearby Connecticut Audubon Society preserves. The center asks that you leave pets at home and that you do not picnic on the grounds.

613 Riversville Road at the corner of John Street (Merritt Parkway exit 28) (203–869–5272). Web site: www.audubon.org/local/sanctuary/greenwich. Open year-round daily 9:00 A.M. to 5:00 P.M. Interpretive building closed Easter, Thanksgiving, Christmas, and January 1. $3.00 adults, $1.50 seniors and children; members of National Audubon Society are free.

Fairchild Connecticut Wildflower Garden

Audubon Center visitors are also welcome to walk the trails of its second parcel just a mile away on North Porchuck Road. This 134-acre tract offers 8 miles of trails. Established by Benjamin Fairchild in the early 1900s as an example of naturalistic landscaping, the garden is especially lovely in the spring. On the two properties, more than 900 species of ferns and flowering plants, 35 species of mammals, and 160 species of birds have been recorded. The Fairchild Garden has no facilities for visitors except for a portable toilet, so bring drinking water if you intend to explore the whole area on a hot day. The mostly flat and easy trails lead through meadow, marsh, and woodlands. Picnicking and pets are prohibited.

North Porchuck Road. Open daily year-round from dawn to dusk. Free.

Bush-Holley Historic Site and Visitor Center
The Historical Society of the Town of Greenwich

If pre-Revolutionary American history or colonial architecture and lifestyles interest you, don't leave Greenwich until you've visited here. A National Historic Landmark run by the Historical Society of the town of Greenwich, the 1732 Bush-Holley House is a classic central-chimney saltbox located beside Strickland Brook in the historic district of Cos Cob. Multiple fireplaces, paneled walls, ornate woodwork, and a double veranda are among its architectural features, but it is most famous as one of the sites on the Connecticut Impressionist Art Trail.

Formerly the home of wealthy farmer and mill owner David Bush and later a boardinghouse operated by the Holley family, the house was once alive with the activities and creativities of one of the first American Impressionist art colonies. Painters and sculptors, including Childe Hassam, J. Alden Weir, and Elmer Livingston MacRae, worked here during the period from 1890 to 1925. A collection of their works as well as an authentic re-creation of MacRae's studio are on display here, along with a fine collection of household implements, tools, furniture, and textiles.

In the Impressionist works, visitors can see the artists' visions of the warehouses, the tidal gristmill, the packet boats and fishing fleet, and the shipyard that once were at the hub of the Lower Landing at the small harbor of Cos Cob.

You can get oriented to the site at the visitor center that traces the development of the landing and the history of the original families of Greenwich and the Bush-Holley house itself. It also reveals the origins of the evolutionary art form that captured nuances of form, light, and shadow and eventually became known as American Impressionism. The visitor center also orients visitors to the history of the art colony and the town; its light- and sound-enhanced tableaus, its hands-on displays designed especially for young visitors, and its special changing exhibitions emphasize local history, art, and architectural and cultural

GARDEN EDUCATION
CENTER OF GREENWICH

Visitors interested in home gardening, landscape design, and other forms of horticulture may enjoy a morning or afternoon at the Garden Education Center on Bible Street in the Cos Cob section of town. This nonprofit organization is located within the 102-acre Montgomery Pinetum, itself a registered historic site and public park. Once the estate of Colonel Robert H. Montgomery, who planted his property with specimens of conifers collected from around the globe, the park is now a lovely spot open to all visitors. Wooded trails throughout the site lead past a pleasing seasonal array of wildflowers and magnificent trees well over a half-century old. A working greenhouse and three outstanding book and gift shops are also within or near this quiet space; the Greenwich Garden Center, with its own shop, is adjacent to the property. If you care simply to walk here, pick up a trail map at the Garden Center. If you are one of the many bitten by the gardening bug, you might rather attend one of the lectures, workshops, programs, or special events offered regularly. Call (203) 869-9242 for a schedule of these events and their fees. The Pinetum is generally open from 8:00 A.M. to sunset daily from April 15 through October 15 and from 8:00 A.M. to 4:00 P.M. Monday through Friday during the remainder of the year. More information can be obtained from the Greenwich Parks Department (203-622-7824).

movements. The site's new Vanderbilt Education Center offers lectures, educational workshops, and special programs for children.

Call to inquire about the ever-increasing activities of this museum. Children, for instance, may attend History Week annually during the month of July to learn about eighteenth-century colonial life and history. The annual Art-in-the-Yard Festival invites artists to paint on the grounds; visitors may reserve a spot in the yard for setting up their own easels, or they may watch as the empty canvases of other guests fill with their artistic impressions. At Christmastime (call for schedule) the house is decorated in a Victorian theme for candlelight tours.

39 Strickland Road in the Cos Cob section of town (203-869-6899). Open from January through March, Saturday 11:00 A.M. to 4:00 P.M. and Sunday 1:00 to 4:00 P.M.;

*April through December, Wednesday through Friday from noon to 4:00 P.M., Saturday
11:00 A.M. to 4:00 P.M., and Sunday 1:00 to 4:00 P.M. Tours of the house, $6.00 adults,
$4.00 seniors and students 12 and older; children under 12 are admitted free. Visitor
center, free to all.*

Putnam Cottage

Built circa 1692, the cottage was formerly known as Knapp Tavern and was
used during the Revolution as a meeting place of military leaders, including
former resident General Israel Putnam, second in command to George
Washington during the war. The cottage has been fully restored to appear
as it might have in 1700. Its unusual fish-scale shingles, its fieldstone fireplaces, and a pretty eighteenth-century herb garden are among its special
features. The cottage's collection includes Israel Putnam's desk, Bible,
glasses, the mirror through which he supposedly saw the British coming,
and the uniform he wore during the war.

The grounds and outbuildings surrounding the house are as beautifully restored as the house itself. Come on the last Sunday in February
to see the reenactment of Putnam's famous ride down the steep stone
cliff to the east of the cottage. Redcoats and rebels in full regalia skir-
mish on the grounds as the actor portraying ol' Put re-creates the general's memorable flourish to Revolutionary history.

*243 East Putnam Avenue, which is Route 1 (203–869–9697). Tours from April
through December on Wednesday, Friday, and Sunday from 1:00 to 4:00 P.M. or by
appointment. Admission $2.00; children under 12 are free.*

Mianus River Park

This 215-acre park straddles the Greenwich-Stamford line and includes
woodlands on both banks of the usually peaceful Mianus River. Several
loop trails through highlands and gorge areas as well as lowland paths
along the river help the visitor to customize a route that fits a day-tripping
schedule. Rough maps are posted at some of the trail junctions, but you can
also pick up a brochure with a complete map at the Greenwich Department
of Parks and Recreation in the Greenwich Town Hall at 101 Field Point
Road. Bring good hiking shoes because the terrain here varies from smooth
dirt or gravel forest roads to knotty footpaths.

Mountain bikers are welcome on the wider gravel paths—as long as
they obey the signs restricting them from the riverside trails. All of the
trails are well maintained, but other than a picnic area, no facilities are
offered for visitors, so be sure to pack in your own water. Freshwater

FOR THE HORSEY SET

World-class polo players from around the globe hit the field at the **Greenwich Polo Club** for high-goal, high-excitement matches that thrill young, old, and in-between onlookers. Matches begin at 3:00 P.M. on selected Sundays in June, July, and September at the club at Conyers Farm on North Street. The public is welcome at a charge of $20 per vehicle, payable at the gates, which open at 1:00 P.M. Special events and displays are planned each week. Call (203) 661-1952 for match dates and to get details about such events as wildlife demonstrations, hat contests, clowns, fashion shows, and more. The people-watching is great, too, as members arrive for the charity luncheons they enjoy before match time. You can bring your own hamperful of picnic goodies or purchase lunch at the concession/bar. Halftime brings divot-stomping fun—come and join the festivities!

anglers may want to bring some tackle. A trout management area is located on the Merriebrook Lane side of the river near Dumpling Pond, where a colonial housewife once quickly dispatched a fresh batch of dumplings rather than feed them to the British who had invaded her space one eighteenth-century afternoon. The policy here is catch-and-release, and a license is needed for anyone over the age of 15.

From Route 1, take Valley Road north to Cognewaugh Road to the parking area at the main entrance between Hooker and Shannon Lanes. To reach the second entrance, take Valley Road across the Stamford line to Mianus Road, then take Westover Road north to Merriebrook Lane; a parking lot is at a dirt turnoff near the one-lane bridge over the Mianus River, marked by a small green sign. For information, call the Greenwich Department of Parks and Trees (203–622–7824) or the Stamford Department of Parks and Natural Resources (203–977–4641). The park is open year-round at no charge from dawn to dusk.

Places to Eat in Greenwich

Dome 253 Greenwich Avenue (203-661-3443). In a stunning landmark setting with a fabulous brick vaulted dome ceiling, this chic establishment is full of surprises, from its electric decor to its architectural presentations of an astonishing array of multicultural cuisines. Marvelous vegetarian choices, inventively garnished seafood, enormous steaks and chops. Open daily for lunch 11:30 A.M. to 3:00 P.M. and dinner 5:30 to 10:00 P.M. $$$-$$$$

Rebeccas 265 Glenville Road (203-532-9270). An excellent choice for aficionados of exquisitely presented food, this simply decorated establishment lets the food take center stage. Rebecca Kirhoffer has invested heart, soul, and a good bit of cash to ensure that patrons can relax over the impeccable artistry and uncompromised quality of dishes created by her husband, chef Reza Khorshidi. Burnished wood floors and white walls and napery are the perfect backdrop for such eye- and palate-pleasing treats as Reza's signature "two-soups-in-one-bowl" to start and warm chocolate cake with mint chips to finish. Come be delighted by the surprises in the main course. Open for lunch Tuesday through Friday from 11:30 A.M. to 2:30 P.M. and for dinner Tuesday through Sunday from 5:30 P.M. $$$-$$$$

Polpo 554 Old Post Road #3 (203-629-1999). An Italian focus here ensures tasty seafood and pasta dishes and nice wines to accompany them. A raw bar and superior antipasto entice the crowds. Open for lunch and dinner daily from 11:45 A.M. $$-$$$

Meli Melo 362 Greenwich Avenue (203-629-6153). This tiny French charmer is a bright spot on the Avenue, sparkling, friendly, and delicious. Crepes are the focus here—our favorites are the banana and Nutella wheat crepes and the fruits rouges crepes. Both are sensational. The onion soup and the sorbets are famed. All are inexpensive. Open daily from 10:00 A.M. to 10:00 P.M. $

Thataway Cafe 409 Greenwich Avenue (203-662-0947). Perfect for taking a break during the formidable task of bargain-hunting in Greenwich, this informal eatery right at the heart of downtown offers burgers, sandwiches, grilled chicken, crisp salads, fresh-daily house-made soups, and good kids' choices like grilled cheese and chicken fingers. Cheerful service; outdoor seating in season. Open daily for lunch and dinner. $-$$

Boat Excursions and Charters

Fjord Brunch and Dinner Cruises (203-622-4020 or 800-925-2622). Fjord Catering and Yacht Charters can provide multiple ways to please folks with a generous handful of clams to rub together. In addition to private parties and clambakes, they offer delightful public cruises from Cos Cob to the western end of Long Island Sound. For $25 per child and $50 per adult, you cruise on a 117-foot luxury yacht from noon to 3:00 P.M. and enjoy a full shipboard brunch of gourmet quality and selection. Full open bar. Board at 11:30 A.M. Call for reservations. Friday evening dinner cruise also available; $80 prix fixe; 7:00 to 9:00 P.M. Check the Web site (www. fjordcatering.com) for complete menus. $$$$

Places to Stay in Greenwich

Stanton House Inn 76 Maple Avenue (203-869-2110). Twenty-four rooms in gracious turn-of-the-twentieth-century mansion close to the heart of town. Most of these immaculate rooms have private baths; some have fireplaces. A small suite has a claw-foot tub and a kitchenette. Outdoor pool, beach passes. Complimentary sherry in the common parlor and a generous continental breakfast in dining room. Open year-round. $$$-$$$$

Homestead Inn 420 Field Point Road (203-869-7500). Handsome 1799 colonial bed-and-breakfast in beautiful Belle Haven neighborhood. In main inn and newer addition, twenty-three antiques-filled suites and double rooms, wicker on wraparound porches, flower beds along flagstone pathways, canopied beds, impeccable service, and complimentary continental breakfast in the award-winning Thomas Henkelmann restaurant. Open year-round. $$$-$$$$.

Harbor House Inn 165 Shore Road, Old Greenwich (203-637-0145). Web site: www.hhinn.com. Twenty-three rooms in Victorian mansion near Greenwich Point Beach. Private baths, some with whirlpools. Coffeemakers and refrigerators in each room. Complimentary breakfast. Nonsmoking; no pets. Bicycles available. $$$$

Cos Cob Inn 50 River Road (203-661-5845). Fourteen beautiful rooms, all with private baths, air-conditioning, refrigerators, data ports, cable TV, voice mail, and much more in gracious Victorian home in historic Cos Cob. Queen-size bed in most rooms. One suite with Jacuzzi. High ceilings, lovely millwork, hand-painted floors, charming nautical touches. Complimentary continental breakfast, passes to beach. $$-$$$$

Hyatt Regency Greenwich 1800 East Putnam Avenue, Old Greenwich (203-637-1234 or 800-233-1234). Luxurious, tasteful, convenient to everything. Fabulous atrium, rooms and suites, restaurants, health club, indoor pool. Sunday brunch. $$$$

Delamar Greenwich Harbor 500 Steamboat Road (203-661-9800). Web site: www.slh.com/delamar. More finery in this eighty-three-room, nine-suite boutique hotel close to downtown and the water. Listed under the Web site for Small Luxury Hotels of the World, the Delamar offers fine European linens, complimentary services such as shoe shines and pressing, a gourmet Mediterranean-Provençal-style restaurant called **L'Escale,** a 600-foot boat dock, and a fitness suite. Plan to pay dearly. Rooms start at $355.

For Further Information

State Welcome Center Merritt Parkway northbound between exits 27 and 28 in Greenwich (203-531-1902). Open daily from Memorial Day through Labor Day, 8:00 A.M. to 6:00 P.M. Restrooms, maps, brochures to attractions.

Metro North Commuter Rail Service (800-638-7646). Trains from New York to New Haven offering stations in Riverside, Old Greenwich, Cos Cob, Greenwich. Call for schedule of service.

Greenwich Commuter Connection (800-982-8420). Shuttle buses between the Greenwich train station and other parts of downtown and elsewhere in Greenwich. Runs every half-hour Monday through Friday during morning and evening rush hours. $1.00 fare.

Greenwich Town Hall 101 Field Point Road (203-622-7700, main number; 203-622-7824, Parks and Trees; 203-622-7817, Beach Card Office). For information on tourist use of Greenwich parks, trails, and beaches. Open 9:00 A.M. to 3:00 P.M. Monday through Friday.

Stamford

Downtown Stamford is a busy hive of activity in all seasons, well established as a business center with a special focus on the financial and banking industries. Dozens of major corporations call Stamford home, and scores of restaurants, clubs, hotels, and a large mall cater to the needs of their employees. The museums, galleries, and performing arts centers sprinkled among the downtown office towers make the city's center sparkle with a vitality that draws travelers into the hub.

Down at the harbor, local sailboats are side by side with yachts from all parts of the globe, and the docks are awash with landlubbers as well as with old tars. Visitors should be sure to tarry awhile near the marinas and beaches or hop aboard a schooner to explore the water up close.

The hills north of downtown lure day-trippers to the hidden pleasures of Stamford's surprising woodlands. Settled in 1641 by families from Wethersfield, the city's farms and fields were once used as an important training ground for soldiers in the Revolutionary War. Today the training grounds and even the farms and fields themselves are overgrown with second-growth forest, cleared only to make room for the suburban homes that characterize the northern section of the city. A unique nature center and a noteworthy arboretum highlight the physical beauty that still remains in this otherwise urban metropolis. From nature center to nightclub, the city offers entertainment for all tastes and ages. Come to Stamford to discover the snappiest side of the Connecticut shore.

The Best of Stamford

Stamford Historical Society Museum

Visitors who would like to begin a city tour with a good sense of place may enjoy a walk through this historical museum. Chockful of furniture, toys, quilts, tools, and other permanent and changing exhibitions on local history, it highlights Stamford's famed citizens and inventions. Seasonal tours of the late seventeenth-century Hoyt-Barnum House (713 Bedford Street), once a blacksmith's residence, can also be arranged through the museum. Stamford's oldest surviving structure, it gives visitors a sense of colonial lifeways before the American Revolution. Return in late summer for the beautiful Antique Quilt Show and Sale, which draws crowds every year.

1508 High Ridge Road (203-329-1183). Web site: www.stamfordhistory.org. Open year-round Tuesday through Saturday, noon to 4:00 P.M.; closed major holidays. Adults $2.00, children $1.00.

Stamford Center for the Arts

The Rich Forum and the Palace Theatre have added more than a dash of panache to Stamford's cultural attractions. From September through June, the Truglia Theater and the Leonhardt Theater in the Rich Forum's lush performing arts complex host highly acclaimed theater productions featuring top performers from around the world. Many of these full-stage performances from Broadway and London are suitable for the whole family.

Designed in the 1920s by noted theater architect Thomas Lamb, the Palace Theatre is an architectural masterpiece with incredible acoustics. With seats for nearly 1,600 patrons, it provides a permanent home to the Stamford Symphony Orchestra, the Connecticut Grand Opera, the New England Lyric Operetta Company, the Stamford City Ballet, and the Connecticut Ballet. Here you might also enjoy short-run performances of music, dance, drama, and other entertainment such as circuses and musical comedies.

In all three theaters ticket prices vary widely, but costs can be cut by taking advantage of group rates, matinee performances, or seats in the upper tiers. Two children's productions are also usually offered at the Palace in the summer. Two performances, at 11:00 A.M. and 1:00 P.M., are given each Wednesday as long as the show runs. Ticket prices start at $6.00.

The Rich Forum (307 Atlantic Street) and the Palace Theatre (61 Atlantic Street). Call the box office (203–325–4466) or the information number (203–358–2305).

Stamford Theatre Works and the Purple Cow Children's Theatre

On the campus of Sacred Heart Academy, a private girls' high school run by the Sisters of Mercy, is a surprisingly contemporary Equity theater that stages not-for-profit and not-always-mainstream professional productions, often lauded as innovative, experimental, and thought-provoking. New and socially relevant works are of primary interest, and a great variety of readings and youth theater programs are staged throughout the year.

The Purple Cow productions are wonderful performances for children ages 3 to 8. Affordable and fun, they are offered twice daily on selected late spring and early summer Saturdays. Reservations are required. Typical fare includes puppet shows, magic, fairy tales, and dramatizations of popular children's literature.

200 Strawberry Hill Avenue (203–359–4414). Web site: www.stamfordtheatre works.com. September through May on Tuesday through Saturday evenings and Saturday and Sunday matinees; tickets $17 to $25. Summer theater (May through July) for children.

Sterling Farms Theatre Complex

The two venues at this community golf/tennis/theater complex specialize in theater for the lighthearted, both at the Ethel Kweskin Theater, housed in a 250-year-old barn that apparently has its own ghost, and across the street at the cabaret-style proscenium stage of the Dressing Room Theatre.

The resident Curtain Call company does four comedy productions each year as well as musicals and dramas. The Players are the pros who produce the bulk of the terrific performances offered at off-Broadway bargain prices; the Half-Pint Players are an energetic company of talented teens with star qualities. Call for a calendar of this year's lineup and inquire as to the appropriateness of individual shows if you'd like to take the whole family. Many are just right for young audiences. Curtain Call also offers theater workshops for adults and youth.

1349 Newfield Avenue: information (203–329–8207) and box office (203–461–6358). Ticket prices are generally $20 adults, $10 students (all performances) and seniors (Sunday only). Open year-round.

Cove Island Park

Located on a small island at the eastern end of the city, Cove Island Park is an eighty-three-acre recreation area right on the Sound. The largest and most popular public park in the city, it is open year-round and offers a wide beach with a pavilion and concessions, picnic areas, fishing areas, horseshoe pits, tennis courts, basketball courts, a softball field, a playground, a marvelous two-lane path for walkers and joggers and for in-line skaters and bicyclists, a marina (no dedicated transient slips), and the Terry Connors Ice Rink. Here too is the **Soundwaters Community Center for Environmental Education** (203-323-1978) at the historic Holly House. Permanent and temporary exhibits on the ecology of Long Island Sound are housed here along with live marine animals in aquariums. (See the Eco-Cruises sidebar on page 20 for further information.)

Try to stay for one of the guided beach walks, sponsored by Save the Sound, Inc., throughout the summer. Midday and evening walks offer a study of the animals and plants of the shoreline. Ask the park attendant for a schedule. If you can't take time for a walk, at least hop aboard the free tram that operates in season, primarily to transport visitors and their beach gear to the sunny or shady spot of their choice. The tram can also be enjoyed just for the pleasure of touring the park and enjoying the water views; the full circuit takes about fifteen minutes. It takes visitors around the perimeter, pausing at picnic areas, the swimming beach and concession, the playground, and so on.

Cove Island Park is at the base of Weed Avenue at the corner of Cove Road. Open year-round from 5:30 A.M. to one hour after sunset. The Environmental Center at Holly House is open Tuesday through Saturday, 10:00 A.M. to 5:00 P.M., Sunday noon to 5:00 P.M. For evening programs, the center opens one-half hour prior to the scheduled *event. From Memorial Day weekend through Labor Day, nonresidents arriving by car can use the park Monday through Friday only, with the purchase of a one-day pass for $15 per vehicle; call the Stamford Parks and Recreation Department (203–977–4692 or 203–977–4641) or the Terry Connors Ice Rink (203–977–4514) for details. Even in season, nonresident walkers or bikers can enter the park at any time at no charge. Off-season, nonresident vehicles can enter daily and at no charge. Nonresident visitors to the Environmental Center may enter in season at no charge if they let the attendant know they are headed there and are preregistered for a program.*

Stamford Museum and Nature Center

Up in the northern reaches of Stamford, this 118-acre park has features like no other nature center in the state. Heckscher Farm is a working nineteenth-century New England farm re-creation that includes a 1750 colonial barn on the rocky pastureland typical of the self-sufficient farms of yesteryear. A garden sowed with heirloom seeds yields a bountiful autumn harvest, and domesticated fowl and livestock inhabit the enclosure. In the midst of the farm is a country store and a tiny gem of an exhibit dedicated to eighteenth- and nineteenth-century farm life and tools.

In addition to 3 miles of woodland trails and a pond habitat with an adjacent picnic area, a 300-foot streamside boardwalk with signs in braille and sensory stations complements the Overbrook Natural Science Center, which houses aquatic tanks that simulate natural habitats of the small creatures that inhabit the woodland and its streams. Outside the center a beautiful brick walkway edges a garden of native plants and flowers.

On the hillside nearest the parking area is the Stamford Museum, which houses seven galleries of changing fine art exhibitions, Americana, nature exhibits, and a permanent exhibit on Native American life and history. Several beautiful dioramas are the highlight of the Native American gallery, which also includes fine artifacts from four major North American Indian groups. The main building of the museum also is home to a planetarium and an observatory, with the largest telescope west of the Mississippi.

The museum has converted a wooded one-acre site to one of the most unusual playgrounds anywhere. Up to 200 children at a time can gain a bird's-eye or chipmunk's view of the surrounding habitat. An 8-foot-high hollow log leading to a hollow branch opens onto a sandpit where kids can dig for fossil replicas. A 6-foot-high hollow stump features copies of insect galleries and honeycombs. Two 7-foot-wide hawks' nests in which to climb, a large-scale chipmunk burrow in which to rest,

ANTIQUES AND HOUSE WRECKERS

You might not plan an all-day excursion to **United House Wrecking** (203-348-5371), but it's such an unusual store that it appears frequently on lists of Stamford attractions. Five acres of land and more than 30,000 square feet of retail space make this a browser's dream-come-true. Architectural salvage—doors, stained glass windows, mantels, claw-foot bathtubs, and chandeliers—is the main seduction for renovators, but the fun only begins there. Furniture of every sort, pottery, jewelry, toys, china, books, and more fill the space to the brim. Mixed with this "normal" stuff is an ever-changing array of truly odd, absolutely fantastical, and downright weird stuff—gargoyles, dentists' chairs, a barbershop pole, jukeboxes, circus posters, subway straphangers—in short, everything under the sun including bells, whistles, and the kitchen sink.

Lovers of the sea and shore may have a special interest in the huge selection of nautical items. Ship wheels, sextants, telescopes, compasses, life rings, clocks, flags, and bridge glasses are just some of the treasures that may add to your collection for boat or home. The store is located at 535 Hope Street. It's open year-round Monday through Saturday from 9:30 A.M. to 5:30 P.M. and Sunday from noon to 5:00 P.M. Closed on major holidays. The store's Web site is www.United-Antiques.com.

Shoppers who can't rest until they locate the perfect one-of-a-kind item might want to peruse the goods at the 22,000-square-foot **Antique and Artisan Center** (203-327-6022), a treasure chest of antiques and fine decorative arts. American furniture forms the core of the enormous selection offered by eighty-five dealers, but artworks, small collectibles, and functional and decorative pieces of every period, style, and description are among the thousands of collector-quality antiques available here. Located at 69 Jefferson Street (near Canal Street), it's open year-round Monday through Saturday from 10:30 A.M. to 5:30 P.M. and Sunday from noon to 5:00 P.M.

and a 30-foot-long otters' slide on which, of course, to slide are among other features. A large water environment area includes play possibilities such as dam construction or boat racing. A treehouse, a beaver lodge replica, and a rope spider's web complete the scene.

Among all of these areas the Stamford Museum and Nature Center staff conducts educational programs, workshops, lectures, festivals, and summer camps. Summer folk concerts, an autumn Harvest Fair, an Astronomy Day, and other annual events such as maple sugaring, ice harvesting, and apple cidering are all on the Nature Center's calendar.

39 Scofieldtown Road (203–322–1646). Web site: www.stamfordmuseum.org. Open year-round Monday through Saturday and most holidays, 9:00 A.M. to 5:00 P.M.; Sunday 1:00 to 5:00 P.M. Closed Thanksgiving, Christmas, New Year's Day. Planetarium shows on Sunday at 3:00 P.M.; adults $2.00 and children $1.00, plus museum entrance fee. Observatory hours, weather permitting, on Friday from 8:00 to 10:00 P.M.; adults $3.00, children $2.00 (no additional entrance fee). The fee to enter the Museum and Nature Center is adults $6.00, seniors and children under 14 $4.00; no charge for children under 4.

Bartlett Arboretum

Just down the road from the Stamford Nature Center is this ever-beautiful sanctuary of oak, maple, and hickory trees interspersed with evergreens, ash, birch, beech, and yellow poplar. Perennial borders, a conifer garden, a native wildflower garden, and a nut tree collection are among the major areas of this gorgeous property.

Five miles of trails lead visitors through the gardens, woodlands, and wetlands. A reflecting pond at the end of the Woodland Trail is a perfect destination for hikers, as is the boardwalk that leads through the Swamp Trail. The self-guided Ecology Trail combines portions of each of these trails. Pick up a guidebook at the visitor center so you can enjoy the descriptions of twenty-seven marked stations. The Arboretum's trails also connect to the Stamford Nature Center's trails, so visits to both areas can be combined.

If you are visiting with a child under 12, borrow a nature activity backpack from the visitor center before you set out on a walk. Crayons, scratch pads, a magnifying glass, and a wonderful set of cards with games, questions, activity suggestions, and educational information enhance the experience for the whole family.

Take a stroll through the greenhouse for a look at the incredible cacti and succulents among the other tropical and temperate plants in the collection. Lastly, stop again at the visitor center, which houses an exhibition hall, an ecology research laboratory, and a lending library of horticultural materials.

The arboretum offers a variety of classes and tours for adults throughout the year. Guided walks for the whole family are free to the public, as are Sunday concerts held approximately every other week in the months of July and August (call for schedule).

151 Brookdale Road (203-322-6971). Open daily year-round, 8:30 A.M. to sunset. The visitor center is open Monday through Friday, 8:30 A.M. to 4:00 P.M., except on holidays. The greenhouse is open every morning from about 9:30 to 11:00. Free.

Places to Eat in Stamford

Beacon 183 Harbor Drive (203-327-4600). Overlooking the marina off Shippan Point, this tri-level restaurant/bar is one of the city's most dramatic dining establishments. Open-fire cooking and a stunning exhibition kitchen are the centerpieces of this casually chic eatery that attracts well-heeled professionals as well as families and tourists. Main courses, such as grilled sea scallops on a rosemary skewer or wood-roasted veal chop are served with grilled and roasted vegetables. Seafood, pastas, salads, soups, and spit-roasted birds and meats are always on the menu; vegetarian choices are easily found or designed from your request. Open for dinner daily; for lunch on weekdays only from noon to 2:30 P.M., and for Sunday brunch, noon to 3:00 P.M. The bar, a popular nightspot, is open daily as well. $$$$

Ocean 211 211 Summer Street (203-973-0494). Situated on two floors of a vintage town house near the heart of the city, this restaurant fairly swims with delicacies from the sea. Tuna, Chilean sea bass, Nantucket bay scallops, lobster-saffron risotto, curried shrimp quesadillas, halibut in truffle sauce, and crab cakes with jicama salad are choices you might find on the changing daily menu. Plenty of sides and salads and a few main courses that originated on land, not sea, will please those who eschew fish. Leave room for dessert—the best-selling chocolate pâté is heavenly. Open for lunch Monday through Friday noon to 2:30 and for dinner from 5:00 Monday through Friday and from 5:30 on Saturday. Closed Sunday. $$$-$$$$

Paradise Bar and Grille 78 Southfield Avenue (203-323-1116). Tropical shirts on the servers set the tone for summer on the docks at this casual eatery at Stamford Landing. Chef Jimmy Myers has created an eclectic menu of pastas, seafood, pizzas, and sandwiches with Cajun, Caribbean, Thai, and southwestern influences. Jimmy's delicious Shipwreck Chowder is as good in winter, when the brass oil lamps on the tables add to the warmth of the fireplace, as it is under the yellow-and-white striped awning in summer. Generous portions mean that you have an excuse to linger in all seasons, where views of the sailboats and the harbor vie with the meal for your attention. Eat out on the deck in warm weather; stay cozy inside near the wall of windows in winter; cool off with a frozen drink at the outdoor **Oasis** bar on a hot summer night. Open for lunch and dinner daily from noon to 9:00 P.M. $$-$$$

Long Ridge Tavern 2635 Long Ridge Road (203-329-7818). If you've tired

ECO-CRUISES

If the smell of the salt breeze draws you away from downtown toward the water, try to catch a ride on the 80-foot *SoundWaters*, a replica of a three-masted sharpie schooner that offers two-hour public eco-cruises from June 1 to mid-October. Led by trained naturalists, the cruises focus on the ecology, history, culture, and future of Long Island Sound. You can help raise the sails, haul in the trawl net filled with creatures from the deep, and examine the catch in four stations that focus on aspects of marine ecology.

Public sails are offered three to five times monthly during the warm season. Special sails, such as a Fireworks Sail in early July, are also open to the public. Call for a schedule or to reserve a place on these very popular cruises. All of the sails require advance reservation and payment.

You'll find *SoundWaters* at 4 Brewers Yacht Haven Marina, at the foot of Washington Boulevard (203-323-1978). Send e-mail to swaters@clubnetct.com. Their Web site is www.soundwaters.org. Adults $25, children 12 and under $15; sunset and fireworks cruises $30 per person. Private charters are also available.

Landlubbers may choose to visit **Soundwaters Community Center for Environmental Education** at Holly House in Cove Island Park (see page 15). Live marine animal talks and changing and permanent exhibits on the ecology and the denizens of Long Island Sound and its estuaries are located here. Programs for all ages are offered year-round; many are free, but some have a small (often $5.00) charge. Salt marsh explorations and beach walks may be among the activities on the schedule. An interpretive self-guiding walking trail is already in place for park visitors.

of the sea and hunger instead for the charm of the New England woodlands, head north in Stamford to this colonial-style tavern in a nineteenth-century horse barn. A gleaming antique bar and a welcoming fieldstone fireplace add to the ambiance of pegged floors and beamed ceilings. Steaming chicken pot-pie, sweet potato bisque, shepherd's pie, rack of lamb with roasted vegetables, and strawberry-rhubarb crisp for dessert are just some of the hearty "new American" dishes you might enjoy here. Musicians and other entertainers enchant the crowd in the tap room Wednesday through Sunday. Open for lunch Tuesday through Saturday 11:30 A.M. to 3:00 P.M. Dinner Tuesday through Saturday from 5:00 P.M. Sunday brunch 11:30 A.M. to 3:00 P.M. $$$

Vuli Two Stamford Forum at the Stamford Marriott (203-323-5300). High above the city is the revolving dining room of this plush Mediterranean restaurant owned by the Vuli brothers. Chef Joseph Vuli will enchant you with Tuscan specialties, delicious seafood, and excellent desserts. The view is equally delightful. Jackets preferred. Open for lunch Monday through Friday; dinner daily; Sunday brunch.

Places to Stay in Stamford

Stamford Marriott Hotel Two Stamford Forum (203-357-9555). Five hundred and seven units, six suites, revolving rooftop restaurant, coffee shop, health club, sauna, jogging track, indoor and outdoor pools, sports court, game room. Lower weekend rates. $$$$

Holiday Inn Select Stamford 700 Main Street (203-358-8400). Three hundred and seventy-five rooms, seven suites, with desks, data ports, cof-feemakers, hair dryers, irons, complimentary newspapers. Restaurant, health club, sauna, indoor pool. $$$$

The Westin Stamford One First Stamford Place (203-967-2222). Four hundred and seventy-six rooms, including thirty-one suites with one or two bedrooms. Full-service restaurant, tavern, health club, heated indoor pool, Jacuzzi, tennis courts, room service. Shuttle to downtown; airport limo. Lower weekend rates. $$$$

Sheraton Stamford Hotel 2701 Summer Street (203-359-1300). Four hundred forty-five units, each with a hair dryer, coffeemaker, clothes iron, and other extras. Atrium restaurant, health club, heated indoor pool, sauna, massage therapy, rooftop tennis courts. Shuttle to downtown, on-site airline ticket office. Lower weekend rates. $$$$

SOMETHING FISHY

One of Stamford's most notable architectural attractions is its fish-shaped First Presbyterian Church, designed by Wallace K. Harrison, at 1101 Bedford Street (203-324-9522). Along with its unique silhouette, the church features the state's largest mechanical-action pipe organ and beautiful stained glass windows by artist Gabriel Loire of France. Visitors are welcome year-round, from 9:00 A.M. to 5:00 P.M. Monday through Friday from September through June and from 9:00 A.M. to 3:00 P.M. on the same days in July and August. A donation is suggested. Free band and carillon concerts are offered on the green during July on Thursdays at 7:00 P.M.

Public Boat Launch

West Beach Park Shippan Avenue (203-977-4641 or 977-4692). Public ramp for boats up to 30 feet; $25.00 daily nonresident fee or $200 nonresident seasonal pass. Residents pay $5.00 daily or $35.00 seasonally. Rest rooms, showers, phone, concession at nearby beach park.

For Further Information

Stamford Chamber of Commerce One Landmark Square, Stamford CT 06901 (203-359-4761). Call for its excellent seasonal calendars of events and its exceptional *Stamford Cultural Guide.*

Coastal Fairfield County Visitors Information Center Level Four at the Stamford Town Center shopping mall. Brochures, maps, calendar, plus tickets for performances at the Stamford Center for the Arts.

Fairfield County Weekly For listings of evening entertainment in Stamford nightclubs and dance clubs, look for a free copy of the *Fairfield County Weekly,* a tabloid newspaper distributed at libraries, restaurants, drugstores, and so on.

Stamford Department of Parks and Natural Resources 888 Washington Boulevard (203-977-4641). Call for information on beaches and on nonresident use of boat launches, tennis courts, and public parks.

Darien

Hugging the shore less than an hour from New York City, the lovely residential town of Darien is safe harbor to throngs of commuters who emerge from the Metro-North trains or exit the highways at the end of the workday. These citizens are not typical worker bees, though: Darien ranks second among the state's 169 towns in per capita income and fourth in cost of homes. Throughout the town, tree-lined avenues flank manicured lawns and beautiful homes, and on the busiest corridors independent shops both classically traditional and trendily contemporary cater to the needs of affluent families. Excellent schools, a noteworthy library, and reliable services give Darien's townsfolk plenty of incentive to stay—but few good reasons for tourists to visit.

The larger cities of Stamford to the west and Norwalk to the east certainly offer more attractions, lodgings, and restaurants and a busier calendar of cultural arts and entertainments. In smaller, quieter Darien, the most exciting event to happen in a *long* time was the British raid on the parish church in 1781, when the Reverend Moses Mather and the men and boys of his congregation were carried right out of the services and carted off to prison for their Patriot sympathies. Since that date the most notable incidents in town have been its separation in 1820 from the town of Stamford and its rapid growth as a suburb after the completion of the New Haven Railroad in 1848.

For many visitors, the most attractive of Darien's features are its miles of Long Island Sound waterfront, fringed with beaches and yacht clubs. Unfortunately, Darien's snug relationship with the sea is closely guarded, and out-of-towners must either pay the hefty daily beach parking fee exacted from Memorial Day through Labor Day or wait until early fall to enjoy Indian summer on the Darien shore. Most day-trippers probably decide to head to less costly beaches in other towns. Stamford's Cove Island Park, Norwalk's Calf Pasture, or Westport's Sherwood Island, for instance, are a fraction of the price even at the height of summer.

Still, a day at the shore in Darien can be a rewarding experience for the traveler willing to patch together a crazy quilt of small adventures chosen from among the following options.

The Best of Darien

Bates-Scofield Homestead

Leave behind Darien's upscale hustle and bustle of the twenty-first century and step into the eighteenth-century world of John Bates and his family. Situated on a small parcel of land not far from the Darien YWCA and the Goodwives Shopping Plaza, this restored saltbox structure is the area's only publicly held example of a pre-Revolutionary farmhouse.

Built in 1736 and once recorded as a "mansion house," perhaps because of its somewhat atypical second story, the homestead in fact exemplifies the simplicity of a modest mid-eighteenth-century Connecticut residence. Around its huge central chimney the house features a formal parlor, a dining room, a kitchen, a buttery, and a number of bedchambers. An interesting variety of domestic tools, porcelain, toys, and wonderful Connecticut-made colonial furnishings are displayed throughout the house. Notable among these are a locally made tall-case clock, a late seventeenth-century painted blanket chest, and a charming baby tender. Although none of the authentic period furnishings are original to the house, they were all collected by the historical society in duplication of the Bates family inventory.

Outdoors to the rear of the house, a garden is planted with heirloom specimens of culinary, medicinal, and fragrant herbs of colonial Connecticut and antique roses found in eighteenth-century Connecticut gardens. Guided tours of the house are given by docents, but visitors are welcome in the gardens at any time year-round. Visitors may also peruse the library and the small gallery of changing exhibitions in the modern wing of the Darien Historical Society, headquartered at this site.

45 Old Kings Highway North (203–655–9233). Open year-round. Research library and Darien Historical Society offices open Tuesday, Wednesday, and Friday from 9:00 A.M. to 1:00 P.M. and Thursday from 9:00 A.M. to 4:00 P.M. Tours of the house are usually Thursday and Sunday from 2:00 to 4:00 P.M. Admission is $2.50 per person for house tours; no charge to use library or view gardens.

Darien Ice Rink

At this privately owned indoor rink, the ice is ready all year long for skaters from beginner to expert. Lessons, a summer hockey camp, frequent hockey games, skating competitions, and other exhibitions are also on the calendar.

One of the most popular events is the five-day Open Figure Skating Competition in April, which brings in as many as 900 skaters from all over the United States. Visitors are welcome to watch these beautiful and exciting performances. Call for this year's dates and admission fees.

The ice rink is on Old Kings Highway North (203–655–8251). The rink is open for public skating every Sunday from 1:00 to 2:50 P.M., plus Monday through Thursday from noon to 1:45 P.M. Adults $5.00, seniors $3.00, children under 12 $4.00; skate rental is extra, $2.00.

Darien Town Beaches

The public beaches of Darien are not actually reserved only for the town's own citizens—it's the *parking* at the beaches that is restricted in the warm months. Residents of Darien purchase seasonal parking passes for the privilege of enjoying their beaches in the most convenient way—that is, to be able to park in the lot near the concessions and restrooms, and so on. Nonresident visitors day-tripping in Darien by means of automobile are welcome to walk onto or bicycle into public beach areas if they can find legal parking for their vehicles elsewhere in town, or they may also pay a daily per-vehicle fee of $30 to enjoy the convenience of parking in the lot at Peartree Point Beach from Memorial Day to Labor Day or at Weed Beach from April through September. Outside of those dates, the parking restriction lifts, as does the daily fee.

If you'd like to explore the beaches, leave I-95 at exit 10 and take Noroton Avenue south to the Boston Post Road (Route 1). To reach Weed Beach, take a right onto the Post Road and a left onto Nearwater Lane, and go south toward the Sound, where the road bears to the right and leads directly to the beach. Lying just south of pretty Holly Pond, which separates Darien and Stamford, Weed Beach faces southwestwardly, across the cove from Stamford's Cove Island Park. The beach is wide and clean and has beautiful views of the Sound and Long Island. To reach Peartree Point Beach, take a left from Noroton Avenue onto the Post Road and a right onto Ring's End Road, cross the small bridge over Gorham Pond and Noroton Bay to Goodwives River Road, and bear right nearly immediately on Peartree Point Road to the beach. This smaller beach faces more directly south and has views of the boat clubs and marinas. A sandy picnic grove has grills and tables, and a simple picnic shelter perched on a small bluff provides a nice place to watch the marine traffic.

Weed Beach (foot of Nearwater Lane) and Peartree Point Beach (Peartree Point Road): Both beaches have picnic areas, rest rooms, and concessions and assess $30 *per-vehicle daily fees for nonresidents in season. For more information, call the Darien Parks and Recreation Department (203-656-7325).*

Darien Arts Center

Founded in 1975, the Darien Arts Council, renamed the Darien Arts Center, followed in the hallowed footsteps of a group established in 1927 and named the Guild of Seven Arts. Today the Arts Center continues to provide an outlet for the dynamic energy of performing and visual artists engaged in a great variety of creative pursuits. Dance, theater, voice, and fine arts in many media are the main areas of focus, but surprising energies of all kinds manifest themselves here with regularity. The center's 2,000-square-foot black-box Weatherstone Studio is the usual site of three dramatic performances each year by the Darien Players; each of these runs two to three weeks and is appropriate for and affordable for (at $10-$15 per ticket) the whole family. The Darien Choraliers offer at least two annual concerts, and guest performances or cabaret productions round out the performing schedule.

An annual juried fine arts exhibition is held each June and is hung in the Weatherstone Studio when the flurry of local dance recitals subsides. Stop in at the center (at the back of the Darien Town Hall) to view the current show. Call for dates and hours.

2 Renshaw Road (203-655-8683).

Boat Excursions and Charters

Rowayton native **Captain Ian Devlin** offers guided wade fishing trips from the Darien shore and eastward to Stratford. A world-record-winning bluefish angler and a certified fly-casting instructor, he also offers chartered flat- and char-fishing trips in the Norwalk Islands from June through November. Contact him at (203) 838-2912.

Places to Eat in Darien

Li's Brothers Inn of Darien 24-48 Old Kings Highway North in the Goodwives Shopping Plaza (203-656-3550). Not a place to rest on a rave reputation as perhaps the best Asian restaurant in the state, Li's outdoes itself seven days a week with wonderful Hong Kong–style dim sum and authentic Hunan and Szechuan specialties. Open for lunch and dinner daily year-round, Li's is as wonderful for adult dining as it is welcoming to families. Relaxing, comfortable atmosphere and gracious service. $$-$$$

DOWNTOWN DARIEN
AND NOROTON HEIGHTS

Shoppers who would rather browse through one-of-a-kind boutiques than shuffle past the same old stuff at chain stores will probably enjoy a spree in Darien's charming owner-operated emporiums. Whether you're caught up in the holiday frenzy or merely window-shopping in any season, try the commercial areas of **Darien center,** which lies mostly along the Boston Post Road, its side streets, and part of Tokeneke Road, and **Noroton Heights,** a neighborhood sandwiched between the railroad, West Avenue, and I-95. Seek and ye shall find unique gift shops, galleries, antiques stores, and cafes.

Among the town's most well-known shops are the **Darien Sport Shop** (1127 Post Road; 203-655-2575), which has provided a few generations with great quality sporting goods and clothing perfect for touring folks, and **The Compleat Angler** (987 Post Road; 203-655-9400) for fine tackle and other fishing gear and gifts, plus excellent advice, instruction, and leads for guided fishing trips. **The Good Food Store** (863 Post Road; 203-655-7355) and **Trader Joe's** (436 Post Road; 203-656-1414) both provide tasty comestibles.

The Black Goose Grille 972 Post Road (203-655-7107). On the south side of the Post Road, basically across from the train station, this restaurant features handsome oak paneling, tin ceilings, and black upholstered booths overhung with etched glass lamps—a lovely, smoke-free setting for casual dining on entrees of seafood, steak, chicken, and pasta and inventive appetizers and sandwiches. A pub room with a fireplace and magnificent bar originally from the Anheuser-Busch Brewery in St. Louis offers dining from the same menu. Smoking is permitted in the bar. Outside dining is possible on the patio tucked along the pretty alleyway that leads to the front door. Open daily year-round for lunch 11:45 A.M. to 2:30 P.M. and dinner from 5:30 P.M. $$–$$$

Dolcetti's 921 Post Road (203-656-2225). Bare wood floors, crisp white napery, and simple wooden furnishings add to the immaculate ambiance of this gracious restaurant known for its fine Italian cuisine as well as for its outstanding pizza. Adults as well as families will feel comfortable here, dining on reasonably priced antipasti, pasta dishes, seafood, veal, and chicken

GRAND PRIX AT OX RIDGE

On a sunny day in early June there can be no more beautiful outing in Darien than an afternoon at the annual **Ox Ridge Hunt Club's Charity Horse Show.** Celebrating nearly seventy years as Connecticut's oldest equestrian tradition, this seven-day event is recognized as one of the top five horse shows in the nation. In a classically country club setting at 512 Middlesex Road off Route 124 (Mansfield Avenue) north of Route 1, this exciting competition showcases the equestrian skills of more than 1,200 horses and riders, including the nation's top amateur and professional hunter/jumper riders from ages 8 through adult.

Benefitting Darien's **Center for Hope** (1003 Post Road; 203-655-4693), a counseling center for children and families dealing with serious illness and bereavement, the Charity Show usually begins on Monday or Tuesday of the first full week in June and continues to the Grand Prix event the following Sunday. The Grand Prix is the United States Equestrian Team Regional Show Jumping Championship. Each day, from about 8:00 A.M. until late in the afternoon, the public is welcome to attend all of the equitation events as well as the other festivities of this benefit. Among these is an arts and crafts show featuring regional artisans and other vendors. A catered concession offers delicious lunches and suppers pleasing to all ages. Guests may also bring their own picnic hampers to enjoy in the stands or on the pretty lawns of this lovely club. Admission is $5.00 per vehicle Tuesday through Friday; $5.00 per adult and $3.00 per senior or child on Saturday; and $7.00 and $5.00 respectively for Sunday's $35,000 Grand Prix main event.

Ox Ridge (203-655-2559) also welcomes visitors to other horse shows throughout the season (typically June through September) and offers introductory horsemanship and riding lessons to the public. Call for further information.

specialties, thin-crust pizza, crusty calzones, Italian sandwiches, and tempting desserts. Open for lunch Monday through Friday 11:30 A.M. to 2:30 P.M. and for dinner daily from 5:00 P.M. $$

Backstreet Restaurant 22 Center Street (203-655-9944). This small eatery is a favorite place for a casual dinner or lunch, especially in warm weather when you can enjoy its back patio. Sit under crisp green market umbrellas and choose from a menu of soups, sandwiches, salads, and appetizers, plus full entrees like steak, chicken, and pasta dishes. Cheerful service; affordable prices; reliably good food with a creative flair. $–$$

Post Corner Pizza 847 Post Road (203-655-7721). Well-recommended for families and casual dining, this local favorite is a sure thing for Greek-style pizza and traditional Italian pasta, seafood, chicken, and veal specialties, plus salads, grinders, and calzones. Open daily year-round for lunch and dinner from 11:00 A.M. to 11:00 P.M. $–$$

Uncle's Deli 1041 Post Road (203-655-9701). If you are here at the crack of dawn, this old-fashioned take-out delicatessen in the heart of the shopping district and not far from the train station is the place to come for breakfast and coffee or, later, to pick up lunch. Open year-round 6:00 A.M. to 5:00 P.M. daily. $

Place to Stay in Darien

Howard Johnson Inn 150 Ledge Road, off I-95 exit 11 (203-655-3933). Seventy-two units, some nonsmoking (but be sure to check first to see if the room meets your standard of smoke-free). Outdoor pool, in-room coffeemakers, hair dryers, irons. Senior citizen rates. Restaurant on premises. $$

For Further Information

Darien Chamber of Commerce 17 Old Kings Highway South (203-655-3600). Monday through Friday 9:00 A.M. to 1:00 P.M. Web site: www.darien.lib.ct.us.

Darien Parks and Recreation Department 2 Renshaw Road in Darien Town Hall (203-656-7325). Information on in-season nonresident use of town beaches and parks. Some Sound-related activities sponsored by the Rec Department may be open to nonresidents if space permits; among the possibilities are swimming, sailing, and sailboarding instruction. Open Monday through Friday 8:30 A.M. to 4:30 P.M. Fishing licenses, call 203-656-7307.

State Welcome Center On I-95 between exits 11 and 13 northbound in the McDonald's rest area (203-655-8289) with food court and restrooms open 24 hours daily. Tourism office open 9:00 A.M. to 6:00 P.M. daily from Memorial

Day to Labor Day; 9:00 A.M. to 5:00 P.M. daily Labor Day to Memorial Day. Maps, brochures, and lodging and restaurant information.

Norwalk

Norwalk's interesting maritime history and attractive position on the Sound make it one of Connecticut's most popular destinations for shoreline travelers. Long famed as a port and as one of the nation's largest producers of oysters, the city is experiencing a marvelous reawakening of its waterfront, a much-lauded revitalization of a small city that began its 350-year history in 1649. A decade or more in the remaking, the South Norwalk neighborhood is now especially redolent of salt air and fresh seafood, as manufacturing in the area has given way to a state-of-the-art aquarium, a visitors' dock, scores of restaurants, galleries, and shops, and a museum celebrating the city's history. Now the sounds of gulls and boat whistles and the rising of the Washington Street drawbridge compete with the happy sounds of the interactions of tourists, shoppers, and entrepreneurs who inhabit the busy streets of SoNo from morning to twilight and beyond.

Down in the quieter enclave of Rowayton near the Darien boundary at the Five Mile River, the sense of the sea is more apparent than in any other section of Norwalk. The quaintly twisting streets are lined with cottages, boatyards, and funky establishments that cater to an eclectic neighborhood of sailors, fishermen, artists, and weekenders from New York City. Just offshore are the sixteen Norwalk Islands, including Sheffield, Goose, and Chimon Islands, which provide habitat for colonial nesting waterbirds as well as migrating neotropical birds. Protected as units of the Stewart B. McKinney National Wildlife Refuge, they are now safe from developers who once eyed the largest islands for their potential value as resort communities. Today Chimon Island is the most productive heron rookery in the state, supporting large populations of a dozen or more kinds of wading birds.

Explore the core and the corners of Norwalk, looking for the contemporary links to its history as a port. You'll have no trouble finding cruises and fishing charters, sailing lessons and regattas, oyster bars and boat shows. You name it—if it involves water, it's in Norwalk.

The Best of Norwalk

The Maritime Aquarium at Norwalk

The flagship, if you will, of the bustling SoNo neighborhood, this aquarium-cum-theater-cum-maritime museum is a celebration of life near, on, and under the sea, particularly Long Island Sound. Located in a restored nineteenth-century foundry overlooking Norwalk Harbor, this major attraction includes twenty-two aquariums filled with nearly 150 species of marine life.

Visitors move from one marine habitat re-creation to another, beginning at the edge of the salt marsh and culminating at a 110,000-gallon tank with 9-foot sharks, stingrays, and other creatures of the open ocean. Harbor seals swim in an indoor/outdoor pool, and river otters tumble and slide in simulated woodlands habitat with underwater viewing windows. Two loggerhead sea turtles share another 15,000-gallon tank. You can handle sea stars, horseshoe crabs, and other tidal pool inhabitants in the tidal touch tank. Interactive and video displays reveal the secrets of the fragile ecosystems of Long Island Sound and its estuaries.

In the maritime museum area, you can watch crafters build wooden boats in the centuries-old tradition of early New England boat builders. Changing exhibitions in the aquarium may feature other creatures of the sea or birds of prey, perhaps. Even the aquarium itself has changed with the opening of an Environmental Education Center, a cafeteria, and an expanded gift shop/bookstore. Before you go home, watch an IMAX film in the six-stories-high theater. Special events, lectures, educational camps, and workshops are commonplace at the Maritime Aquarium; call to ask for a calendar of programs.

10 North Water Street (203–852–0700). Web site: www.maritimeaquarium.org. Open daily year-round, except on Thanksgiving and Christmas Day. Regular hours are 10:00 A.M. to 5:00 P.M.; from July 1 to Labor Day, hours are extended until 6:00 P.M. The IMAX theater runs on the hour from 11:00 A.M. to 3:00 or 4:00 P.M. and is also open for Friday and Saturday evening shows. Admission is charged to the center alone, to the IMAX alone, or to both together. Adults are $8.75, $6.75, or $13.25, respectively. Seniors are $8.00, $5.75, or $11.50, and children 2 to 12 are $7.25, $5.00, or $10.00; under 2 are free. Parking is available at municipal lots adjacent to the facility at an additional cost.

The Norwalk Museum

The innovative albeit small Norwalk Museum seeks both to educate and entertain visitors by presenting the last hundred or so years of Norwalk history from a commercial and retail point of view. Located in the grandly restored 1912 former City Hall building, just a block from the Maritime Aquarium, the museum focuses on the late nineteenth century and the first half of the twentieth. The museum's centerpiece gallery, Merchants' Court, is created to bring to mind authentic businesses, industries, and artisans of earlier times. Celebrating the great number of goods invented or manufactured in Norwalk, it showcases dozens of products that added to the economy of the city while satisfying the needs of the populace.

Curator Susan Gunn creates varied changing exhibitions in the museum's Lockwood Gallery; these often feature Norwalk or Connecticut themes. Recent displays have included a collection of Norwalk-made chairs, the work of Civil War photographer E.T. Whitney, and items related to abolitionist John Brown.

A small gift shop completes the scene for tourists; a reference library is available to researchers.

41 North Main Street at the corner of Marshall (203–866–0202). Open Tuesday through Sunday year-round, except on holidays, from 1:00 to 5:00 P.M. Free.

Lockwood-Mathews Mansion Museum

A National Historic Landmark, this lavish Victorian stone mansion is true extravagance. Originally built in 1864 as a summer home for Norwalk native Legrand Lockwood, Wall Street investment banker and railroad magnate, this remarkable four-story château redefines splendor and elegance as it displays the craftsmanship of the finest American and European artisans of the time. Incredibly fine inlaid woodwork, marble columns, frescoed walls, gold-leafed ceilings, crystal chandeliers, sweeping staircases, and decorative arts of all kinds are found throughout the fifty rooms that surround the mansion's magnificent skylit octagonal rotunda.

Hour-long guided tours of the mostly restored first and second floors are preceded by a short film describing the painstaking ongoing restoration. A Victorian gift shop and lovely grounds are also available for browsing and strolling. Annual events include a Victorian Ice Cream Social in early summer and a crafts fair in mid-July.

295 West Avenue, just a hair north of SoNo and I–95 (203–838–9799). Open mid-March through December, Wednesday through Sunday from noon to 5:00 P.M. Closed on major holidays. Last tour an hour prior to closing. Adults $8.00, seniors and students $5.00, children under 12 free.

SONO HISTORIC DISTRICT AND SONO ARTS CELEBRATION

The restored waterfront area called South Norwalk is listed on the National Register of Historic Places, and its comeback from decay is a tribute to the City of Norwalk. Centered on Washington, Water, and South Main Streets, SoNo is a picturesque neighborhood of boutiques, restaurants, art galleries, and other attractions. In addition to the Maritime Aquarium, you'll find the dock for the eco-cruise boat *Oceanic,* and the Norwalk Museum. Lining the streets of SoNo are shops selling beads, dollhouses, hand-painted pottery, funky light fixtures, and everything else under the sun.

If you like the arts, come to SoNo during the first full weekend in August for the three-day **SoNo Arts Celebration,** held annually for more than twenty years (203–866–7916). Hundreds of juried fine artists exhibit their work in a sidewalk show spanning several blocks. Continual live-music performances, an antique auto parade, dance exhibitions, a silent film fest, and an extraordinary giant puppet parade are all part of the midsummer festivities. A children's area offers entertainment and hands-on projects specially designed for young artists.

Stepping Stones Museum for Children

Based on the idea that children learn best through interactive, hands-on investigation and discovery, this marvelous, state-of-the-art interactive learning center is a "Please touch" fantasyland located on its own five-acre space in Mathews Park, just steps away from the Lockwood-Mathews Mansion Museum. Firmly rooted in down-to-earth philosophies regarding the nourishment and encouragement of a child's sense of wonder and curiosity, Stepping Stones branches upward and outward from the point of view that kids love and need to use all their senses as they learn.

In diverse exhibits that incorporate elements of the arts, science and technology, and culture and heritage, children (and their caregivers) can immerse themselves in irresistible, sensory-rich environments guaranteed to educate as well as entertain. The museum's only permanent exhibit is its entrancing Color Coaster, a 27-foot-tall kinetic sculpture.

Mesmerizing visitors with an ever-changing interplay of color, light, and shape, this giant mechanical toy is in constant motion near the entrance to this wonderland. Beyond it, in a variety of learning labs, galleries, theaters, and outdoor celebration areas, are such changing exhibits as Toddler Terrain, Waterscape, I Spy Connecticut, Express Yourself!, and In the Works.

The youngest visitors entering the tot-friendly Toddler Terrain can crawl into a giant tree or cross a carpeted "pond"—on stepping stones, of course. Or, they might check out the Busy Wall of mirrors, gears, doors, and noisemakers. There's even an Infant Oasis for truly tiny patrons. In Waterscape, children enter the gallery under a giant see-through umbrella that protects them from an overhead rainstorm, the runoff from which is channeled into model streambeds, dams, and waterwheels. Here children learn about such concepts as flotation and currents as they play in the interactive greenhouse environment. I Spy Connecticut invites kids to take simulated helicopter, train, and submarine rides to see the state by air, land, and sea. Through such props as mechanical devices, mazes, musical instruments, and puzzles, Express Yourself! and In the Works encourage experimentation, problem solving, and the development of varied verbal and nonverbal communications skills.

Special community and museum events, theater performances, workshops by artists and educators, a center of resource materials for parents and teachers, and a year-round calendar of outdoor activities are among the unique aspects to look for in this museum's bright future. One of the best such learning environments in the country and the only one of its kind in Connecticut, Stepping Stones is definitely a don't-miss-it sure bet for families with young children.

303 West Avenue, in Mathews Park, near the junction of I–95 (exit 14 north or exit 15 south) and Route 7 (203–899–0606). Web site: www.steppingstonesmuseum.org. Open Tuesday through Saturday 10:00 A.M. to 5:00 P.M, Sunday noon to 5:00 P.M. Also open on Monday from 10:00 A.M. to 5:00 P.M. in the summer, and on Monday holidays. Closed Christmas, Thanksgiving, and New Year's Day. Admission $6.00 per person; children under age 1 are free.

Seaport Islander *Cruises to Sheffield Island*

The clean and comfortable forty-four-passenger, U.S. Coast Guard–approved *Seaport Islander* offers a thirty-minute cruise to the outermost of the Norwalk Islands, where one can disembark for an hour, an afternoon, or a whole day of beachcombing, bird-watching, sunbathing, picnicking, hiking, or touring the beautiful 1868 stone lighthouse.

The friendly and knowledgeable *Seaport Islander* crew and captain offer a lively narration on the trip to the island. Once on dry land out at the island, passengers are free to spend their time as they choose. Most folks take the fifteen- to twenty-minute tour of the ten-room lighthouse, of course. Several of its rooms have been restored, and four flights of stairs lead to a lovely black-capped light tower. If you have time to spare, bring a picnic and spread a blanket under the oaks in the picnic grove for a leisurely lunch or brunch. No concessions are on the island, so bring your own snacks. Wear bathing suits and sunscreen so you can swim or comb the beach. A new environmentally friendly bathroom is on the island.

The sixty-acre island also includes the secluded **Stewart B. McKinney National Wildlife Refuge.** Within its boundaries is a 2,000-foot nature trail with observation deck, or you can encircle the refuge by walking the perimeter of the island. The last cruise departs the island at 5:30 P.M. on weekdays and 6:00 P.M. on weekends and holidays. The seating area on the *Seaport Islander* is covered to protect you from sun, wind, or inclement weather. A bathroom and a snack-and-drinks bar add to your comfort. The island is also open to private boaters. A dinghy service transports sailors from moorings to the island dock at a charge of $4.00 per adult, and $2.00 for children.

Board the Seaport Islander *at Hope Dock at the corner of Washington and Water Streets. Schedule and information (203–838–9444); special charters (203–334–9166). Web site: www.seaport.org. Weekends and holidays only from early May until the third week of June, with cruises at 11:00* A.M. *and 2:00* P.M.

AW, SHUCKS! OYSTERS!

The famed **Norwalk Oyster Festival** is held annually on the weekend after Labor Day. The huge waterfront festival celebrates Long Island Sound and its seafaring past, as well as the delicious bluepoint eastern oysters that have made Norwalk's oystermen among the most successful farmers of the sea in history. Festival events include entertainment, an arts and crafts show, tall ship tours, an oyster shucking contest, and the typical foods and hoopla of summer festivals. Don't deny yourself the pleasure (203–838–9444).

From late June through Labor Day, cruises depart at 11:00 A.M. and 2:00 P.M. on weekdays; on weekends and holidays, cruises depart at 10:00 A.M., 1:00 P.M., and 4:00 P.M.. Sunset cruises also offered in season at 7:00 P.M. Seating is first-come, first-served. Adults and seniors $15.00; $2.00 discount on Monday and Tuesday for seniors. Children under 12, $12.00; children under 3, $5.00. Thursday evening New England clambakes (late June through late September, 6:00 to 9:40 P.M.) on the island are $45 per person.

Boat Excursions and Charters

Oceanic Eco-cruises From the Maritime Aquarium dock at the Norwalk River (203–852–0700, extension 206). The Maritime Aquarium offers two-and-a-half-hour cruises on its research vessel, the 40-foot trawler *Oceanic*. On weekends from December through March, weather permitting, public cruises set out to see the harbor seals that inhabit the Sound during the coldest months. Naturalists explain the marine plant and animal life and the laws protecting them. Summer cruises have onboard educators who explain the ecology of the Sound as participants study the marine life by collecting water samples, hauling a trawl net, examining the catch in the shipboard touch tank, and using a video microscope to view the tiny plants and animals that sustain life throughout the Sound. These Marinelife Study Cruises are daily at 1:00 P.M. from July 1 through Labor Day and on Saturday and Sunday only in May, June, and September. All adults and children pay $17 for both summer and winter cruises. Reservations recommended.

Island Princess 144 Water Street (203–852–7241). Sailing from its dock at the Norwalk Cove Marina, this vessel is the only two-deck side-wheeler in the Northeast; from May through October Captain Wendy offers daily one-and-a-half-hour harbor cruises of the Norwalk Islands and out to the Green Ledge lighthouse.(adults, $15; children $10; under 3 free; private charters for up to 140 passengers). The enclosed, climate-controlled main deck has a full bar and galley; the upper open-air promenade deck is covered and can be curtained in case of inclement weather. Cocktail and dinner cruises. Call for a public sail schedule or for further information on charters.

Odyssey Norwalk Cove Marina. On a beautiful sailboat, book half-day and full-day outings or extended overnight adventures. Up to six passengers. Sea kayaks on board. Web site: www.sailodyssey.com

White Creek Expeditions 99 Mayanos Road, New Canaan (203–966–0040). Freshwater and saltwater canoeing and kayaking; guided trips and instruction.

ROWAYTON

One of Connecticut's most charming shoreline communities is Norwalk's tiny village of Rowayton, which hugs the border of Darien and edges out into the Sound at Noroton Point. A bare square mile of quaint seaside streets, it is lined with residences, from delightfully unique renovations to traditional New England cottages dating from before the turn of the twentieth century. Boatyards, marinas, and beaches rub shoulders with pocket parks, art galleries, and a small selection of restaurants and delis.

If you happen to be in Darien, follow Tokeneke Road across the Five Mile River to Cudlipp Street, then south on Rowayton Avenue to reach the diminutive center of "downtown" Rowayton. Or from South Norwalk, take Washington Street to Dr. Martin Luther King Jr. Boulevard to Wilson Avenue (Route 136 South) and wander into the enclave through the back door. An especially picturesque route is down Wilson Avenue to Bluff Avenue to Westmere, then a block south on Yarmouth, a right turn on Crescent Beach Road, a right turn up Ensign Road, a left on Pine Point to a right on Roton Avenue, and then a left on Crockett Street to Rowayton Avenue. This route is wonderful for bikers, walkers, and drivers, taking visitors through the Bell Island and Roton Point sections. Allow time for stops at **Bayley Beach** or the tiny waterfront park near the base of Rowayton Avenue.

Linger for a meal at the outstanding **Restaurant at Rowayton Seafood** (see Places to Eat), the bright and artsy **Bistro du Soleil** (162 Rowayton Avenue; 203-855-9469), or the **Rowayton Food Market** (157 Rowayton Avenue; 203-852-0011), for gourmet-quality take-out and picnic fare. (*Pssst:* Take your meal out to the market's back porch overlooking the Five Mile River; it's one of the prettiest spots in the village.) **Pinkney Park** is a special delight in summer; if you are lucky you may catch its annual **Summer Arts Festival** or see one of its annual **Shakespeare in the Park** productions, held for four or five days in late June at 7:30 P.M. (call 203-851-1657 for information). Be sure to stop by the three galleries of fine art at the **Rowayton Arts Center** (145 Rowayton Avenue; 203-866-2744). If the sirens of the sea lure you, rent a kayak from **Below Deck** at the Market and take to the water.

Small Boat Shop 144 Water Street (203-854-5223). Guided sea kayak tours of Norwalk Harbor and the Norwalk Islands, weekends and holidays from mid-May through October, weather permitting. No experience necessary; reservations required.

Sound Sailing Center 54 Beach Road (203-838-1110). Private and group sailing instruction for all ages at all levels, plus rentals of sailboats, catamarans, and cabin cruisers. Adventure sailing trips from three hours to a full week.

Overton's Boat Livery 80 Seaview Avenue. Rentals of 16-foot dories for sightseeing and fishing from May through October, weather permitting.

Places to Eat in Norwalk

Harbor Lights 82 Seaview Avenue (203-866-3364). On the east side of the Norwalk River opposite the SoNo riverbank is this reasonably priced, cheerful establishment serving generous portions of fresh seafood, pastas, crusty breads, redolent soups and chowders, and house-made desserts. Excellent mussels; perfect lobster. Porch open in summer, heated and closed in winter, for year-round delights. Open for lunch and dinner daily. $$-$$$$

Silvermine Tavern 194 Perry Avenue (203-847-4558). For romantic dining on New England–style cuisine in an eighteenth-century setting, reserve a table here. Antiques and folk art, crackling fireplaces in winter, and alfresco summertime dining on a tree-shaded deck overlooking the pond are some of the features that lure regulars and travelers, the latter of which can stay overnight in the inn's guest rooms (see *Places to Stay*). Inn Late Jazz nights year-round on Friday and Saturday from 9:00 P.M. to midnight; New England Buffet dinner ($17.95) every Thursday from 6:00 to 9:00 P.M., with Dixieland jazz. Open year-round Wednesday through Saturday for lunch from noon to 3:00 P.M. and dinner from 6:00 P.M., plus Sunday champagne buffet brunch 11:00 A.M. to 2:30 P.M. and Sunday dinner 3:00 to 9:00 P.M. $$$

The Restaurant at Rowayton Seafood 89 Rowayton Avenue (203-866-4488). For outstanding seafood, great views, and an unbeatable ambiance overlooking the Five Mile River, try the restaurant adjacent to the fish market in the lovely hamlet of Rowayton. For lunch, try the barbecued shrimp sandwich on a Portuguese roll with Monterey Jack cheese and onions; for dinner indulge in oysters, scallops, salmon, and other seafood dishes, plus salads, appetizers, and more. Open daily year-round for lunch and dinner, plus Sunday brunch. $$$-$$$$

LIFE-IN-CONNECTICUT WPA MURALS

Norwalk is home to yet another treasure, this one located right in its City Hall at 125 East Avenue. The hallways here are hung with a series of murals that are one of the nation's most important collections of Depression-era art. Bright and beautiful, these **Life-in-Connecticut murals** were a federal art project sponsored by the 1930s Works Progress Administration. Several of the nearly twenty restored paintings feature scenes of Connecticut history, from the Indians selling land to Roger Ludlow to such events as the Great Connecticut State Fair at Danbury.

Contact Ralph Bloom, the city's historical curator (203-866-0202), if you'd like to arrange a $3.00 per person guided tour. The murals can be visited without a tour year-round, Monday through Friday from 9:00 A.M. to 5:00 P.M., unless City Hall is closed for a major holiday.

River Cat Grill 148 Rowayton Avenue (203-854-0860). Most dishes here come in appetizer-size portions, so it's easy to indulge in a sampler of great food at moderate prices. In the dining room, out on the terrace, or in the bar, try the Maryland crab and cod cake with mango, red onion, and red pepper relish or the pan-roasted duck breast with a lemon, honey, and peppercorn glaze, or maybe fettucine with mussels and scallops in a saffron lobster broth. Save room for the exquisite desserts; chocolate freaks won't be disappointed here. Come back for brunch; the raisin French toast is tops. Open for lunch and dinner from 11:30 A.M. Tuesday through Sunday. $$-$$$

Match 98 Washington Street (203-852-1088). The wood-burning oven turns out incredible thin-crust pizza, to be sure, but much more awaits sophisticated diners here. Ultra-chic minimalist/industrial decor; vibrant colors to match the stylish, young clientele that comes to eat, then stays late to party. Excellent roasted chicken, grilled swordfish, handmade ravioli; mouth-tantalizing desserts. Open for dinner only, daily. $$-$$$$

Ocean Drive 128 Washington Street (203-855-1665). Casual but oh-so chic and right on the pulse of all that is hot in SoNo, this joint is hoppin' on two levels, with windows wide open in summer to the street scene outside. A fabulous oyster bar features twenty-five varieties shipped from around the world. Five kitchen areas prepare fresh fish, pasta dishes, grilled "shish" of chicken, shrimp, and steak, chops and burgers and lobsters done just about every way imaginable. Private cabanas in a wraparound balcony and a fabulous Dale Chihuly glass chandelier go a long way in adding to the dynamic ambiance here. Open daily for lunch and dinner and beyond. $$$

New York Pizzeria and Trattoria 58–60 North Main Street (203–866–9068) The best pizza in town is found in the heart of SoNo. Jack and Nick Chiaramonte make fantastic, authentic New York–style pizza, all kinds of traditional Italian pasta dishes, salads, wraps, calzones, grinders, and much more. You'll be happy and well fed no matter what you order. Bring the whole family—the fare is a bargain. Open daily for lunch and dinner. $–$$

Places to Stay in Norwalk

Courtyard by Marriott–Norwalk 475 Main Avenue (203–849–9111 or 800–647–7578). One hundred forty-five units with one king-size or two double beds, plus twelve suites. Restaurant, lounge, health club, whirlpool,

AN ISLAND GETAWAY

During the 1800s and early 1900s many families lived on the Norwalk Islands. One farmer raised his sheep on Sheffield Island and separated the ewes from the rams by driving the males across the sandbar at very low tide to a neighboring island, which soon became known as Ram Island. Once used by Mormon missionaries as a place to baptize converts without being bothered by onlookers, Ram Island was also the site of one of several noxious fish-oil rendering plants. Early environmentalists protested the smoke and odor that wafted from the island to the mainland, and the plants were shut down in the late 1880s. The island has been renamed Shea Island in honor of Norwalk's Vietnam War hero Daniel Shea. Home to sparrow hawks, herons, and egrets, the city-owned island has a swimming and picnic area that can be enjoyed by visiting boaters. Camping is allowed on the eastern shore near Ram Historical Park. Call the Norwalk Parks and Recreation Department (203–854–7806) for information.

indoor pool, laundry facility, dry cleaning service. Moderate weekend rates; discounts for seniors. Complimentary breakfast buffet. $$$-$$$$

Norwalk Inn & Conference Center 99 East Avenue (203-838-5531 or 800-537-8483). Seventy-one units, including three suites, restaurant, lounge, coffee shop, outdoor pool. Senior citizen rates. $$$$

Four Points Hotel by Sheraton 426 Main Avenue (203-849-9828 or 888-806-4786). One hundred twenty-seven units with two suites, restaurant, lounge, exercise room. Lower weekend rates and senior discounts. $$$

Club Hotel by Double Tree 789 Connecticut Avenue (203-853-3477 or 888-444-2582). Two hundred sixty-eight units, restaurant, lounge, indoor pool, sauna, fitness room. Club Room with self-service business center and personal office space. Senior discounts; lower rates on weekends. $$$$

Silvermine Tavern 194 Perry Avenue at Silvermine Avenue (203-847-4558). This rambling 1785 country inn is set on the banks of the Silvermine River by a waterfall that lulls happy dreamers to sleep at night. Ten guest rooms, all with private baths, some with antique canopied double or queen-size beds, some with two single beds—all equally charming and immaculate. Award-winning restaurant (see *Places to Eat*) serves traditional New England cuisine; guests receive a complimentary continental breakfast featuring the tavern's famed honey buns. $$$-$$$

Public Boat Launch

Norwalk Visitors' Dock Veterans Memorial Park (203-849-8823). Public boat launch ramp, water, pump-out service, snack bar, bait, dockage for twenty transient boats.

For Further Information

Norwalk Seaport Association 132 Water Street, South Norwalk 06854 (203-838-9444 or 888-701-7785). Information on boat charters, excursion cruises, special events in South Norwalk, events on Sheffield Island, public clambakes, and annual festivals such as the Oyster Festival (the weekend after Labor Day), the SoNo Arts Celebration (the first full weekend in August), and Norwalk Harborsplash (the third weekend in May), an annual festival celebrating the waterfront with harbor tours, walking tours, clam chowder cook-offs, boating activities, and performing and visual arts.

Norwalk Parks and Recreation (203-854-7806). Information on nonresident use of the parks and beaches. **Cranbury Park** on Grumman Avenue has 8 miles of hiking and mountain biking trails, plus picnic areas and lawns for games and ball-playing. Nonresidents are welcome at any time at no charge. Nonresidents can park at **Calf Pasture Beach** at any time at no charge in the off-season and for $15 daily from Memorial Day to Labor Day. No cooking is allowed at Calf Pasture. Adjacent **Shady Beach** allows cooking but does not offer nonresident parking. If you want to cook, park at Calf Pasture and walk to Shady Beach.

Westport

Westport usually needs no introduction. Long famous as a haven for writers, actors, artists, and other glitterati, it is well-known as the suburb of suburbs, with a dash of panache rivaled only by its imitators. Though more crowded with high-priced automobiles than ever before, it still has the same old zing. Travelers are often drawn to Westport by the hype about its astonishing shopping opportunities and its famed residents. The truth lies somewhere in the midst of the many lines of hyperbole—you *might* be seated next to Paul Newman at his favorite Italian restaurant, and you *might* run into Redford or some other seasonal resident at the Baskin Robbins ice cream emporium, but chances are you won't. Better to enjoy the shops, the restaurants, and the entertainments for what they can more obviously offer to you.

Travelers intent on discovering the natural wonders of Westport will be attracted to its beaches and woodlands. While few of the town's typical tourists would start a tour of Westport in its quieter corners of nature, most would agree that once the thrill of browsing and buying in the shops wears off, the spirit is restored by the more prosaic qualities of the woodlands and wetlands. In whatever order you choose to enjoy Westport's attractions, be sure to save time for an evening performance at one of its equally famed stages. More than in any other place on the Connecticut shore, the stars come out in Westport.

The Best of Westport

Earthplace: The Nature Discovery Center

Open 365 days a year from dawn to dusk, this outstanding nature haven features the sixty-two-acre Wildlife Sanctuary with 2 miles of trails for all ages. A Swamp Loop Trail, an open field habitat, and a trail for the blind are among the several options outside. A universal-access nature trail welcomes all visitors, including those with special challenges. A lovely wildflower courtyard and a bird and butterfly garden showcase both native and introduced plants.

Inside Earthplace's 20,000-square-foot museum, a large live-animal hall with many species of indigenous animals is often the site of live animal demonstrations. A Discovery Room with changing displays on ecology and animal biology, a native plant court, a working water-quality lab, a wildlife rehab center, a variety of dioramas and aquariums, a marine touch tank, and a great gift shop are all here. Plans are underway to re-create the Exhibit Hall with interactive areas such as the "Tiny Treehouse" and the "Explorer's Clubhouse."

Perhaps best of all, though, are the special events, workshops, guided walks, outdoor classes, and summer camp programs. Beach walks, maple sugaring, bird banding, Earth Day activities, junior naturalist groups, a holiday fair, and more are open to all visitors. Some are free; others require reservations and tuition. If none of those options appeal, still come to this little slice of wilderness—wild turkeys, pheasants, red foxes, deer, hawks, songbirds, and more await you. Weekends are best in summer, when the popular weekday activities are not in session.

10 Woodside Lane (203–227–7253). Web site: www.naturecenterwestport.org. Open year-round. Grounds, 7:00 A.M. to dusk; building, 9:00 A.M. to 5:00 P.M. Monday through Saturday, 1:00 to 4:00 P.M. Sunday. Closed on major holidays. Adults are invited to donate $2.00; children, $1.00.

Sherwood Island State Park

One of the state's most popular sites on the Sound, this park's mile-and-a-half-long beach is preceded by 234 acres of open space, two picnic groves, and several sorts of drives, footpaths, and walkways. Swimming, fishing, and scuba diving or snorkeling are permitted (scuba divers must register at the ranger station) at all times, but lifeguards are on duty only from Memorial Day to Labor Day; during this time they won't let you bring inflatable water toys, boats, canoes, or kayaks into the water.

Come here for saltwater shore fishing and clamming, kite-flying, volley-ball, badminton, horseshoes, softball, bocce, and bicycling. Bring your own equipment for all of the above. No animals are allowed in the park in the summertime. From September 30 to April 15 you can bring them, but dogs must be leashed.

The park's appeal to lovers of Long Island Sound is enhanced by a self-guided interpretive nature trail that points out flora, fauna, and special areas of interest on the Sound, its freshwater estuaries, and its shoreline. Just a half-mile long, the trail is perfect for seniors and fami-lies with young children. A small and very good nature center includes a touch tank, live-animal exhibits of native reptiles and amphibians, and shorebird specimens; it is linked by a handicapped-accessible foot-path to one of the park's brand-new bathhouses, located at the eastern and western ends of the beach. The bathhouses, built by United Stone America, include new lifeguard stations, first aid offices, and outdoor showers. The nature center is open 10:00 A.M. to 4:30 P.M. between Memorial Day and Labor Day, except on Mondays. A bird observation deck provides an overview of the shore habitat; bird-watchers are wel-come year-round. More than 280 bird species have been recorded here.

The park provides public rest rooms, changing rooms, and showers at no additional charge. Only the rest rooms function in the winter. The concession stand at the beach's large pavilion offers food, drink, candy, and some souvenirs, and folks are welcome to picnic or barbecue.

Off I–95 exit 18. Turn south at the end of the ramp and drive directly into the park (203–226–6983). Open daily year-round, 8:00 A.M. to one half-hour before sunset. Admission per vehicle, $5.00 with Connecticut plates, $8.00 with out-of-state plates from Memorial Day to Labor Day on weekdays. On weekends and holidays from Memorial Day to Labor Day these rates are $7.00 and $12.00, respectively. Off-season parking is free, except on weekends in May and September, when the charge is $5.00 Connecticut and $8.00 out-of-state.

Westport Country Playhouse

For nearly seventy-five years, this wonderful summer-stock playhouse has offered hundreds of professional productions starring such legends as Henry Fonda, Helen Hayes, Jessica Tandy, Gene Kelly, Liza Minnelli, Cicely Tyson, and many, many others. Located in a cow barn-turned-tanning factory and now a rustic country theater with post-and-beam construction and red-cushioned bench-style seating, the playhouse is a Fairfield County fixture and one of the few remaining professional stock theaters in the Northeast.

ON THE SCENE DOWNTOWN

Go ahead and get the urge out of your system—trendy and upscale downtown Westport is the ideal place for an all-day shopping spree in any season. Both national chain stores and one-of-a-kind boutiques are densely but pleasantly packed into a relatively small area, also crammed with dozens of eateries purveying everything from egg creams and bagels to lobster thermidor. From army-navy surplus to haute couture, the clothing shops are filled with an array of goods matched only in Greenwich. If you can't put your finger on what you want in the environs of Main Street, Riverside Avenue, and the immediate stretch of the Post Road East near these two north-south arteries, you probably won't find it anywhere. If compelled, however, amble or drive a while farther along the east-west Post Road any distance from Norwalk to Fairfield—this route is basically wall-to-wall stores and nary a mall in sight.

Bargain-hunters should be sure to come to Westport in summer (for the exact dates, call the Westport Chamber of Commerce at 203-227-9234) for the **annual sidewalk sale.** The best of its kind probably anywhere, it is an unbelievably popular event with amazing goods sold at deeply discounted prices. Real detectives may want to peruse the famed racks of the **Westport Goodwill** (203-259-3943) on the Post Road, where a black cashmere Ann Taylor sweater can be salvaged for $5.00 as easily as a $30.00 Armani suit. For renewal at the end of an exhaustive spree, Sal Gilbertie's famous herbs, flowers, essential oils, and other wholesome garden goods are all on display and for sale in the beautiful greenhouses and shop (203-227-4175) at **Gilbertie's Herb Garden** on Sylvan Avenue off Riverside Avenue.

Now in the process of an exciting plan to redirect and refurbish, the playhouse is growing under the expert guidance of such theater greats as Paul Newman, as well as the creative talents of executive director Alison Harris and artistic director Joanne Woodward. Their collective dream is to infuse the playhouse with renewed energy and new voices to build upon the classic fare also treasured here. With the pluck, passion, and formidable intellects of these folks at work, theater lovers may even be able to enjoy the playhouse year-round one day soon. Construction of the new facilities and refurbishment of the old is slated for fall 2003. For now, approximately five shows per season, from early June until mid-September, bring musicals, comedies, dramas, and classics to the stage. Refreshments are served outside in the playhouse courtyard. Preshow performances by local musicians greet theatergoers as they arrive.

If you have young children in your party, call for a schedule of the theater's second most famous productions—its Children's Summer Theatre. For eight weeks in the summer of 2002, for instance, a new show was staged each week from mid-June through August 23. Shows were Fridays at 11:00 A.M. and 2:00 P.M. Fairy tale productions, magic shows, and sing-along concerts were among the productions. Tickets are about $10 (depending on which part of the theater you'd like) per ticket for children and adults.

25 Powers Court, just off Route 1 (203–226–0153 or 203–227–4177). Web site: www.westportplayhouse.org. Ticket prices vary; subscriptions as well as single tickets are sold for the season's series.

White Barn Theatre

The brand-new works of well-known as well as up-and-coming playwrights and performers are staged at this fifty-year-old converted rustic country barn venue run like an English theater club. All performances are at 8:00 P.M. on Friday, Saturday, and Sunday; a Saturday matinee is staged at 4:00 P.M. The Sunday evening show includes a post-performance reception that allows the audience to mingle with writers and actors.

452 Newtown Turnpike (203–227–3768). Web site: www.whitebarntheatre.org. Tickets are $30 and $35, subscriptions for the six-show season are $150 to $180. Student rush tickets are $10 per show, available thirty minutes before curtain.

Levitt Pavilion for the Performing Arts

Don't miss the festival atmosphere at the Levitt. Right on the banks of the Saugatuck River, this open-air series has offered approximately sixty evenings of entertainment every summer, from late June through late August, for the past thirty years. Bring a blanket and a picnic to the lawn in front of the band shell and enjoy the absolutely free performances.

Tuesday is Potpourri night—maybe swing, maybe the community band, maybe stories for children. Wednesday is Family and Children (theater, mime, puppetry, magic, storytelling, sing-alongs). Thursday is Classical/Cabaret/Theater; Friday is Party Time (maybe folk, reggae, bluegrass, or classic rock 'n' roll); Saturday is Pop/Rock/Blues; and Sunday

SAUGATUCK VALLEY TRAILS

A cooperative effort of Westport's Aspetuck Land Trust, the Bridge-port Hydraulic Company, the Connecticut Audubon Society, and the Nature Conservancy, with support from the towns of Weston and Redding, has resulted in the limited development of protected lands for hiking and some horseback riding in areas surrounding the Saugatuck River and its beautiful reservoir. Available to the public at no charge, the trails are open year-round. Open meadows, shaded mountain laurel groves, cascades and pools, marshes, and forested uplands are among the habitats and features in twenty-four separate preserves. Free maps of these areas are mailed to interested hikers who write to Aspetuck Land Trust, P. O. Box 444, Westport CT 06880. The trail map is considered a hiking permit, and all users must have one. Day-trippers can find the maps at the Westport Town Hall or the local libraries of Westport, Redding, or Weston. The maps show the location of parking areas and toilets. Adequate footwear is a must for these easy to strenuous trails.

is Big Band/Blues/Jazz. On most Mondays, there is no show, and occasional special events (usually just two per season) do have an admission charge. Call for a calendar.

Showtimes vary slightly, but Wednesday performances are always at 7:00 P.M. and most others are at 8:00 P.M. Fridays and Saturdays are designated as alcohol-free evenings. Park in one of the municipal lots in back of the Westport Public Library on Jesup Road off the Post Road East (Route 1) and walk up the gravel path toward the brownish band shell at the side of the river.

Jesup Road, behind the Westport Public Library (203–226–7600 for a calendar or 203–221–4422 for recorded information on the concert hotline). Web site: www.levittpavilion.com.

Boat Excursions and Charters

Longshore Sailing School 260 South Compo Road (203–226–4646). In addition to lessons with sailboats, catamarans, and sailboards for all skill levels from ages 9 and up, this well-reputed sailing school offers rentals of sailboats, canoes, sea kayaks, sailboards, and rowboats. Available June through August.

My Bonnie Captain Sal Tardella (203-866-6313) Village Creek Dock. Charter fishing trips, up to six passengers.

Middlebank Captains Lauren and Timothy Griffith (203-655-5918). Cove Marina. Full- and half-day trips.

Places to Eat in Westport

Miramar 2 Post Road West (203-222-2267 or 800-628-4255). This restaurant consistently presents award-winning continental cuisine and impeccably elegant style. Open for dinner Tuesday through Sunday, this four-star establishment is an unforgettable albeit expensive experience. After your meal, take a stroll along the riverfront boardwalk in this restored historic wharf area on the Saugatuck River. Patio in season. Reservations a must. $$$$

Da Pietro 36 Riverside Avenue (203-454-1213). This self-described romantic storefront cafe transports patrons to the south of France or the north of Italy with the award-winning menu of owner/chef Pietro Scotti. A relaxing and enticing dining experience rated excellent by the *New York Times* and voted best Italian in the state by readers of *Connecticut* magazine. Open for dinner only, Monday through Saturday. $$$-$$$$

Splash 260 Compo Road South (203-454-7798). Rave reviews continue for this refreshing contemporary restaurant in Longshore Club Park. Pacific Rim cuisine means lots of fresh seafood and other dishes with a creative, tropical flair. Outdoor dining on a wraparound porch in warm months; a cozy new dining room perfect for winter evenings; the **Patio** bar with live music on Sundays from 4:00 to 8:00 P.M. Views of the Sound indoors and out. Open daily for lunch 11:30 A.M. to 2:30 P.M. and dinner from 5:30 P.M. $$$-$$$$

Tengda 1330 Post Road (203-255-6115). My new favorite in Westport is the marvelous Asian fusion restaurant that offers superior sushi plus excellent Thai, Malaysian, and Chinese dishes in a snappy contemporary setting that used to be one of the most romantic Italian restaurants in the county. The transformation is complete and delicious. Don't hesitate to go in a group and share. Open for lunch and dinner daily. $-$$$

Bridge Cafe 5 Riverside Avenue (203-226-4800). Casually elegant continental

A TASTE OF WESTPORT HISTORY

The 1795 **Wheeler House** is the home of the Westport Historical Society, the docents of which would be happy to let visitors in on some of the local lore and legend. Westport enjoyed quiet beginnings in the mid-seventeenth century, with settlements in what were then parts of both Fairfield and Norwalk. Not too much happened in the area except some nasty dealings with the natives and some fairly efficient forest clearing and farmstead building. During the Revolution, a little action came to Westport in the form of a notable raid by the Brits on Compo Beach and some handy efforts at retaliation on the parts of the colonial minutemen, some of whom followed the Redcoats to the Battle of Ridgefield and skirmished with them again in Westport after their retreat from Danbury.

After that first Fourth of July, Westport went back, for the most part, to farming, small manufacturing, shipping, and warehousing goods bound for other parts of the world. For a hundred years or so, not a lot changed until the railroad brought the cityfolk to town, and Westport became a New York suburb with a flair for the dramatic.

The Wheeler House re-creates the nineteenth century pretty tidily in its restored Victorian parlor, bedroom, and kitchen, its costume collection, its unusual octagonal-roofed cobblestone barn, and its changing exhibitions on Westport history from prehistoric to contemporary times. The museum is open year-round Tuesday through Saturday from 10:00 A.M. to 3:00 P.M. (203–222-1424). A donation is suggested.

restaurant on the Saugatuck River serving exceptional seafood, delicious veal, poultry, and beef, creative pastas, and outstanding desserts. Tile floors and stuccoed walls in soft colors inside; outdoor patio in warm seasons. Open for lunch Monday through Friday 11:30 A.M. to 2:30 P.M. and Saturday and Sunday until 3:00 P.M. Open for dinner Monday through Saturday from 5:30 P.M. and Sunday from 5:00 P.M. $$$-$$$$

Acqua 43 Main Street (203-222-8899). Marvelous Mediterranean menu with an emphasis on seafood. Excellent appetizers, wonderful pastas, inventive thin-crust pizzas made in a wood-burning oven. In the heart of the downtown shopping district, this casual but sophisticated restaurant has

THE GREAT RACE

One of the most entertaining Westport festivities is the annual Great Race on the Saugatuck River. A series of small-craft competitions for canoes, kayaks, and racing shells underscores the serious side of the race, but an amusing collection of homemade vessels of every description adds a whole lot of levity to the spectacle. Judged for the creativity and originality of their appearance and for their propulsion method, the watercraft ride the tides sometime in mid-July, often coinciding with the excellent two-day **Westport Outdoor Art Show** in downtown Westport and along the banks of the Saugatuck. The put-in point for the race is usually somewhere close to the Post Road bridge across the river; the best viewing spots are in the riverside park on the eastern bank (behind the Westport Public Library at the Levitt Pavilion) or from various vantage points along Riverside Avenue on the western shore. Call for further information on the race (203-454-6564) or the art show (203-226-4261).

an upstairs bar with views of the river. Open for dinner Monday through Saturday from 5:30 P.M. Closed Sunday. $$-$$$$

Places to Stay in Westport

Westport Inn 1595 Post Road East (203-259-5236 or 800-446-8997). Web site: www.westportinn.com. Full-service hotel with 116 units, heated indoor pool, fitness center, whirlpool, sauna, Gennaro's restaurant, lounge, entertainment. Newly renovated traditional country rooms in the inn's original wing; check to be sure your room has been updated. Senior discounts and weekend packages. $$$$

The Inn at Longshore 260 Compo Road South (203-226-3316). Formerly a summer estate, built in the 1890s, this seaside inn at town-owned Longshore Club Park offers lodging right on the Sound. The twelve comfortably decorated rooms (including three one-bedroom suites) have a New England flair. All have private baths and air-conditioning. Some rooms have wide-angle views of the Sound; others offer limited seascapes. Among the extras are two outdoor pools and beach swimming, boating, tennis courts, a golf course with guest privileges and options for cross-country skiing in the winter, and a children's playground. Complimentary continental breakfast. Adjacent restaurant for lunch and dinner (see Splash, page 48.) $$$$

The Inn at National Hall 2 Post Road West (203-221-1351 or 800-628-4255). Web site: www.innatnationalhall.com Fabulously luxurious inn in historic 1873 National Register Italianate brick building overlooking the Saugatuck River in the heart of downtown. Fifteen rooms, including seven suites, each equally stunning but all unique. Top-of-the-line everything is everywhere; this inn is a cut above the cream of the crop. Massage services can be arranged; guest privileges at the Westport YMCA are complimentary, as is continental or full breakfast. AAA five-diamond award. Award-winning Miramar restaurant on the first floor (see Places to Eat, page 48). $$$$

Public Boat Launch

Saugatuck River Ramp Access on eastern bank under I-95. Take Route 136 south onto Compo Road; first right to launch area. Parking for twenty-five cars. Seasonal weekend and holiday parking fee.

For Further Information

Westport Chamber of Commerce (203-227-9234). Maps, brochures, information on lodging, restaurants, annual events.

Westport Parks and Recreation (203-341-5090). Information on nonresident use of beaches and parks. Policy has been $10 per car for nonresidents on weekdays and $25 per vehicle on weekends and holidays. Inquire about use and launching of car-top boats. The beach parks at Compo Beach and the Longshore Club have playgrounds, snack bars, showers, changing rooms, rest rooms, grills, and picnic tables. For information on use of golf course at Longshore Club Park, call (203) 341-1833.

Westport Community Theatre 110 Myrtle Avenue (203-226-1983). Nearly half a century of comedies, musicals, and classical and contemporary drama by such playwrights as Hellman, O'Casey, Wilde, Shakespeare, and Williams. Intimate theater located in back of the Westport Town Hall. Call for a calendar of September through June productions and ticket information.

Westport Arts Center 431 Post Road East, Suite 8 (203-226-1806). This center for the performing and visual arts offers exhibitions, performances, and workshops throughout the year. Call for information on programs and special seasonal and annual events.

Fairfield

Fairfield's position on the coast of Long Island Sound was no mere coincidence when it was settled by the English in 1639. A string of such settlements along the shore had sprung from the importance of the estuary as a maritime highway in a time when sailing vessels provided the quickest means of transporting people and goods. In the seventeenth century, bedraggled colonists traveling by land struggled through Connecticut's swamps and marshes, hacked their way through forests, and depended on rudimentary ferries to carry them across rivers. When Captain John Mason and Roger Ludlow, deputy governor of the Connecticut colony, arrived in the native village of Unquowa after harrying the Pequots from Mystic all the way to the swamp at Sasqua, they were no doubt exhausted. Apparently a fair amount of adrenaline, combined with a belief that the Divine Lord *wanted* the English to destroy the fearful Pequots, helped Ludlow complete the colony's mission of decimating the tribe's remaining eighty warriors. Ludlow and his compatriots spared the 200 old men, women, and children who hid in the thickets of the swamp, then promptly claimed the land for the colony and renamed its native villages Fairfield and Southport.

Beleaguered area tribes (who had themselves suffered at the hands of the dominant and often vicious Pequots) were all too happy at the time to give land to the triumphant English who had subdued their enemy. At the completion of the negotiations, Ludlow had secured the nearly 140 square miles of shoreline and woodland that made up Fairfield. Soon the fair fields of Unquowa and Sasqua had been sown with English seed, and farming and shipping interests replaced the less intrusive lifeways of the natives. Fairfield's entrepreneurial citizens capitalized on its location on the Sound, and by the eighteenth century the development of water-powered mills and shipping wharves led to the growth of the grain, lumber, cider, textile, and shipbuilding industries.

Populated mostly by farmers, tradesmen, sailors, and shipbuilders through much of the eighteenth century, the town was burned in 1779 by Hessian troops under the command of British Major General William Tryon. Rebuilding was slow but determined, and soon the community had rallied as the busy Southport and Black Rock harbors helped to reestablish Fairfield's place as an important port of entry.

Two centuries later, Fairfield's shoreline location still influences life in this thriving, comfortable community. Today the interstate highway system, railroads, and air transportation relieve the town's dependence on the Sound, leaving its coastline open for mostly recreational activities. The onion fields that once flourished in Southport are long gone; the mills and factories supported by an immigrant workforce are mostly closed. Now largely residential, Fairfield attracts newcomers looking for a suburban setting within commuting distance of larger cities. As one of Connecticut's oldest towns, Fairfield holds beautiful historical homes and still-quaint village centers within its now 30 square miles. These classically New England sights, plus 8 miles of shoreline and sophisticated options for entertainment, dining, and shopping, keep Fairfield on the map for shoreline day-trippers.

The Best of Fairfield

Ogden House and Gardens

An excellent historical site for those interested in pre-Revolutionary life, Ogden House is a 1750 saltbox farmhouse furnished to portray the lives of its first inhabitants, Jane and David Ogden. Owned by the Ogden family for 125 years, the house has been meticulously restored and accurately outfitted with artifacts mentioned in the original household inventory. An eighteenth-century kitchen garden and a native wildflower woodland garden are also on the picturesque property overlooking Brown's Brook near Mill River.

In addition to annual events celebrating the gardens and the seasons, Ogden House offers workshops, lectures, and activities for visitors of all ages. A Hands-On History Camp for children 8 to 11 is held annually during the second week in July, and high school students can make reservations to participate in the archaeological dig that takes place on the property from time to time.

1520 Bronson Road (203–259–6356 or 203–259–1598). Public tours of the house and gardens are offered from May through mid-October on Saturdays and Sundays from 1:00 to 4:30 P.M. Adults $2.00, children $1.00.

THE DOGWOOD FESTIVAL

While you visit the northern reaches of Fairfield, explore the neighborhood a bit. Graced by vintage homes as well as more modern mansions, the winding country roads take you through lightly populated residential enclaves and into a perfect antique village center punctuated by one of the nation's most stately Congregational churches. Known as Greenfield Hill, the area is heavily planted with dogwoods and is famed for its annual **Dogwood Festival** in mid-May.

To celebrate the gorgeous pink and white blossoms that open on more than 30,000 dogwoods, the Greenfield Hill Congregational Church (1045 Old Academy Road) plans a weeklong schedule of festivities that include an arts and crafts show, a plant sale, walking tours and sit-down luncheons, musical programs, a children's games and crafts area, and a white elephant sale. Buy food here or bring a picnic. For information, call the Fairfield Town Hall and ask for the current Festival Committee telephone number.

Fairfield Historical Society

In its Georgian-style brick home near the town green, this wonderfully curated small museum offers seasonal changing exhibitions as well as a permanent collection of paintings, prints, maps, costumes, furnishings, and fine decorative arts. Three spacious galleries showcase objects from pre-Revolutionary vintage to contemporary significance. In addition to household implements, tools, locally made furniture, and toys, are artifacts that relate to the town's role as a seaport during the eighteenth and nineteenth centuries. Notable among the museum's collections are its textiles, costumes, and an intriguing assortment of walking sticks.

636 Old Post Road (203–259–1598). Open 10:00 A.M. to 4:30 P.M. Tuesday through Saturday and from 1:00 to 4:30 P.M. on Sunday. Closed on Monday and major holidays. Suggested donation, adults $3.00, children $1.00.

Connecticut Audubon Birdcraft Museum and Sanctuary

This six-acre enclave was founded in 1914 as the first songbird sanctuary in the United States. Documented records of more than 120 species of birds have been kept for this vest-pocket site. Huge maples and century-old rhododendrons are along the trail that runs through the woodlands and across a beautiful wooden boardwalk above a shallow pond. A quarter-mile handicapped-accessible trail opens the property to all visitors. Sit awhile at the gazebo and listen to the birds and frogs. Look for the nesting night herons.

A vintage cottage on the property has been restored as the complex's visitor's center; a stop here will ensure that you are oriented to the varied attractions. In addition to a gift shop, a library, and rest rooms, it offers a hands-on nature observatory designed especially for families, with scopes, terraria, aquaria, and other tools for enjoying wildlife.

Inside the turn-of-the-century museum, designated as a National Historic Landmark, browse through galleries featuring the birds and mammals of New England, grouped in diorama displays by habitat and by seasons, and of Africa. The murals here are exceptional.

You can stroll through the Birdcraft on your own or take a one-hour guided tour, arranged by appointment. Be sure to plan a visit for the second Saturday of May and enjoy the annual International Migrating Bird Day. This is a festival of bird-watching, with crafts, a book sale, and lessons on how to landscape your own yard to attract birds.

314 Unquowa Road (203-259-0416). Web site: ctaudubon.org/centers/birdcraft/birdcraft.htm. Museum and sanctuary open year-round Tuesday to Friday from 10:00 A.M. to 5:00 P.M. and Saturday and Sunday from noon to 4:00 P.M. Adults $2.00; children under 14, $1.00.

Roy and Margot Larsen Bird Sanctuary and Connecticut Audubon Center at Fairfield

Created on reclaimed farm property, this 160-acre tract of New England woodland in the north end of town was built as a model wildlife sanctuary juxtaposing habitats and trails to allow people maximum opportunity to experience the diversity without disturbing the refuge. Marsh, wetlands, streams, vernal pools, meadows, coniferous forest, and second-growth areas of mature hardwoods are among the sanctuary's habitats. Laced throughout the property are 7 miles of trails, including a Trail for the Disabled. A butterfly meadow designed to attract native butterfly species and other indigenous insects features native vegetation that had been supplanted by invasive imported plants.

On site is the Connecticut Audubon Center at Fairfield (with natural science exhibits, a discovery room, a solar greenhouse, a non-circulating library, live animal displays, and an excellent gift shop/bookstore) and the Educational Birds of Prey Compound of non-releasable animals that the Audubon Society has rehabilitated. An Algonkian wigwam replica is also on site. Summer camps, workshops, naturalist-guided walks, junior naturalist programs, field trips, and a regular schedule of special events are open to visitors.

2325 Burr Street (203–259–6305). The Audubon nature center is open year-round, Tuesday through Saturday, from 9:00 A.M. to 4:30 P.M. and Sunday (except in July and August) from noon to 4:30 P.M. Closed on Mondays and major holidays. Admission is free. The bird sanctuary is open daily, year-round, from dawn to dusk; adults $2.00, children under 12, 50 cents.

Quick Center for the Arts

This facility on the campus of Fairfield University brings nationally and internationally acclaimed performers to the stage throughout the season from September to June. From student productions featuring the university choral groups and instrumental ensembles to such star talents as Emanuel Ax, Arlo Guthrie, Shawn Colvin, or the Urban Bush Women, the Quick Center offers single tickets and series subscriptions to its music, dance, and theater productions. A Young Audience series provides entertainment ranging from puppetry and magic shows to interpretations of classic literature and folk storytelling.

The Quick Center also has an outstanding gallery for fine arts exhibitions. Called the Thomas J. Walsh Art Gallery, it focuses on the works of contemporary painters, printmakers, sculptors, and photographers as well as exhibitions showcasing masterpieces of past centuries.

At Fairfield University; enter on North Benson Road (Box office: 203–254–4010; 877–ARTS–396 for ticket information or for full calendar of events and exhibitions.) Walsh Gallery open Tuesday through Saturday 11:00 A.M. to 5:00 P.M. and Sunday from noon to 4:00 P.M. Web site: www.quickcenter.com.

J. Russell Jinishian Gallery

Visitors with an appreciation for the beauty of the sea and ships may enjoy a visit to this outstanding gallery of marine and sporting art. Although the works are all museum-quality, this gallery is not, of course, a museum. The artworks are for sale and typically range in price from $500 to $50,000. Appreciative browsers are welcome to enjoy a look at these magnificent pieces before they find good homes.

At the Greenwich Workshop Gallery, 1657 Post Road (203–259–8753). Open to the public Tuesday through Saturday from 10:00 A.M. to 5:00 P.M. and by appointment. No charge to visit the collection.

BEACHIN' IT

Public access to Long Island Sound has long been a priority for the town of Fairfield. Five public beaches allow residents and visitors to enjoy fishing, swimming, boating, and beachcombing throughout the year. From Memorial Day to Labor Day, nonresidents must pay a day-use fee to park at either Jennings or Penfield beaches, payable in cash at the gate of either beach: $20 per vehicle on weekends, $12 during the week. To get a seasonal pass for unlimited use of the beaches throughout the summer season, purchase a windshield sticker ($75) at Independence Hall next to the Fairfield Town Hall at the corner of Beach Road and the Old Post Road. For further information, call the Fairfield Parks and Recreation department (203-256-3144).

Penfield Beach (Fairfield Beach Road) and **Jennings Beach** (South Benson Road) are the only two beaches open to nonresident vehicles. Both facilities have pavilions, concessions, rest rooms, showers, and playgrounds. In addition to its other amenities, Jennings Beach features the Sandcastle, a play structure for children; it is also a great place to watch the annual fireworks extravaganza on or near the Fourth of July.

Southport Beach (Pequot Avenue) is less crowded and has great sandbars for young children, rest rooms, and a small concession area. Its parking area is restricted to resident vehicles, but walkers and bikers are welcome. This beach is just past the pretty historic village center of Southport—a pleasant place to stroll and shop. For picnic goodies, pick up traditional American delicatessen staples at the classic **Southport Market** (203-259-8377; open 8:00 A.M. to 6:00 P.M. daily), on Pequot Avenue, or at the **Spic and Span Market** (203-259-1688; open 7:30 A.M. to 6:00 P.M. Monday through Saturday) across the way for goods with a gourmet flair. You can take your picnic to picturesque **Perry's Green** on Harbor Avenue adjacent to the Pequot Yacht Club, a five-minute walk from the village center, or park (at no charge) along the street.

PEQUOT LIBRARY BOOK SALE

If you are in Southport in late July, stop at the **Pequot Library's annual five-day book sale.** Nearly 100,000 books are collected each year, and the selection is fantastic. On the first day, book dealers and casual collectors alike arrive in droves to vie for the most desirable volumes. On this day (Friday), buyers pay twice the marked price; big spenders laying out $250 or more receive 20 percent off the doubled price. On Saturday and Sunday, the books are priced as marked; on Monday they are half of the marked price; and on Tuesday, all remaining books are free!

No admission is charged; the tents and doors open at 9:00 A.M. daily. On Friday the dash for the best titles ends at 8:00 P.M. On Saturday, Sunday, and Monday, the feeding frenzy is stopped at 5:30 P.M., and on Tuesday, you and your wheelbarrow have to be out by 3:00 P.M.

Built in 1887, the recently restored Romanesque revival library (203-259-0346) is a Southport landmark, located at 720 Pequot Avenue just before you round the bend to Southport Beach.

Places to Eat in Fairfield

Voila! 70 Reef Road (203-254-2070). This "bistro française" is Fairfield's most charming eatery, tiny and lace-trimmed, French-owned and utterly delicious. Soft pink walls and black-and-white napery give a pleasing and promising message that lovely surprises will follow—and they do. Try the coquilles St. Jacques Provençale, the marvelous cheese soufflé, or the panfried monkfish. Perfect crusty breads, excellent desserts made in the patisserie at the rear of the same building, and a well-chosen wine list make lunch or dinner here a complete delight. Open Monday through Saturday for lunch from 11:30 to 2:30 P.M. and dinner from 5:30 to 10:00 P.M. $$$

St. Tropez 52 Sanford Street (203-254-8094). Why have only one excellent French bistro in town when you can have two? Chef Etienne Menozzi transports diners to the loveliest harbor on the Mediterranean, setting the scene with a mural depicting Saint-Tropez and presenting dishes redolent of the sea. The traditional bouillabaisse Tropézienne, the escargots Provençal, and the outstanding crusty baguettes would meet the standards of any epicure. The desserts are exquisite. The ambiance is sunny and warmly welcoming. Open for lunch Monday through Saturday, noon to 2:00 P.M. Open for dinner from 5:30 P.M. Monday through Saturday and on Sunday from 5:00 P.M. $$$-$$$$

Sarabande 12 Unquowa Place (203-259-8084). This little charmer has some bistro-like qualities including reasonably priced, appropriately sized portions of good, well-seasoned food. Tasty seafood, nice appetizer-size pizzas, pleasing desserts. Try the sour cream cheesecake; it's luscious. Open for lunch Monday through Saturday and dinner daily. $$$

Firehouse Deli 22 Reef Road (203-255-5527). Major sandwiches, grinders, tacos, salads, quiche, soup, bagels, cheesecake, giant cookies, much more. Take-out or sit-down self-service. Outside seating in nice weather. Open Monday through Saturday 7:00 A.M to 6:00 P.M. and Sunday 8:00 A.M. to 5:00 P.M. $

Paci 96 Station Street (203-259-9600). On the eastbound side of the Southport train station in a renovated freight depot originally built in the 1880s, this marvelous establishment is a winner of the National Award of Excellence in Architecture and Interior Design from the James Beard Foundation. Airy and minimalist in decor, with a dramatic watch face projected on its main dining room wall, the restaurant allows a focus on its fabulous classic Italian dishes, homemade pastas, and fresh sauces created from market-fresh produce. Smoke-free. Open for dinner Tuesday through Saturday 5:30 to 10:00 P.M. $$$-$$$$

Places to Stay in Fairfield

Fairfield Inn 417 Post Road (203-255-0491). Convenient, clean, cream-of-the-crop motor inn. Eighty units, outdoor pool. $$$

Merritt Parkway Motor Inn 4180 Black Rock Turnpike (203-259-5264). Perched atop a hill at north end of town. Forty units, restaurant, continental breakfast. $$

Seagrape Inn at Fairfield Beach 1160 Reef Road (203-255-6808). Web site: www.seagrapeinn.com. Fourteen suites in an impeccably renovated Fairfield landmark that hasn't always enjoyed a crystal-clean reputation. Today the entire place sparkles in its new incarnation. A kitchenette, balcony,

SOUND REFLECTIONS

Although thousands of residences crowd nearly rafter to rafter in private beach areas, most of the five million people who live along the shores of Long Island Sound only occasionally consider that America's Mediterranean, as it has been called, is a precious treasure that needs vigilant protection.

Fairfield is a good place from which to reflect on the importance and value of the ecosystem to which we also belong. Notable for its commitment to preserving public ownership and stewardship of coastal areas, Fairfield also is home to a large population that actively uses the Sound for recreation and transportation. Sit a while on Jennings Beach and notice the many indications of the complex issues that affect the future of the Sound: the busy commercial and recreational boat traffic, the signs of air and water pollution especially common in the western end of the estuary, the erosion of wildlife habitats as humans jostle for space along the sand and attempt to control the sea with jetties and seawalls. Juxtapose these concerns with the pleasures of listening to the rustling grasses on the restored dunes, breathing the fresh salt air, watching the sun rise on the eastern horizon, sifting through the sand for simple treasures like sea glass and shells.

Remember that this waterway teems with life and that human behavior constantly impacts the health of its plants, animals, and the water itself. In Fairfield and everywhere in the Long Island Sound watershed, human responsibility is essential to the preservation of this sea and all of its gifts to us.

and sitting room is in every immaculately redecorated suite. A renovated restaurant is also on the premises. Daily, weekly, and monthly rates. Open year-round. $$$$

Public Boat Launches

South Benson Marina in the Jennings Boat Basin on the inside of Ash Creek Harbor to the west of Black Rock Harbor. Town-owned ramp for resident use primarily; nonresidents cannot purchase day-use permits, but seasonal permits ($80) are available by prior arrangement at the Parks Department

(203-256-3010) at Independence Hall at the corner of Beach and Old Post Roads. Bring driver's license, vehicle registration, and boat registration.

Ye Yacht Yard at Southport Harbor (203-259-1384). Public boat launch ramp that operates exactly like the one at South Benson (see entry above).

For Further Information

Fairfield Conservation Trust (203-256-3071). For a map of 650 acres open for low-impact hiking, fishing, swimming, and mountain biking on Conservation Trust land. Areas of special interest may be Lake Mohegan and the Cascades, for swimming, hiking, fishing, and, with a permit, primitive camping; **Ash Creek,** for salt marsh, meadow, and creek habitats as well as a children's playground, walking trails, and opportunities for boating and fishing; **Brett Woods,** for a stocked trout pond and horseback riding trails; **Springer Glen,** for walking, fishing, picnicking; and **Pine Creek Marsh,** for boating and fishing at a 113-acre tidal salt marsh with wildlife.

Fairfield Parks and Recreation Department Independence Hall at the corner of Beach and Old Post Roads (203-256-3010). Information on beaches, parks, tennis, golf, boating, and permits for public boat launch ramps.

Fairfield Chamber of Commerce 1597 Post Road (203-255-1011). Maps, brochures, and information on lodging, businesses, and restaurants.

Bridgeport

Heavily industrialized Bridgeport is unlikely to be the first municipality that comes to mind when travelers consider a visit to a coastal Connecticut town. At first glance, its virtues seem limited to manufacturing ventures, and its connection to the Sound appears a wholly unromantic one.

And yet, the state's largest city is also one of its busiest ports, its harbor offering dockage to massive tankers and cargo vessels loaded with goods destined for shipment to all of New England. Its beaches and salt marshes make up the longest public waterfront in the state, and its many marinas and yacht clubs offer slips and moorings equal to the best of the better-known sailors' ports along the coast. One of the nation's oldest lighthouses is in Bridgeport, and, although its beacon is extinguished now, it once guided to safe anchorage the commercial fleet that still plies the offshore fishing grounds for lobsters and Connecticut's famed bluepoint oysters.

If you decide to forgo a visit to Bridgeport, you will miss a wealth of activities linked to the city's golden history as a center of industry, culture, and trade. Bridgeport has more designated historic districts than any other Connecticut municipality (including 3,000 structures on the National Register of Historic Places) and among its many greenswards are two expansive parks designed by famed landscape artist Frederick Law Olmsted.

Settled in 1639 on the site of a Native American village known as Pequonnock, or "cleared field," after the cultivated acreage north of the natural harbor, Bridgeport was, for more than a hundred years, a scant collection of perhaps a dozen houses between the larger towns of Stratford and Fairfield. The deepest port between New York and New London was at Bridgeport's Black Rock. Consequently, Bridgeport's early economy focused on maritime trade, whaling, and shipbuilding.

During the Industrial Revolution, inventors, entrepreneurs, and major manufacturers flooded the "cleared field," establishing the city as a center of industry and a mecca for the immigrant population in search of jobs. Elias Howe had his sewing machine mass-produced here, Alexander Graham Bell's gramophones burst into song here, and Frisbie's pies made history first for their culinary excellence and later for the clever recycling of their tins as the world's first Frisbees.

Ethnic enclaves enriched the city's cultural life, public parks and monuments punctuated wide boulevards lined with mansions and magnificent public buildings, and trains and trolleys brought visitors from the suburbs to the city's theaters and restaurants. Unfortunately, all that glittered was not gold. Greed, graft, and a notorious political patronage system, along with street crime, overcrowding in substandard schools, and poorly constructed housing hastily built to shelter immigrant laborers led to the deterioration of the gilded city.

Finally, in the last quarter of the twentieth century, much was done in Bridgeport to polish up the urban landscape. Royal-blue street signs now help usher visitors to the best-kept secrets of life in this reawakening shoreline city. Notwithstanding worrisome headlines about the current politics, it's not too early to celebrate the renaissance of Bridgeport. The city's seaside parks, its excellent museums and theaters, the state's only zoo, and the diverse ethnic communities infuse the culture of the city with energy and vitality.

The Best of Bridgeport

Discovery Museum

Hands-on in nearly every way, this family-friendly museum contains more than 100 interactive exhibits in the areas of art, science, and a smattering of industry. Although all are of general interest to visitors of all ages, the displays have been specially designed for the entertainment and education of children ages 4 to 12.

Built to represent an artist's studio, the first floor's Interactive Art Gallery offers lessons about color, line, and perspective. You can "paint" with a computer, spin color wheels to "mix" new colors, shift stained "glass" puzzle pieces to create mood changes, or duck into a cavelike structure that plays red, blue, and yellow music.

Upstairs, past the fine art gallery, visitors learn about nuclear energy, electronics, electricity, magnetism, and light. Take a simulated bumper car ride to test your reaction time, hear Alexander Graham Bell's first telephone transmission, measure your height electronically under the giant Stanley Powerlock measuring tape, and use your body to create a swirling wall of color in the Pepsico Light Gallery.

The lowest floor includes a gallery of simple machines and the Discovery House, a learning space for children under 5, with simplified hands-on science and art for the youngest visitors. The lower level is also home to the **Henry B. Dupont III Planetarium.**

The museum is also the site of one of the nation's sixteen **Challenger Learning Centers,** a computer-simulated mission control and space station where participants perform experiments and collect data as astronauts would. Afternoon mini-missions are offered to the public on weekends; these thirty-minute sessions are limited to visitors older than age 10. Five-hour missions, also for visitors age 10 and up, are planned for selected Saturdays throughout the year. For either option, call ahead for prices and reservations.

4450 Park Avenue (exit 47, Merritt Parkway) (203–372–3521). Web site: www. discoverymuseum.org. Open year-round Tuesday to Saturday 10:00 A.M. to 5:00 P.M. and Sunday noon to 5:00 P.M., and on Mondays 10:00 A.M. to 5:00 P.M. in July and August. Closed on major holidays. Adults $7.00, seniors and children ages 3 to 18, $5.50; children under 3 are free. Extra fee for Challenger missions.

The Beardsley Zoological Gardens

This 52-acre zoological park inside 130-acre Beardsley Park specializes in rare or endangered species of North and South America, including red wolves, scarlet ibises, sandhill cranes, golden lion tamarins, spectacled bears, and ocelots. A beautiful trio of Siberian tigers also lives here, an unusual departure from the Americas theme—and a lucky one for zoo visitors who admire this magnificent species. Among the 120 other species are river otters, toucans, timber wolves, and macaws. A New England farmyard enclosure is a petting zoo that features bunnies, goats, geese, sheep, a red-headed pig, and a Scottish Highland cow. Inside the New World Tropics building is an outstanding South American rain forest re-creation. Woolly monkeys, tortoises, and marmosets live with tropical birds in this excellent open-aviary exhibit.

The zoo's small size and accessible facilities plus frequent special events such as the ZooFolk concert series and teddy-bear picnics make Beardsley Zoo a popular site for families. Pony rides, a children's stage, a gift shop, a snack bar, and a large picnic grove are on the grounds. Also here is a marvelous pavilion housing exhibits from the beautiful antique **Pleasure Beach carousel** as well as its operating modern replica. It is open seasonally from 10:30 A.M. to 4:00 P.M.

Plan to return soon: New exhibits are under development for an Asian plateau theme and an Arctic tundra theme. As you leave the zoo, ask the parking attendant for directions back to Route 8/25 South (which takes you to Route I–95 north or south) or North (which takes you to the Merritt Parkway north or south). It's a different route out of the zoo than in because of a one-way street or two.

1875 Noble Avenue (203–394–6565). Web site: www.beardsleyzoo.org. Open daily from 9:00 A.M. to 4:00 P.M., except for Thanksgiving, Christmas, and New Year's Day. New World Tropics Exhibit is open 10:30 A.M. to 3:30 P.M. daily. Adults $6.00, children ages 3 to 11, $4.00; under 3 are free. Zoo-only visitors do not have to pay the parking fee ($3.00 for Connecticut vehicles, $6.00 for out-of-state vehicles) charged to users of Beardsley Park.

Barnum Museum

Located in the heart of downtown on Main Street a block south of State Street is one of the best small, themed museums between New York and Boston. If you have only one day to spend in Bridgeport, make sure this "Greatest Show on Earth" is one of your stops. Refueled by the energies of a new executive director, the Barnum is currently launching a series of changes designed to immerse the visitor in the experience of its exhibits, creating the effect of a journey back in time. Renovations and new interactive displays are slated for installation in the next couple of years. Be sure to step right up and see them.

THE BARNUM FESTIVAL

The annual **Barnum Festival** is a multifaceted celebration that culminates with the Great Street Parade and the Seaside Park fireworks on or near each Fourth of July. Among parades held across the nation, Bridgeport's has historically been second in size only to Macy's Thanksgiving Day extravaganza. A fabulous marching band competition called Champions on Parade, a Jenny Lind voice competition, and a children's Wing-Ding parade and carnival at Beardsley Park are among other festival events that out-of-town visitors can enjoy. For a schedule, call the **Barnum Festival Society** (203-367-8495).

Those visitors charmed by the beguiling Mr. Barnum and his tiny companion, Tom Thumb, may wish to visit **Mountain Grove Cemetery** on Dewey Street at North Avenue, the final resting place of Barnum and Charles Stratton, the tiny man who toured the world as General Tom Thumb. Call for hours and directions (203-336-3579). Open year-round at no charge.

Dedicated to the life and times of Phineas Taylor (P. T.) Barnum, the museum also celebrates the industrial heritage of Bridgeport and the culture of the circus in general. The first floor concentrates on Barnum the showman, entrepreneur, politician, and journalist. The successful juggler of half a dozen careers during his eighty-one years, Barnum bragged that his circus was "the most expensive and marvellous combination of the world's wonders ever brought together." You'll be easily drawn in to his magic from the minute you step inside the museum.

Stop for a while to watch the excellent clip from the movie *Barnum* so you get a fix on who Barnum was. Born in 1810 in Bethel, Connecticut, Barnum was a study in contradictions—hoaxster of outrageous proportions when it came to entertaining (and bilking) the masses, the clever Barnum was also mayor of this city, responsible for one of its greatest periods of growth and the conservation of its valuable parklands.

On the third floor, you'll enter the circus. See Barnum's Fejee Mermaid, the two-headed calf, a real Egyptian mummy, Tom Thumb and Lavinia Warren's clothing and furniture, clown props, memorabilia of singer Jenny Lind, and the incredible five-ring Brinley's circus, hand-carved completely to scale and massive even in miniature.

820 Main Street (203–331–1104). Web site: www.barnum-museum.org. Open year-round Tuesday through Saturday 10:00 A.M. to 4:30 P.M. and Sunday noon to 4:30 P.M. Also open Monday in July and August, 11:00 A.M. to 4:30 P.M. Adults $5.00, seniors $4.00, children 4 to 18, $3.00; under age 4 free.

The Housatonic Museum of Art

In the midst of the magnificently restored neighborhood surrounding lovely McLevy Green is Bridgeport's Housatonic Community-Technical College, which houses a small art museum with a noteworthy collection of 4,000 pieces. American and European artists of the nineteenth and twentieth centuries are represented here, along with African and Asian ethnographic collections, contemporary Latin American art, and works by Connecticut artists.

Among the paintings, graphics, prints, photos, masks, wood carvings, and sculpture are works from Cassatt, Miró, Rodin, Cézanne, Matisse, Picasso, Marsh, Lichtenstein, Rauschenberg, De Kooning, and Warhol. When you visit, you will see only a portion of the whole collection in the galleries as you walk into the main building at 900 Lafayette Boulevard. New shows are hung in this space every several weeks. Look for the wall racks that hold self-guided tour brochures to the rest of the collection in various campus sites.

900 Lafayette Boulevard (at State Street) on the downtown campus of Housatonic Community-Technical College (203–332–5000). Open September through May, Monday through Friday, from 8:30 A.M. to 5:30 P.M. Closed during college recess in summertime and midwinter. Free, but donations are appreciated.

Downtown Cabaret Theater

This theater produces professional, award-winning shows from Broadway hits to original musical revues every weekend of the year. Matinee and evening performances are given cabaret-style; patrons sit at round tables and bring their own picnics and refreshments or purchase snacks and setups from a concession. Many of the evening performances are suitable for children older than 8.

An enormously successful slate of musical productions for children ages 4 to 12 is offered every weekend from October through May. A great bargain for exposing youngsters to theater are the subscriptions to all six shows each season. Security parking ($2.00) for all performances is available in the City Hall lot on Golden Hill Street, directly across from the Cabaret.

263 Golden Hill Street (203–576–1636). Open year-round; performances Friday

HARBOR YARD BALLPARK AND ARENA

The continuing revival of Bridgeport is apparent in the stadium constructed in 1998 as part of the sports arena and transportation complex rising over the next few years near the city's waterfront. The Bridgeport Bluefish are the Park City's Class A baseball team playing in the Atlantic League, a professional minor league club.

The 5,300-seat ballpark squats on the former site of the Jenkins Brothers Valve Company just blocks from the water and a mere stroll away from downtown. It has fine views of the Sound and the ferry docks, and its box seats, club seats, and even skyboxes ensure a great view of the game. A supervised play area, a barbecue picnic area, food and souvenir concessions, rest rooms, and on-site parking ($2.00) add to the park's appeal. This too is the home park of the major league lacrosse team, the Bridgeport Barrage, playing from June through August. Also in this complex is the Arena at Harbor Yard, where the Bridgeport Sound Tigers of the American Hockey League took to the ice in 2001 as the premiere affiliate of the New York Islanders. Their season runs from October through April. Not since the 1940s when the lights went out on the Bridgeport Bees, who played in the old Colonial League in the North End's Candlelight Stadium, has Bridgeport been this excited about sports.

The complex is located at 500 Main Street (off exit 27 on I-95). Call the Bluefish Ticket Office at (203) 345-4800; for lacrosse games, call the Bridgeport Barrage at the same number; for hockey games, call the Sound Tigers at (203) 334-GOAL.

at 8:00 P.M., *Saturday at 5:30 and 8:30* P.M., *and Sunday at 5:30* P.M. *Single tickets generally range from $16 to $25; subscriptions available for whole season. Children's matinee series October through May; performances Saturday at noon and 2:30* P.M. *and Sunday at noon. Single tickets $9.50; subscriptions available to part of or whole series.*

The Polka Dot Playhouse

Called by the *New York Times* "the quintessential community theatre," Bridgeport's oldest continuously running live performance company is proudly celebrating its own renaissance as a professional theater. For more than forty years, the playhouse staged four productions each summer season from its island home at Pleasure Beach Park. Tragedy struck in 1996 when the charming, white wooden bridge to the island went up in flames.

Now relocated to an amazingly revitalized area in the heart of downtown, the Polka Dot's curtain is up in a fabulous 223-seat theater created inside a magnificent 1911 bank building in one of Bridgeport's historic districts. Just a block from the Barnum Museum and the Housatonic Museum of Art, the Polka Dot is now a year-round venue, offering stand-up comedy, musical revues, Broadway hits, and dramas as well as monthly performances specifically aimed at families with young children. Here in this incredibly transformed district is an affordably priced opportunity to enjoy great theater. In 2002, tickets were $25 and $30 for adults. Family shows called Polka Dot Kids Productions were $10.

167 State Street (203–333–3666). Web site: www.polkadotplayhouse.org. Performances usually on Friday and Saturday at 8:00 P.M. and Sunday at 3:00 P.M. All ages. Call for a program of the current season.

The Bridgeport to Port Jefferson Steamboat Company

The huge white boats at the pier just a block from the downtown transportation terminal offer ferry service across Long Island Sound 365 days a year. Still more excursion boats than commuter transportation, these ferries can be used as a pleasure cruise or as a means of getting by car to the prettier parts of Long Island more quickly than you could via New York City or the Throgs Neck Bridge.

You can go on foot, with bicycles, or with your car to Port Jefferson, New York, a village of shops and restaurants that cater to day-tripping crowds from the ferry. Theatre Three (516–928–9100) on Main Street in Port Jefferson presents live summer theater including reasonably priced, well-known hits suitable for the whole family. Special children's matinee productions are offered in July and August.

The sailing time on the ferry is about an hour and twenty minutes each way. From Bridgeport, the boats usually depart every hour on the half-hour between 6:30 A.M. and 9:30 P.M. The ferries have enclosed passenger decks plus topside sun decks, rest rooms, lounges, and food service in onboard restaurants and bars. Charters, moonlight cruises, and dance cruises are among the special services and events offered.

Water Street Dock, Bridgeport (888–443–3779) or 102 West Broadway, Port Jefferson (516–473–0286). Operates year-round. Rates and schedules vary. Call for reservations, brochures, or information on Port Jefferson attractions.

SEASIDE PARK

At the city's southernmost tip at the shore of Long Island Sound lies Seaside Park, a 325-acre expanse donated to the city by P. T. Barnum and designed by famed partners Frederick Law Olmsted and Calvert Vaux. The park is reached through the magnificent Perry Memorial Arch over Park Avenue. Designed by Henry Bacon in the same year (1916) he designed the Lincoln Memorial in Washington, the arch is the gateway to the small peninsula that features a shoreline drive, a wide, white-sand beach, playing fields, a band shell, concessions, walking paths, and rest areas.

Nonresidents wishing to drive through or spend a day at the park and beach must stop at a checkpoint to purchase a day-use pass. Connecticut vehicles are charged $5.00, out-of-state vehicles are charged $10.00, from Memorial Day weekend through Labor Day weekend. Swimming is occasionally limited in the summer season due to pollution, but the water is usually perfect for wading and cooling off, and the sand at Seaside is exceptionally fine and clean.

If you're in the mood for beach walking, follow the walkway along the long spit westward to Fayerweather Island and its nineteenth-century lighthouse. The perfect place for watching the boat traffic to the small marinas in the area, this site also offers a view of the sewage treatment plant and the now-grassy city landfill. Despite these inconsistencies, Fayerweather Island is a pretty place, offering great views of the Sound, the seaport, and St. Mary's-by-the-Sea. A public boat launch ramp is out this way, as is a public fishing pier. The park is widely used year-round and is open from dawn until sunset. Call the Bridgeport Parks Department (203-576-7233) for more information.

Captain's Cove Seaport

One of the notable examples of Bridgeport's gradual recovery from blighted pockmark to merry dimple in the cheek of the Sound is this busy place at the edge of historic Black Rock Harbor. Part marina, part museum, and part shopping arcade, Captain's Cove was originally the baby of Kaye Williams, the friendly and imaginative Black Rock native and lobsterman who began the cleanup of this derelict area in the early 1980s. Along with the totally

ST. MARY'S-BY-THE-SEA

In Black Rock, close to the city's border with Fairfield at Ash Creek, **St. Mary's-by-the-Sea** is one of the prettiest spots along the Connecticut coast. Below a natural bluff, a seawall edged with riprap keeps the waves from washing over the grassy shoreline park and promenade that borders the Sound. Across the curving boulevard that separates the park from the adjacent residential neighborhood are some of Bridgeport's most beautiful mansions.

Once the site of a small wooden church called St. Mary's-by-the-Sea, the park is now popular with walkers and joggers of all ages, families pushing strollers, and lovers ambling hand in hand. The cement promenade with a low wooden rail overlooks a wide-open vista across the Sound. Linger here, if you can, to watch the sun set and the moon rise and the lights come on across the water on Long Island. Benches along parts of the park and promenade provide a place to rest, but no other facilities are here. Small beaches lie at either end of the walkway, so you can add beachcombing to the simple pleasures you can enjoy at this lovely spot. Parking in the summer season is limited to Bridgeport residents and is strictly enforced. If you have been to Seaside Park earlier in the day, however, you can use your day-use pass at both parks. Otherwise, come from Labor Day to Memorial Day to savor the sights and smells that are free to all visitors.

To reach the mile-long park, take Fairfield Avenue (Route 1) west from downtown Bridgeport or east from Fairfield to Courtland Avenue. Go south on Courtland one long block to Gilman Street. Take a right on Gilman and follow it along the curve of Ash Creek and the salt marshes. As the road curves to the left near the mouth of the creek, it becomes Grovers Avenue, which is the wide boulevard that stretches along the promenade. Stop if you can, then continue along Grovers Avenue to Brewster Street. Take a left there to return to Fairfield Avenue.

refurbished marina with new docks and slips and a boat repair shop are a 500-seat restaurant, a fish market, and a charming boardwalk filled with tiny boutiques and galleries, most of which are open only in the warm months.

Among the vessels at Captain's Cove is one of the U.S. Coast

Guard's former lightships, the *Nantucket*, which once served to protect other vessels approaching the treacherous Nantucket Shoals. The only U.S. lightship stationed in international waters, the *Nantucket* was nicknamed *Liberty of the Sea* because she was often the first sight of American property seen by European immigrants heading toward Boston or New York. Tours (adults $3.00; children $2.00) are given in the summertime; call for times.

The seaport also includes a small museum on the first floor of the restored Victorian Dundon House. Exhibits are on the maritime history of Black Rock Harbor as well as the environment and economy of Long Island Sound and its fisheries and oyster beds. Photographs depict the history of three local lighthouses that guided sailors and fisherfolk, and a collection of interesting items salvaged from nearby waters provides an eye-opening look at nautical litter. Admission is $2.00 for adults, $1.00 for children.

The surprises that await you at Captain's Cove are as variable as the New England weather. Sea chantey sing-alongs, band concerts, food festivals, and other events are planned daily. Harbor cruises and chartered fishing trips are easily arranged here. Harbor cruises on passenger launches, such as the 40-foot Navy launch *Chief*, for instance, are generally offered on Saturday and Sunday from noon to 5:00 P.M. (about $5.00 per adult, $4.00 for seniors, and $3.00 for children under 12). Private charters can also be arranged on some of these tour boats. Call the Seaport Office for more information or contact the Web sites of the *China Clipper* (www.thechinaclipper.com) or Black Rock Sailing (www. brsailing.com).

One Bostwick Avenue (203–335–1433). Web site: www.captainscoveseaport.com. Seaport stores open roughly April 1 to October 1 from 11:00 A.M. Closing time varies with the day, the crowds, and the weather. Restaurant, bar, and fish market open year-round; call for off-season schedule. Free admission to seaport. Small fees for entrance to boats and Dundon House.

Boat Excursions and Charters

Harbor tours at Captain's Cove 1 Bostwick Avenue. Narrated public cruises around historic Black Rock, Burr Creek. For further information, call the office at Captain's Cove Seaport (203–335–1433) to ask for telephone numbers of the captains currently offering cruises or private charters. Most recently, the following boats offered sightseeing tours or fishing charters:

Chief (203-355-1433). Forty-foot Navy launch offers guided one-day tour of Black Rock Harbor; see Black Rock, Fayerweather, and Penfield lighthouses. Mid-May through late October.

Daystar Captain Bob Bociek (203-615-0070). Departs Captain's Cove Seaport mid-April through November.

Somertime Captain Bill Somers (203-438-5838). Departs Captain's Cove mid-April through November.

Coastal Charter Company Captain Richard Scofield (203-334-9256). Web site: www.thechinaclipper.com. The 53-foot Hatteras motor yacht *China Clipper* offers lunch/dinner cruises, sightseeing; overnight cruises for up to six passengers. April 15 to November 15.

Places to Eat in Bridgeport

Take Time Cafe 211 State Street (203-335-7255). This downtown coffeehouse/bagel bakery is close to the museums, theaters, and ballpark. Its nautical decor is a great backdrop for its outstanding array of breakfast, lunch, and picnic foods, such as bagels and spreads, sandwiches, muffins, and scones. Official suppliers of coffee for the Bridgeport Bluefish, Take Time also offers cappuccinos and lattes. Open weekdays from 6:30 A.M. to 3:00 P.M. $

Bloodroot 85 Ferris Street (203-576-9168). Tucked at the edge of Cedar Creek, this unassuming little place near Black Rock harbor is a marvelous place for wholesome-food lovers. Nourishing soups, crispy salads, whole-grain breads, and tasty vegetarian and vegan casseroles made with organic produce, aromatic grains, and root vegetables are some of the reasons a loyal following will come from out of state just to enjoy the food and the enlightened spirit that infuses the casual dining room. Enjoy a look at the terrific bookstore focusing on women's literature, poetry, health, and spirituality; it's to the left of the dining room as you walk in. Open for lunch Tuesday and Thursday through Sunday from 11:30 A.M to 2:30 P.M. and for dinner Tuesday and Thursday from 6:00 to 9:00 P.M. and Friday and Saturday from 6:00 to 10:00 P.M. $-$$

La Scogliera 697 Madison Avenue (203-333-0673). Bridgeport's Little Italy is centered on Madison Avenue at Capitol Avenue and is also known as the MAMA district, truthfully an acronym for Madison Avenue Merchants Association but symbolically a reminder of the great home cooking available at the many Italian restaurants, markets, and bakeries near this intersection. Just a few blocks south of the intersection, this restaurant on Madison between Capitol and North has offered authentic Italian cuisine for twenty years, and rumor is that no one has been disappointed yet. Housemade pasta, flavorful sauces, and tasty seafood and poultry dishes are what you might try before indulging in the delicious desserts. Open for lunch and dinner year-round, Tuesday through Thursday 11:30 A.M. to 10:00 P.M., Friday and Saturday 4:30 P.M. to midnight; Sunday noon to 9:00 P.M. $$

Ye Olde Tollgate Steakhouse 360 Fairfield Avenue (203-337-9944). If you're a true-blue carnivore, you'll be mighty pleased here. Fine prime beef is the star here; chicken, pasta, and some seafood and salads are also offered. Open for lunch on weekdays and dinner daily. $$-$$$

Places to Stay in Bridgeport

Bridgeport Holiday Inn 1070 Main Street (203-334-1234). Full-service hotel in convenient downtown location. Two hundred thirty rooms, including two suites. Health club, indoor pool, restaurant, P.T.'s lounge, coffee shop. Sunday brunch from 9:00 A.M. to 1:00 P.M. Kids stay free. Inquire about senior citizen rates and weekend packages. $$$

Trumbull Marriott 180 Hawley Lane, Trumbull (203-378-1400). Convenient to Merritt Parkway and Route 8 and all Bridgeport attractions. Health club with sauna, indoor and outdoor pools, piano lounge. Three hundred twenty rooms with data ports, hair dryers, coffeemakers, and more; children stay free. Two restaurants, including award-winning Ashley's Grille and Gratzi; Sunday brunch from 10:30 A.M. to 2:00 P.M. Half-price meals for kids 5 to 12 and complimentary meals for those under 5. $$$

Public Boat Launches

Seaside Park Ramp I-95 exit 27, south on Park Avenue, right on Waldemere Avenue to Barnum Dyke (203-384-9777). City launch ramp. Park is open roughly at dawn; gates lock at sunset. $5.00 fee for non-city residents. Parking for sixty cars.

Brewster Street Ramp Call Bridgeport harbormaster (203-576-8107) or Bridgeport Port Authority (203-384-9777). Improved ramp near Black Rock Harbor; no fee.

For Further Information

Bridgeport Convention and Visitors Commission 303 State Street (203-576-8491). Calendar of events, maps, brochures for attractions, information on lodging, dining, and transportation.

Bridgeport Parks Department (203-576-7233). Information on park hours, fees, special events.

Bridgeport Chamber of Commerce (203-332-1995). Maps; brochures on local attractions and businesses.

Stratford

This small municipality often gets lost in the shuffle as travelers and commuters rush past it on I-95, but an afternoon here offers a few rewards for the educated tourist. It's true that few folks traveling through on the interstate highway would pick Stratford out as one of the most picturesque towns along the Sound, even though it has had ample time to establish itself as such. One of Connecticut's earliest English settlements, founded along with Fairfield in 1639, Stratford actually predates the hulking city of Bridgeport across the Pequonnock River. In those early days Bridgeport was a mere dozen houses in a place called Newfield, and Stratford was far more important as the place where the ferryman brought Post Road travelers across the wide Housatonic on its eastern border.

Although today much of Stratford maintains a close link to the quiet charms of the sea and busies itself with the simple commerce of a largely residential suburb, during the nineteenth century Stratford grew along with Bridgeport as a center of industry. Well known for its production of machine products, brake linings, hardware, and chemicals, the city also celebrates its unquestionable role in aviation history as the workshop of Igor Sikorsky, inventor of the first practical single-rotor helicopter. Today dwarfed by Bridgeport, Stratford still stays on the map as producer of the magnificent whirlybirds of Igor's imagination at the Sikorsky Aircraft Division of United Technologies. From its earliest days to the present, Stratford has enjoyed only a modest reputation in

Connecticut history in spite of its notable bird. A closer look reveals a few little-known attractions at the edge of the Sound.

The Best of Stratford

Captain David Judson House and the Catharine B. Mitchell Museum

Visitors curious to discover exactly what Stratford has been all about these past 350 years should come here to its town museum. The home of the Stratford Historical Society, this small complex between Stratford's Main and Elm Streets includes two buildings open to visitors. A walk through the past is the main treat at the handsome red home of Captain David Judson. Built about 1750 on the site of his great-grandfather's 1639 stone homestead, this carefully restored post-and-beam, central-chimney colonial has a beautiful broken-scroll pediment doorway, a huge kitchen fireplace, paneled walls, and many examples of original Stratford-made furniture.

The Catharine Bunnell Mitchell Museum adjacent to the Judson House contains permanent exhibits on Stratford history and changing exhibitions taken from the collections of the historical society. Among its artifacts are a fine collection of baskets, objects from the Native Americans who inhabited the area prior to European settlement, and items from early African American history.

967 Academy Hill (I-95 exit 32, Rte. 15 exit 535; 203–378–0630). Open mid-May through October 31, Wednesday, Saturday, and Sunday from 11:00 A.M. to 4:00 P.M. and other times by appointment. Genealogy library open Tuesday and Thursday from 9:00 A.M. to 2:00 P.M. year-round. Guided tours of the Judson House; self-guided tours of Catharine Bunnell Mitchell Museum. Adults $2.00; seniors and students $1.00.

Short Beach Park

On the east-facing cove that cups the mouth of the Housatonic River, Stratford's city-owned Short Beach lies just north of the beach community of Lordship at the southernmost part of town. Popular with town residents as well as visitors, Short Beach offers tourists the best day-tripping bargain of all the public beaches along the Connecticut shore.

Ballfields, a playground, a nine-hole golf course, a miniature golf course, and tennis, basketball, and paddle tennis courts are all here.

Picnic tables and grills help to make a visit a daylong affair. If barbecuing seems like too much of a chore, buy snacks at the concession (summer months only).

Short Beach Road (Stratford Parks and Recreation Department: 203–385–4052). Open year-round dawn to dusk. Lifeguards mid-May through Labor Day. Concession, rest rooms, outside showers. Nonresident day use fee $5.00 per vehicle; season pass $100 per vehicle for unlimited use from Memorial Day to Labor Day.

The Garbage Museum

If young children are in your party, a visit to this innovative museum may be a worthwhile lesson. Twenty-two interactive exhibits teach children about the importance of recycling and the responsible treatment of garbage. One of the exhibits is a soft-sculpture compost pile in which children can crawl around in a simulated worm tunnel to see how organic matter decomposes into soil. The museum's mascot of sorts is Trash-o-saurus, a 24-foot-long dinosaur constructed from trash.

Visitors to the museum generally spend about an hour at the hands-on exhibit area, then take a tour of the next-door Southeastern Connecticut Regional Recycling Plant, where recyclables are sorted and prepared for sale to remanufacturers. Often a visit here ends with a return to the museum area for creation of a craft made from recycled or reusable material.

1410 Honeyspot Road Extension (I-95 exit 30; 203–381–9571). Open to school groups daily throughout the academic year; open to families from 10:00 A.M. to 4:00 P.M., in July and August Tuesday through Saturday and during the academic year Wednesday through Friday from noon to 4:00 P.M. Four special events on occasional Saturdays; call for schedule. Admission is free.

Long Beach Skateland

A whirl around this old-fashioned roller-skating rink is sure to lift the spirit and raise the heart rate of every visitor, young or old. Owned and operated by the same family for the past forty-plus years, the rink now welcomes the kids of the kids who skated here in the fifties and sixties. To protect their specially coated wooden floor, the owners allow only traditional quad skates—no new-fangled in-line skates. Bring your own skates if you still have them or borrow a pair here, then let the rhythm of the music set your pace around the rink. You might want to consider your taste in tunes when choosing a time to visit: Most sessions feature contemporary Top Forty hits that kids and teens seem to love, but Sunday evenings feature the charming

ANTIQUES BONANZA

Perhaps the artifacts of the Judson House have whetted your appetite for furnishings and accessories of days past. If so, head to the **Stratford Antique Center** (400 Honeyspot Road; 203-378-7754), an enormous blue warehouse filled to the brim with the wares of more than 200 dealers. Located not far from exit 31 off I-95, this group shop covers more than 16,000 square feet with furniture, statuary, jewelry, glassware, pottery, thousands of collectibles, and one-of-a-kind artifacts both functional and decorative. Open at no charge daily from 10:00 A.M. to 5:00 P.M. year-round, and until 9:00 P.M. on Thursday evenings in November and December. Closed Thanksgiving, Christmas Day, and Easter Sunday.

lilts of organ music harking back to the heyday of roller-skating dance competitions. A competition team practices here still, and you may get to see their graceful artistry if you come on Sunday evening.

Washington Parkway (203–378–9033). Open year-round, Friday 7:00 to 9:00 P.M., Saturday 2:00 to 4:00 P.M. and 7:30 to 10:00 P.M., and Sunday 2:00 to 4:00 P.M. and 7:00 to 9:00 P.M. Admission $4.50 per person regardless of age. Skates available at no extra charge. Snack and soda machines.

Stratford Shakespeare Festival Theater

Sadly, theater lovers will have to wait even longer than expected for the revival of this landmark. Set in the midst of fourteen beautiful acres on the banks of the Housatonic, the Stratford Festival Theater was commonly known as the Shakespeare Theater from its opening in 1955 to its closing in 1982. Renowned during that time for its full-stage productions of the works of Shakespeare, the theater itself was modeled after the design believed by scholars to most closely resemble the bard's own Globe Theatre in London. When the theater's stage darkened in the early eighties, deterioration of the theater as well as its surrounding parkland began.

Restoration of the park and renovation of the theater includes plans to add two new theaters to the original structure. Theater workshops and dramatic arts classes may one day accompany the main stage productions of classic plays by famed dramatists and perhaps Broadway musical hits and other twentieth-century works.

*1812 Elm Street. Call 203–378–1200 or 203–381–1600 for the latest informa-
tion on this long-awaited reopening. You can also contact the theater's Web site
(www.stratfordfestival.com).*

Boothe Memorial Park and Museum

This thirty-two-acre park overlooking the Housatonic River was once the
site of an estate most recently shared by two wealthy but apparently eccentric brothers whose family had successfully farmed the site for more than
300 years. Today the park includes two of the original Boothe home-
steads, plus a trolley station, a tollbooth plaza, a model lighthouse, a
miniature windmill, an icehouse, an outdoor basilica with an organ
house, an 1844 chapel, a barn with a weaving loom and other objects
related to nineteenth-century farm life, a working blacksmith shop that

LONG BEACH

The sand spit at Long Beach offers some of the best beach walking
in Fairfield County—and also demonstrates some of the powerful
ways natural erosion, storms, and artificial beach "armor" like
boulders, groins, and jetties can affect the condition of a beach.
Park at the base of Washington Parkway among the restaurants
near Marnick's Motel and walk from Point No Point, at the eastern
end of the seawall, toward the west, where Stratford's Long Beach
stretches toward Bridgeport's Pleasure Beach.

The armor of boulders at **Point No Point** that protects the Lordship residents from storm tides also robs its beach of sand. A walk
along here from east to west reveals how the beach widens from only
yards across to more than a quarter-mile across as the sand stretches
westward. At the western edge of the spit, a 700-foot-wide inlet was
cut between Long Beach and Pleasure Beach by the hurricane of 1938.
Closed over a period of years by the construction of a series of
groins and by renourishment of the beach through the dumping
of hundreds of thousands of cubic yards of sand, this inlet, known
as Lewis Gut no longer threatens the Great Meadows marsh or its
nearby human residents. Shoreline conservationists predict that
another catastrophic storm is likely to destroy the spit, but for now,
beachcombers enjoy the wind and the wildlife in this secluded spot.

boasts forty-four corners and forty-four vertical outside walls, a clock tower museum, and an amazing redwood monument called the Technocratic Cathedral. Did I mention that the brothers were eccentric? Surrounding this intriguing conglomeration are acres of park grounds offering a beautiful rose garden, walking paths, picnic groves with tables, barbecue grills, shelters, a children's playground, ball-playing areas, and rest rooms. The buildings and rest rooms close in November, but ice-skating and sledding are permitted in the off-season when the weather cooperates.

134 Main Street, in the Putney section of town (203–381–2046 or 203–381–2068). Park grounds open year-round daily from approximately 8:00 A.M. to dusk. Buildings open for guided or self-guided tours May 1 through November 1; schedule is generally Tuesday through Friday 11:00 A.M. to 1:00 P.M. and on weekends from 1:00 to 4:00 P.M. Call ahead. Free.

Boat Excursions and Charters

Reel Thing Boat Charters (203–375–8623). Operates from Brown Boat Works, 638 Stratford Avenue. Chartered fishing trips May 1 through November 1. Capacity up to sixteen passengers; day trips 7:00 A.M. to 3:00 P.M.

Mako (203–261–8821). The *Mako* docks at Birdseye Street municipal ramp at Beacon Point. Chartered fishing trips April to mid-November.

Places to Eat in Stratford

Outriggers Broad Street in Brewers Stratford Marina (203–377–8815). Among the boats and gulls, dine on classics like cherrystone clams, grilled shellfish and flatfish, salads, pasta, sandwiches, and chowder. Casual, busy place overlooking the waterfront. Open for lunch and dinner daily, except Monday. $$$

Knapp's Landing 520 Sniffens Lane (203–378–5999). Knapp's Landing sits at the mouth of the Housatonic at Sniffens Point, just north of Short Beach. Delicious continental cuisine, a charming sunken fish pond left from its former incarnation as a Japanese restaurant, and an open deck with patio seating in warm weather make this a great place to enjoy lunch or dinner on the Sound. The chef offers an eclectic menu of chicken, seafood, and pasta dishes, plus steaks, sandwiches, and salads. Open for lunch and dinner year-round, Tuesday through Sunday. $$

Allen's East 60 Beach Drive (203-378-0556). A classic seafood restaurant basking in the sun at Long Beach in Lordship, Allen's East is a spin-off from the famed Allen's Clam and Lobster House in Westport, now closed. Overlooking the Sound, with gorgeous views from inside as well as from its beautiful outdoor patio, Allen's is well known for its outstanding seafood, its delicious Boston-style clam chowder, and its fast, friendly service. Full bar; lunch and dinner daily year-round. $$$

White Lilac Tearoom 2410 Main Street (203-378-7160). This tiny tea parlor is a sweet spot for an old-fashioned lunch, tea, or dinner. Open for lunch Tuesday through Saturday; dinner Friday and Saturday (BYOB). $-$$$

Plouf! Le Bistro de la Mer 14 Beach Drive (203-375-2149). This elegant waterfront cafe adds a definitively French flair to its creative seafood and other dishes. The lively, colorful decor is well matched by the tasty, perfectly seasoned French dishes with traditional and contemporary presentations. Chef Roger Martin enjoys his genius and is happy to share the fun with patrons. Located just steps away from the Lordship seawall, Plouf is dramatic in all seasons, and you can walk off the indulgences after your meal. Open for lunch Monday through Friday and dinner daily. $$-$$$

Places to Stay in Stratford

Nathan Booth House B&B 6080 Main Street (203-378-6489). In the Putney section of town, south of the Merritt Parkway, this beautifully restored 1843 Greek Revival farmhouse on the National Register of Historic Places offers four lovely guest rooms decorated with period antique furnishings. A full country breakfast for all guests each morning may include fresh eggs from the innkeepers' own chickens, fresh honey collected from their honeybees, and treats like banana-blueberry pancakes, decadent French toast, or herb-baked eggs, plus juice, coffee, and teas. Smoke-free; no pets or children under age 13. $$$$

Marnick's Motel 10 Washington Parkway (203-377-6288). Updated and redecorated with a fresh face for the new century, this waterfront motel has been family owned for thirty-plus years. Of its twenty-nine simply but comfortably furnished rooms, all those facing the Sound have balconies, microwaves, and refrigerators. All rooms have private baths, cable color TV, and either two double beds or a king-size bed. Some rooms are reserved for nonsmoking guests. Rollaways and cribs available. Private beach for swimming and shore fishing. Casual family restaurant serves three meals daily year-round; American fare ($). $$-$$$

Ramada Inn Stratford 225 Lordship Boulevard (203-375-8866). One hundred forty-five rooms, restaurant, lounge, Friday and Saturday night live entertainment. Indoor pool. Senior citizen rates. $$$-$$$$

Staybridge Suites 6905 Main Street (203-377-3322). Studio, one-bedroom, and two-bedroom suites; complimentary breakfast buffet. Fitness center, laundry room, convenience store. Pool. Fully equipped kitchens in each room. $$$$

Public Boat Launches

Stratford Municipal Ramp Birdseye Street to Beacon Point (203-377-9114). Permit required; inquire about day and season use.

Knapp's Landing Sniffens Lane at Sniffen's Point (203-375-6184). Seasonal ramp with gas/diesel dock; restaurant.

For Further Information

Stratford Parks and Recreation Department (203-385-4052).

Milford

Settled in 1639 by families from New Haven and Wethersfield, this community is Connecticut's sixth-oldest municipality. Now home to enough citizens to qualify as a small city, Milford nonetheless retains the charm of a New England shore town. In fact, Milford revels in its connection with the sea and the rivers that lap its 17 miles of freshwater and saltwater shoreline.

On the town's western border, the wide Housatonic River empties its freshwater into the Sound near beautiful Milford Point after making the 148-mile passage from its headwaters in the Berkshires. On Milford's eastern border with West Haven, the boundary is formed by the Oyster River, once the site of native encampments and later oystering concerns. In the center of town, the Wepawaug and Indian Rivers flow gently into Milford Harbor and Gulf Pond before adding their waters to the Sound, providing quiet shelter and safe anchorage for the thousands of anglers and boaters who play here nearly three-quarters of the year. Even the duck ponds and waterfalls that characterize downtown remind the visitor of Milford's undeniable link to the water.

Back in 1639 one Thomas Tibbals literally stumbled upon Milford when he and a few others were busy chasing the Pequots from Mystic to Fairfield. He hurried back to his congregation and told them of the fair harbor and rich and goodly meadowlands he had found at the banks of the Wepawaug. The congregation set out by land and by sea to their new home, which they purchased from the Paugusset for the typical assortment of kettles, cloth, axes, and such. A year later, the English built a gristmill near the narrows between the river and the harbor and named their plantation Milford.

By the late seventeenth century Milford was well established as a mill town, with two gristmills, a sawmill, and two fulling mills for the production of cloth. By 1690 it had begun construction of its first shipbuilding wharf and sent its brigs to establish a brisk West Indies trade. Later the town gained a reputation as a producer of fine quality seed, straw hats, carriages, boots, shoes—and oysters.

Milford has made remarkable efforts to protect or restore its most valuable assets near the shore. Its coastal wildlife sanctuary is one of the most important tidal salt marsh refuges on the Sound, and its shellfish beds are among the healthiest and most productive in the state.

The Best of Milford

Connecticut Audubon Coastal Center at Milford Point

This pristine 840-acre habitat of salt marshes that border the Sound and the mouth of the Housatonic River provides visitors the opportunity to see one of the last surviving unaltered coastal properties in Connecticut. Opened in 1995, the Coastal Center is located at the very end of Milford Point Road.

A pathway provides access to the area's beach, a serene and secluded place for exploring and enjoying the native flora and fauna. Observation platforms at the beach edge help you gain a better view of the shorebirds and other wildlife. This is not a park, so no picnic areas or trash receptacles are provided. Swimming is prohibited, as are collecting and dune walking.

At the coastal environment education center, you can climb to the top of a marvelous observation tower for a crow's-nest view of this land-and seascape. The displays inside the center include a 300-gallon saltwater tank with a diamondback terrapin and other specimens native to the area, along with exhibits on shells, eggs, birds, and Long Island Sound ecology. Inquire about the lecture series, summer camp programs, and family activities.

Among the most popular events here are the naturalist-guided canoe trips through the Charles E. Wheeler State Wildlife Management Area, which is the official name for all this beautiful wetland and waterway system that surrounds the Coastal Center. Reservations are strongly recommended for the day and evening trips from mid-May through late September. Fees are $8.00 for Audubon Society members, $12.00 per nonmember, if you bring your own canoe. If you borrow center-owned canoes, the fees are respectively $10 or $14 per person.

One Milford Point Road, off Seaview Avenue (203-878-7440). Web site: www.ctaudubon.org/centers/coastal/coastal.htm. Open year-round. Outdoor areas open dawn to dusk at no charge. Center open Tuesday through Saturday from 10:00 A.M. to 4:00 P.M. and Sunday noon to 4:00 P.M. Adults $2.00; seniors and children 3 to 12 $1.00; under 3 free; family rate $5.00. Free bird walks from 9:00 to 10:00 A.M. every second and fourth Saturday, year-round.

Milford Landing

At the head of Milford Harbor at the mouth of the Wepawaug River is an establishment that bends over backward to be the best of its kind anywhere. An all-transient docking facility for visiting boaters, this city-owned marina features fifty slips for vessels up to 65 feet, a launch ramp, 30- and 50-amp service, free pump-out service for overnight dockage, concierge service, and trained dock staff to assist at tie-up and so on. Handicapped access, rest rooms, shower facilities, ice and water, and a Laundromat help make visitors comfortable. Six public tennis courts, basketball courts, and a picnic pavilion are in the adjacent Wilcox Park.

37 Helwig Street. For slip reservations and further information, call Operations Director Dick Hosking (203-874-1610) or reach him by fax (203-874-1619).

MILFORD BEACHES

Milford offers out-of-towners a chance to enjoy its public beaches for active fun.

Gulf Beach Gulf Street. Visitor parking $5.00 per vehicle from Memorial Day through Labor Day. Concession, rest rooms, lifeguards, bird-watching/fishing pier.

Walnut Beach Corner of East Broadway and Viscount Drive. Parking $5.00 or free street parking. Large beach, small pavilion, rest rooms, picnic tables, lifeguards. Nice, wide-open views and convenient location adjacent to Silver Sands State Park. Officially open on weekends only from 11:00 A.M. to 3:00 P.M. from Memorial Day to July and from mid-August through Labor Day; open daily from 10:00 A.M. to 4:00 P.M. between July 1 and mid-August. These are the hours when the concession operates and lifeguards are on duty. From here you can walk across the sandbar to Charles Island, about half a mile offshore, at low tide. This adventure is not recommended by officials for nonswimmers but is perfectly doable even for adult-supervised children if you're aware of the tides. Be aware that a swift current crosses the fully submerged bar when the tide rises. On the partly wooded isle you can observe seabirds and look for signs of the legendary treasure of Captain Kidd, supposedly buried somewhere on the south side of the island. Off-island, you can go oystering. The island is closed to the public during nesting season.

Silver Sands State Park (Call the Western Division of the state DEP at 860-485-0226). Off Mayflower Avenue between Robert Treat Drive and Nettleton Avenue. Contiguous with Walnut Beach, this property of approximately 310 acres of shoreline includes Silver Sands Beach. Ongoing development at this state-owned property is making this a popular destination; a first aid station and rest rooms are among the slated projects. Lifeguards, portable toilets, and a lovely wooden boardwalk across the top of the beach and into the saltmarsh are the current amenities; bring your own drinking water, picnic foods and beverages, and trash bags. No charge.

Anchor Beach Beach Avenue off Chapel off Merwin Avenue in the Woodmont section of town. Free (but limited) street parking, no concession, toilets. Small, pretty crescent beach in mostly residential beach neighborhood.

Historic Wharf Lane Complex

Revisit the past through a visit to the three historic eighteenth-century homes maintained by the Milford Historical Society. Named for the old street that once ran from the old town wharf near Milford Harbor to the Milford Green, the Wharf Lane site was once a busy place lined with warehouses, tanneries, and general stores. Today a peaceful spot on a small bluff overlooking the harbor at the lower end of High Street, Wharf Lane is now but a road back in time. Featuring the 1700 Eells-Stow House, the 1780

THE MILFORD GREEN

The Milford town green, the second largest in Connecticut, was used in colonial times to graze cattle and sheep. Today the green, which lies between North and South Broad Streets in the center of town, is used mostly for cultural events like craft fairs, art shows, and annual festivals. Free concerts are held on selected Friday nights from mid-June through August. Visitors are welcome to join town residents at these relaxing hourlong events. Call the **Milford Chamber of Commerce** (203-878-0681) or the **Milford Fine Arts Council** (203-878-6647) to obtain a schedule of the fairs and seasonal entertainment.

One of the green's best-known events is the **New England Arts and Crafts Festival,** held in early July, usually on the weekend following Independence Day. This colorful fair celebrates the creativity of scores of the region's finest crafters and fine artists. Visitors can enjoy musical performances and other entertainment throughout the two-day festival. A food court set up on the green by area restaurants helps keep the crowds happy. The festival hours are 9:00 A.M. to 5:00 P.M. both days.

The green is surrounded by boutiques and restaurants, so even without a planned activity, visitors will have no trouble finding ways to enjoy this pretty spot. Browse too on nearby River Street, where you'll find pleasures galore at **Sweet Designs** (58 River Street), a bakery with exquisite cakes and fresh-baked scones and muffins. **Rainbow Gardens Inn** (203-878-2500) at 117 North Broad Street is a nice place to rest for lunch, dinner, or a full night. (See Places to Eat and Places to Stay for details.)

Clark Stockade House, and the circa-1785 Bryan-Downs House, the complex portrays three centuries of life in New England through the furnishings, artifacts, and tours given in the trio of homes.

The **Eells-Stow House** is claimed to be the oldest surviving house in Milford. Built by Samuel Eells, this home has some significant architectural details and Milford-made eighteenth-century furnishings. See Eells family artifacts and portraits, and hear the story of second owner Stephen Stow, who gave his life in an effort to minister to 200 American soldiers returned from a British prison ship with smallpox.

The **Bryan-Downs House** contains the Claude C. Coffin collection of Native American artifacts, touted as one of the finest archaeological records ever gathered in the state of Connecticut. Baskets, pottery, and stone tools are among the outstanding specimens providing clues to 10,000 years of prehistory in a coastal community. Also in the Bryan-Downs House is a re-creation of a general store, with barrels of candy and wooden toys, local histories and lore and walking tour guides. Outside the house is a period garden planted with herbs and flowers popular in the 1700s.

The **Clark Stockade House** was the first house in Milford to be built outside the original stockade. Moved to this site from its original location near the western end of the green, the house served as Milford's first hospital and also as a teahouse. Enjoy the thrill of walking down the same stone steps that General Washington trod when he visited Clark's Tavern during the Revolution.

34 High Street (203-874-2664). Open Memorial Day through Labor Day on Saturdays and Sundays from 2:00 to 4:00 P.M. Free; donation appreciated. Call to inquire about walking tours, Christmas in July festivities, and candlelight tours in December.

Center for the Arts

In a landmark railroad station just north of Broad Street and the green is the Milford Fine Arts Council's own Center for the Arts, site of an ongoing schedule of events in the arts. Full dramatic productions by the **Eastbound Theater Company** have included such popular shows as *A Lion in Winter* and *The Butler Did It*; among children's performances staged in the summertime have been *A Secret Garden* and other productions taken from classic literature. Poetry readings, coffeehouses on the last Friday of each month, a jazz concert series in the fall, a fine arts exhibition in October, and a photography exhibition in April are among the events visitors might enjoy here.

CHRISTMAS IN THE MANSION

A unique Milford tradition is the annual holiday fair at Lauralton Hall, a private Catholic girls' high school of the Sisters of Mercy. The school's picturesque campus a short distance north of the town green was originally a country estate owned by Charles Hobby Pond, who built his early Victorian mansion there in 1864.

The school's principal fund-raiser takes festive advantage of the romantic ambiance of the mansion. Christmas in the Mansion, held on the weekend following Thanksgiving weekend, is a three-day arts and crafts fair. Decorated with luminaria, garlands, living wreaths, and thousands of lights, the mansion's rooms and hallways are filled with the wares of dozens of talented regional artisans. A Chinese auction allows visitors to take a chance on beautiful themed Christmas trees created by local decorators and florists, and the festival includes complimentary wassail and an affordable self-serve luncheon of quiche, soup, and sandwiches.

Lauralton Hall is located at 200 High Street. For further information, call (203) 877-2786.

If you visit in summer, ask about the council's annual sandcastle competition planned in July or August according to the best tide. Inquire also about the council-sponsored summer concerts (at Fowler Field near Milford Landing on Fridays at 7:00 P.M., June through August) and festivals on the green.

40 Railroad Avenue South (203-878-6647). Open Monday through Friday from 9:00 A.M. to 1:00 P.M. plus other times for exhibitions, coffeehouses, and performances. Free exhibition center; special performances $10.00 for adults; $8.00 seniors and students; $5.00 for children's performances.

Places to Eat in Milford

Stonebridge Restaurant 50 Daniel Street, off Broad Street at the memorial stone bridge (203-874-7947). Just a short walk from either the green or the harbor, this pretty restaurant overlooking the Wepawaug River and its waterfall offers casual patio dining in the summertime, plus intimate seating in the cozy inside dining room, open year-round. Salads, sandwiches, seafood, chicken, steaks, and vegetarian dishes are the mainstay here, as is evening entertainment in the pub room. Open Sunday to Thursday from 11:30 A.M. to 10:00 P.M and Friday and Saturday until 2:00 A.M. $-$$$

Scribner's 31 Village Road (203-878-7019). Tucked into a mostly residential beach community called Woodmont, Scribner's serves the freshest fish available anywhere. Wood-paneled dining rooms and a booth-lined lounge offer a comfortable ambiance for enjoying fine seafood and other culinary treats. Lighter fare dinners served throughout the evening offer smaller portions at a reduced price.They leave plenty of room for indulging in a cup of Scribner's famed clam chowder. Open daily for dinner year-round from 5:00 P.M.; lunch Monday through Friday from 11:30 A.M. to 2:30 P.M. $$$

MILFORD OYSTER FESTIVAL

Slap on the sunscreen and load your wallet with cash for the irresistible fun at this annual celebration of the gustatory delights of the homely but delicious oyster. Why all the fuss for a simple shellfish? Well, Milford is famed for its oyster beds. The Paugusset tribe gathered oysters for centuries not far from the Wepawaug riverbank where their village was located, and the colonists became oyster gatherers too. By the mid-1800s, oystering had become big business in Milford.

The second full weekend in August is the usual date of the Oyster Festival, which draws tens of thousands of visitors to the harbor, the green, and Fowler Field on New Haven Avenue a block or so east of the green. An arts and crafts fair, a classic car show, entertainment, children's activities, a canoe race, a moonlight music and dance party, and a food court featuring oysters, of course, as well as many other treats from the sea are all part of the fun.

Admission to the Oyster Festival is free, but the food and the crafts will cost you at least a little something. Call (203) 878-5363 for more information.

Jeffrey's 501 New Haven Avenue (203-878-1910). From inventive appetizers to delicious entrees, Jeffrey's offers one taste sensation after the other. Located just east of the center of town near Old Gate Lane, the restaurant overlooks the salt marshes bordering Gulf Pond. Open year-round for lunch Monday through Friday from 11:30 A.M. to 3:00 P.M., dinner Monday through Saturday from 5:30 P.M. $$$

Rainbow Gardens Inn 117 North Broad Street (203-878-2500). Across from the gazebo on the green, this colorful Victorian inn serves equally colorful and delicious meals year-round at lunch and dinner. Creatively multicultural meals measure up to their intriguing names: Discover the culinary delights of Rising Sun Stir Fry, Bayou Bliss, Medallions of Gold, or Heaven and Earth. Open for lunch Monday through Saturday 11:00 A.M. to 3:00 P.M.; dinner is served Tuesday through Thursday 5:00 to 9:00 P.M., Friday and Saturday until 10:00 P.M., and Sunday 4:00 to 8:00 P.M. $$$

Café Atlantique 33 River Street (203-882-1602). This coffee bar with a European touch is a good choice for breakfast, lunch, and light dinners. Choose from espressos, lattes, pastries, salads, wraps, crepes, and soups. Enjoy the artwork, poetry and open mike nights, and the outdoor area in season. Open Monday through Thursday 7:00 A.M. to 7:00 P.M., Friday from 7:00 A.M. to midnight, and Saturday 9:00 A.M. to midnight.

Places to Stay in Milford

Comfort Inn 278 Old Gate Lane (203-877-9411 or 800-221-2222). One hundred twenty units, including four suites; sauna, indoor and outdoor hot tubs, continental breakfast. $$

Hampton Inn–Milford 129 Plains Road (203-874-4400 or 800-HAMP TON). One hundred forty-eight units; continental breakfast. $$$

Fairfield Inn Milford 111 Schoolhouse Road (203-877-8588 or 800-288-2800). One hundred four units; outdoor pool, continental breakfast. $$

Howard Johnson Lodge 1052 Boston Post Road (203-878-4611 or 800-IGO-HOJO). One hundred sixty-five units with three suites; restaurant, coffee shop, lounge, in-room refrigerators, health and exercise facilities, sauna, whirlpool, playground, indoor and outdoor pools, miniature golf. Airport limo; senior citizen rates. $$

Rainbow Gardens Inn 117 North Broad Street (203-878-2500). This beautifully restored 1855 Victorian home on the green offers three cheerfully decorated rooms with antique furnishings, special luxuries like down pillows, a full country breakfast, and room service. For a truly indulgent treat, guests can arrange for a massage, facial, or aromatherapy. The inn is smoke-free and air-conditioned. Dinner & Stay packages are available. Open year-round. $$$$

The Lily Pad B&B 44 Prospect Street (203-876-9996). Built in 1820, this French Colonial with a mansard roof offers three guest rooms and two baths. Lily and Charles Flannigan welcome you to enjoy their gardens, gazebo, and lawn swing in this charming property on the Wepawaug River. Smoke-free. Continental-plus breakfast served in the dining room at guests' convenience. $$$-$$$$

Public Boat Launches

Housatonic River State Boat Launch Ramp and parking area in Devon section of town on Naugatuck Avenue north of Route 1, under the I-95 bridge between Stratford and Milford. Access upriver as far as the dam in Derby; downriver through the Charles E. Wheeler Wildlife Refuge and out to Long Island Sound. Parking fee in summer only.

Milford Town Dock near Milford Landing at the head of the harbor (203-877-9990). Boat launch ramp; daily or seasonal fee.

For Further Information

Milford Chamber of Commerce (203-878-0681). 5 North Broad Street, 06460. Open 8:30 A.M. to 4:30 P.M. Monday through Friday. Web site is www.milfordct.com. Maps, brochures, information on lodging and dining.

West Haven

Nearly 60,000 residents share West Haven's 10 square miles, leaving little room to entertain tourists in this suburb of New Haven. Settled by the English in 1648, this area was at first called West Farms and was considered part of the New Haven Colony. By 1711, West Farms had formed a separate parish with the area now called Orange, and eventually the two sections became known as the town of Orange. Late in the nineteenth century, a borough called West Haven was created, and in 1921 it became a town.

Today, rows of modest homes with neatly groomed yards characterize many neighborhoods; in others, commercial establishments are flanked by apartment complexes and condominium developments right down to the shoreline. Nevertheless, the foresight of the city planners reserved a wide swath of beach for the use of all residents—and, thankfully, out-of-town guests. On your way to towns with sexier attractions, pause for an hour or so to savor the seascape.

The Best of West Haven

Bradley Point Park and West Haven Promenade

Grab a picnic cooler and a colorful kite and ride down to the West Haven shore to enjoy one of the most wide-open views of Long Island Sound accessible to the public. Along West Haven's Ocean Avenue and Captain Thomas Boulevard, walkers, bicyclists, and motorists can soak up the sounds and smells of the waves and the sea breezes as they explore 3-plus miles of roadway, pathway, and beach.

Today, by comparison with past decades, the completely restored and redeveloped West Haven Public Beach is a quiet place, and the promenade that stretches across the former site of Savin Rock amusement park (see next entry) is frequented mostly by gulls wheeling overhead, seniors playing bocce at the John Barone Bocce Court, and anglers waiting patiently at the fishing pier for a tug on their lines. On breezy days the sky here is often filled with the merry dance of literally dozens of kites. Come with your own kite, or just watch the beautiful aerial acrobatics of other flyers. Stroll Sculpture Mile, an outdoor display of large works by American artists. Bring a picnic (leaving out anything that requires cooking—open flames are prohibited), beach gear, and bicycles to enjoy a full day here.

Food vendors often set up in or near the park, and several restaurants along the boulevard provide sit-down meals of all descriptions. Another public park lies farther east of the promenade, after Captain Thomas Boulevard shifts south one block and becomes Beach Street. Called Morse Park, it has a playground and pavilion and is not far from the town boat launch ramp and the marinas that dot the western edge of New Haven Harbor. At this turning point, Beach Street becomes First Avenue, which heads northward to hug the harbor shore. To leave West Haven, follow First Avenue right up to I-95.

Bradley Point Park is on Captain Thomas Boulevard at Bradley Point (203-937-3651). Take exit 42 off I-95 and follow the signs for Route 162 South, to Platt Avenue, and then south to the shoreline. The park, the promenade, and West Haven Public Beaches (Ocean Avenue and other sites; 203-937-3510) are open dawn to dusk year-round. Parking in lot or on side streets; constable on duty from Memorial Day to Labor Day; nonresidents pay per-vehicle fees of $10.00 per day or $5.00 after 4:00 P.M.

Savin Rock Museum and Learning Center

In the first half of the twentieth century, the West Haven beach area was home to one of the Northeast's most famous amusement centers. At the height of its popularity, from 1927 to 1957, the Savin Rock amusement park, once called White City, included dozens of carnival rides. One of the world's highest Ferris wheels was there, and a colossal—and scary—wooden roller coaster called the Thunderbolt took its screaming fans right out over the water. After ninety years of happy, dizzying activity, the park became dilapidated and a center for activities of a more unsavory nature, and it finally was bulldozed in the early 1960s.

Now a new museum recaptures the magic of that milelong entertainment extravaganza and the culture and customs of that era. Located at the Savin Rock Conference Center on Rock Street near Jimmie's Restaurant at the intersection of Captain Thomas Boulevard and Kelsey Avenue, the museum features hands-on exhibits, interactive video displays, and park memorabilia.

Savin Rock Conference Center (203-937-3566). Open year-round; limited hours; call ahead. Expanded hours in summer. Adults, $4.00, children and seniors, $2.00.

Places to Eat in West Haven

Chick's Drive-In 183 Beach Street (203-934-4510). A shoreline classic established in 1950, this quintessential drive-in seafood shack is the perfect place to stop if you want to be as close to the beach as possible when you celebrate summer with an orgy of fresh fried clams, a brimming lobster roll, or a plate of soft-shell crabs. If seafood doesn't float your boat, pair one of Chick's famed West Haven split dogs with an order of excellent home-style onion rings. Indoor and outdoor seating. Open daily year-round. In-season hours Sunday through Thursday from 10:00 A.M. to 11:00 P.M.; Friday and Saturday until midnight. Winter hours shorter. $

Beach Street Waterfront Grille 343 Beach Street (203-934-3554). Star-studded fiber optic ceilings, colorful murals, and a wide-open view of the Sound accompany pastas, grilled seafood, shrimp pesto, a raw bar, and much more. Entertainment in the bar on Friday and Saturday nights; open daily for dinner year-round; lunch also on Friday and Saturday, plus the dinner menu from noon onward on Sunday. $-$$$

Captain's Galley 19 Beach Street (203-932-1811). Some folks say this is the best of all the seafood restaurants nearby; it certainly is delicious. Fresh seafood almost any way you like it; house-made chowders, fresh salads, plus chicken, prime rib, and pastas. Inside dining and outside patio in warm weather. Open year-round for lunch and dinner daily. $$

Jimmie's of Savin Rock 5 Rock Street (203-934-3212). Probably the most widely known of all the seafood restaurants along this part of the shore. Long lines attest to its popularity. All the shore seafood favorites, plus lots of other American standbys. Overlooks the Sound, but no outdoor seating. Open year-round for lunch and dinner daily. $$

Biagetti's Restaurant 77 Campbell Avenue (203-934-7700). Not far from the beach but with no view, this restaurant has offered fine Italian-American cuisine for nearly thirty years. If you love good food, trade the view for wonderful specialties just like Mama made. Everything is home-made, from sauce to soup, and the family-style ambiance keeps the place comfortable and affordable for adult as well as young diners. Open year-round for dinner Tuesday through Saturday from 5:00 P.M. and Sunday from 1:00 P.M. $$

FUN AFTER DARK OR DINNER

Fireworks over the Sound are special in West Haven on or near the Fourth of July. Launched from a barge offshore, the twenty- to thirty-minute pyrotechnic extravaganza is among the best in the state. Plan to arrive early in the afternoon and stake out your place on the beach or promenade for the best views. Along with your beach chairs and blankets, be sure to bring a bit of extra cash for balloons, ice cream, and neon necklaces. Call the West Haven Park and Recreation Department (203-937-3651) for information on this year's display.

If you arrive in town on a summer evening, stay for the free outdoor concerts on the West Haven green in June and in Old Grove Park from July through September. Performances begin at 7:00 P.M. Call for the exact schedule at (203) 937-3566.

Places to Stay in West Haven

Courtyard by Marriott New Haven/Orange 136 Marsh Hill Road, off I-95 exit 41 in Orange (203-799-2200). One hundred twenty-one rooms, including six suites, some with a Jacuzzi and balcony; outdoor pool, health club, breakfast restaurant. $$$$

Best Western Executive Hotel–New Haven 490 Saw Mill Road, off I-95 exit 42 (203-933-0344 or 800-528-1234). One hundred units; restaurant, lounge, indoor pool, whirlpool, fitness center. Senior citizen rates; shuttles to airports. $$$

Public Boat Launch

West Haven Public Ramp At foot of Monahan Place off First Avenue. Floating dock and launch ramp (203-946-8546).

For Further Information

West Haven Chamber of Commerce 259 Elm Street, second floor (203-933-1500). Open year-round Tuesday to Thursday 11:00 A.M. to 2:00 P.M. Maps, brochures, and listings of businesses, lodgings, restaurants.

New Haven

Since its earliest days an important center of industry, education, and culture along the Connecticut shore, New Haven also remains one of the most vital cities in the state. Although Connecticut's capital city of Hartford is also steeped in history and strongly rooted in the arts and education, New Haven sports a more sophisticated, cosmopolitan style. Perhaps its location on I-95 between New York and Boston contributes to this ambiance. Undeniably, its inseparable association with Yale University enriches its artistic and intellectual aspects, and its diverse community of citizens adds to its cultural panache.

Long a center of life for the Native Americans who once fished its waterways and hunted along its traprock ridges, New Haven has also been home to European newcomers for the better part of four centuries. Once the site of a village called Quinnipiac, which means "long river place," New Haven was renamed by the five hundred English settlers who arrived from Boston in 1638 and established a colony here in 1640. Led by a charismatic Puritan minister named John Davenport and a wealthy Puritan merchant named Theophilus Eaton, the New Haven colonists were better off financially than any other group of settlers in New England. Their wealth showed in the stately homes they built around the New Haven Green, and their confidence defined their settlement as one of great importance. From 1701 to 1875, in fact, New Haven served, with Hartford, as joint capital of the Connecticut Colony and then of the state.

New Haven became known best for the superior quality of its products. By 1810 and for more than fifty years, for instance, New Haven was famed as the producer of the country's finest carriages, and America's first assembly line was right here in James Brewster's Carriage Factory. Perhaps the city's most notable manufacturer was Eli Whitney, Yale-educated lawyer and inventor. Whitney's cotton gin changed the economy of the South—as well as contributed to the rise (and tragedy) of slavery—and was produced in his New Haven factory.

Simultaneously with all this activity, New Haven's Yale College developed its reputation as one of the nation's finest educational and research institutions. By 1810, it had established a medical school and the nation's first school of science. Shortly thereafter, it added other professional schools, including one of the country's first law schools and what is to this date the oldest continuous forestry school in the

DING! DING! DING!

The Greater New Haven Transit District rolled out four red and green electric trolleys in the summer of 2002 to provide free transportation to passengers throughout downtown. From Monday through Saturday from 10:00 A.M. to 6:00 P.M., the trolleys travel a downtown circuit that stops at normal bus stops. Another route provides rush-hour service only from 7:00 to 9:00 A.M. and 4:00 to 6:00 P.M. on weekdays.

United States. In 1832, it established the nation's first university art museum and the nation's first art school. Be sure to spend at least a few days exploring this fascinating urban campus.

The Best of New Haven

West Rock Ridge State Park

If the layout of the city mystifies you, you might want to start a tour of New Haven high above the urban clamor. Overlooking the entire city, West Rock is one of two ridges of basalt forced skyward through volcanic action some 200 million years ago. The state park here runs along the top of the western ridge and has hiking trails, a fishing pond, and a picnic area.

A scenic drive traverses parts of the park. Its southern portion is open to motor vehicles only on a seasonal basis, usually April through November; call for opening dates. The northern section is closed to vehicles but open to hikers, cyclers, and skiers year-round. Folks in cars wishing to hike when the scenic drive is closed can park at the West Rock Nature Center on Wintergreen Avenue. The park entrance is about 200 feet south of the nature center, also on Wintergreen Avenue.

The park's blue-blazed main trail, called **Regicides Trail**, is accessible at the top of the ridge via the scenic drive, or you can walk in off-season from the nature center. Situated just off the roadway that also leads to the park's South Overlook, this 6.3-mile footpath begins near a parking area close to the summit at Judges Cave. It follows the crest of the West Rock Ridge range northward, ending at its junction with the Quinnipiac Trail, which leads to Sleeping Giant State Park in Hamden. The trail offers beautiful views of the harbor and, of course, leads through pretty woodlands. Wear proper footgear because the path, although not consistently strenuous, can be difficult in some spots.

The most infamous site on the trail is the **Judges Cave,** where in 1661 Edward Whalley, John Dixwell, and William Goffe hid from bounty hunters (agents of Charles II) who were hoping to claim the reward for their capture as traitors against the Crown. Charles II intended to execute the men, who had been among nearly sixty Englishmen who had signed the death warrant against Charles I many years earlier. The trio eluded the pursuers, and each of the men lived in New Haven for at least some time after the agents gave up the search. Today, three of the city's avenues are named for the regicides.

Wintergreen Avenue (203–789–7498). Open year-round daily from 8:00 A.M. to sunset. Entrance fee for cars, in season, $1.00.

West Rock Nature Center

Owned and operated by the city and visited most frequently by school-children, this separate area just north of the entrance to West Rock Ridge State Park on Wintergreen Avenue covers forty acres. Short nature trails take visitors along the Wintergreen Brook ravine, over Wintergreen Falls, past a small pond, and so on. Winter is also pretty here. If you come on a snow day with sleds and toboggans, a guaranteed good time awaits.

1020 Wintergreen Avenue, at Baldwin Drive, not far from exit 59 off Route 15 (203–946–8016). Closed holidays. Grounds open dawn to dusk daily, year-round. Free.

East Rock Park

The twin of West Rock, East Rock is on the other side of the city, recognizable by its matching sandstone and traprock cliffs. The 425-acre park is best known for its spectacular views of the city and harbor from its monument-topped summit. Long-range binoculars, benches at the scenic overlook, and a large picnic area with barbecue grills add to your enjoyment.

An environmental education center called the Trowbridge Environmental Center contains displays about local wildlife and plant life. Guided nature walks and workshops appropriate for all ages are scheduled at this center, which is located in College Woods with the ranger station.

Elsewhere in the park, walk on the 10 miles of hiking trails, including the cliff-side ascent called the Giant's Steps Trail. A bird sanctuary, a self-guided nature trail, picnic pavilions, playgrounds, an ice-skating

YALE UNIVERSITY VISITOR INFORMATION AND WALKING TOURS

As you might guess from its worldwide reputation, Yale is a wonderful university to tour. See the gloriously Gothic splendor of the Sterling Memorial Library. Walk through Phelps Gate into the Old Campus quad and listen to the bells in Harkness Tower. Stop at the statue of Yale grad Nathan Hale outside the 1750 Connecticut Hall, where Noah Webster, Nathan Hale, and William Howard Taft perfected their studies. Learn about the development of the university into a world-class research and education center.

You can join a free, student-guided **Yale University Walking Tour** on Saturday and Sunday at 1:30 P.M. and on Monday through Friday at 10:30 A.M. and 2:00 P.M. (but not on Thanksgiving, Christmas Eve, Christmas Day, New Year's Eve, or New Year's Day). The one-hour tour leaves from the **Yale Visitor Information Center** (203-432-2300) at 149 Elm Street, across from the north side of the New Haven Green. No reservations or tickets are necessary; simply arrive about ten minutes prior to departure. (Keep in mind that this tour is the one prospective students and their parents take.) You can also pick up a self-guided tour pamphlet from the visitor center (open year-round, Monday through Friday from 9:00 A.M. to 4:45 P.M. and Saturday and Sunday from 10:00 A.M. to 4:00 P.M.) and tour the campus on your own.

A second tour option is the perfect complement to the university tour; offering a special focus on the city's history and architecture, the **New Haven Walking Tour** covers important downtown sites near the New Haven Green. Those tours are given from April through October on Thursdays at noon. Plan to arrive at the Yale visitor center five minutes or so before noon. No reservations or tickets are necessary for this tour either, but you may call for information (203-432-2302).

rink, a basketball court, and opportunities for sledding, fishing, and kite flying are also located within the park boundaries. Stop at the ranger station for a map.

Enter from East Rock Road in New Haven or Davis Road in Hamden. Playground, environmental center and ranger station in College Woods at the corner of

Cold Spring and Orange Street (203–946–6086). Park open daily year-round from sunrise to sunset. Summit Road open daily from April 1 to October 31, 8:00 A.M. to sunset, and at the same time on Fridays and weekends only from November 1 through March. Two other roads are closed to vehicles but open to cyclists, in-line skaters, and walkers. Hiking trails are closed to mountain bikes. Free.

Yale University Art Gallery

Founded in 1832, this is the oldest university art museum in the United States, and its 100,000-piece collection provides an excellent overview of the history of art from ancient to modern times. Come here to see objects from ancient Egypt, elsewhere in the Middle East and Africa, the Pacific islands, and the Far East. The American paintings and decorative arts are exquisite, as are the collections of American furniture and silver. O'Keeffe, Kandinsky, and Pollock are among the twentieth-century artists, but earlier treasures abound, including masterpieces of the Hudson River School and American Impressionists. The European collection includes Van Gogh, Manet, Monet, Picasso, and many more famed artists.

In addition to special exhibitions of works from the permanent collection, the museum hosts changing exhibitions of work that may never again be collected in one place in this area. The museum also offers tours, lectures, and concerts.

1111 Chapel Street at York Street (203–432–0600). Open Tuesday through Saturday from 10:00 A.M. to 5:00 P.M and Sunday from 1:00 to 6:00 P.M. Closed Monday and on major holidays. One-hour guided gallery tours throughout the season, usually on Wednesday and Saturday at 1:30 P.M., plus other dates with special speakers. Free; donation suggested.

Yale Center for British Art

Home to the largest collection of British art outside Great Britain, the center exhibits magnificent oil and watercolor paintings, drawings, prints, rare books, decorative arts, and sculpture from the Elizabethan period to the present. Works by Stubbs, Gainsborough, Hogarth, Turner, Constable, Blake, and Reynolds are among its treasures. Aligned with a research institute, a reference library and photographic archive, and a paper conservation laboratory, the museum has a serene and serious aura, but visitors of all ages are most welcome. Although the museum's calendar of lectures, symposia, gallery tours, Sunday afternoon concerts, and films are specifically directed to art students and adult aficionados, programs suitable for children often appear on this schedule.

THE AUDUBON ARTS DISTRICT

Tucked primarily into the two short blocks of Audubon Street between Whitney Avenue and State Street, the Audubon Arts District is a small neighborhood with a focus on the visual and performing arts. In this enclave, galleries, studios, and art and music schools attract visitors as well as serious artists and aspiring students. Serving their other needs are a fair number of restaurants, cafes, and boutiques with a personal flair. In addition to the **Creative Arts Workshop** (203-562-4927) at 80 Audubon Street, visitors may want to visit or inquire about special exhibitions and/or performances at such establishments as the **Educational Center for the Arts** (203-787-5191) at 55 Audubon Street, the **Neighborhood Music School** (203-397-2709) at 100 Audubon Street, the **Small Space Gallery** (203-772-2788) at 70 Audubon Street, and the **Wave** gallery and shop at 15 Whitney Avenue.

Of particular note in the neighborhood is **Artspace** (203-772-2377), at 70 Audubon Street. Its studios usually hum with the vibrations of creative energy, and its gallery and some studios are open to visitors Tuesday through Saturday from 11:00 A.M. to 5:00 P.M. (summer hours may differ).

The **John Slade Ely House** (203-624-8055) at 51 Trumbull Street is just a block north of Audubon Street between Whitney Avenue and Orange Street. Housed in a 1905 mansion, this center for contemporary visual arts and humanitarian activities offers eight galleries displaying works from New Haven's oldest art guilds. The center is open at no charge from September through June from Tuesday through Friday 1:00 to 4:00 P.M. and Saturday and Sunday 2:00 to 5:00 P.M.

1080 Chapel Street at High Street (203–432–2800). Open year-round Tuesday through Saturday 10:00 A.M. to 5:00 P.M. and Sunday noon to 5:00 P.M. Closed Monday and major holidays. Free.

Beinecke Rare Book and Manuscript Library

In the midst of the Yale campus and bordered by a sunken courtyard garden featuring the sculpture of Isamo Noguchi, the Beinecke Rare Book and Manuscript Library contains remarkable treasures within its dimly lit galleries. The only natural light that enters this nearly sacred space is filtered through translucent slabs of Vermont marble, which protect the manuscripts, illuminations, and rare prints from the damage of solar radiation. One of the largest rare book collections in the world, the Beinecke contains well over 500,000 printed volumes and several million manuscripts. Among the library's most famed holdings are a Gutenberg Bible, the prints of artist and ornithologist John James Audubon, and the original collection of the Yale College Library. Along with these are amazing medieval illuminated manuscripts, priceless volumes printed before 1500, and journals, first editions, and rare editions of books by the world's greatest authors. Awe-inspiring and yet welcoming to visitors of all ages, the library presents four special changing exhibitions annually.

121 Wall Street (203-432-2977). Open year-round Monday through Friday from 8:30 A.M. to 5:00 P.M. and Saturday from 10:00 A.M. to 5:00 P.M. Closed on Sundays, major holidays, and on Saturdays in August. Free.

Carillon Concerts at Harkness Tower

If you are in New Haven in the summertime on Friday night at 7:00 P.M., grab a blanket and a picnic dinner and head to Harkness Tower near the Old Campus between Chapel and Elm Streets. Enter the quad from High Street and there in the Branford College courtyard relax a while and listen to the incredible music of the 221-foot-tall tower's fifty-four chromatically tuned carillon bells. Students of the art as well as international artists play here several times each summer for about an hour. Don't pack anything crunchy and noisy in your picnic and make sure you close your eyes for the full and unforgettable effect of the glorious classical and popular pieces on each concert's program.

For a schedule of these free performances, call the Yale Guild of Carillonneurs (203-432-2309) or Yale Events Hotline (203-432-9100). In case of rain, a listening room is opened in Phelps Hall at 344 College Street.

Yale Peabody Museum of Natural History

The Peabody, built in 1866, houses one of the nation's oldest and largest natural history collections. Just imagine dinosaurs, dinosaurs, dinosaurs, plus fossils, birds, insects, seashells, rocks, shrunken heads, minerals, meteorites, mummies, mastodons, and mammals. An enormous mural in the Great Hall depicts scientists' best guesses as to how the dinosaurs might have looked. (Called *The Age of Reptiles,* this Pulitzer Prize–winning mural painted by Rudolph Zallinger from 1942 to 1947 has also been partially reproduced on one of the oil storage tanks near New Haven Harbor.)

In other galleries, excellent wildlife and cultural dioramas from many habitats and periods include studies of Neolithic, Pacific, Mesoamerican, ancient Egyptian, and Connecticut Native American peoples. Of interest to those traveling with children may be the Discovery Room, which has been designed especially for young visitors who need to touch, feel, and smell the displays.

Changing exhibitions and tons of special events, classes, workshops, and hands-on activities are offered throughout the year. The museum has a gift shop and rest rooms but no food concession.

170 Whitney Avenue (203–432–5050). Open year-round daily, Monday through Saturday 10:00 A.M. to 5:00 P.M. and Sunday noon to 5:00 P.M. Adults $5.00, children 3 to 15 $3.00.

New Haven Colony Historical Society

This beautiful building designed by famed architect and architecture historian J. Frederick Kelly expressly as the museum of the New Haven Colony is alone worth a visit. A Colonial Revival masterpiece built in 1930 in the late Georgian style, it has a lovely skylit rotunda, marble staircases, an alluring salmon-colored ballroom, and magnificent moldings at every doorway. The exhibits focus on the history of the colony, the development of the city, and the inventions and industries begun in New Haven County. See Eli Whitney's cotton gin, Charles Goodyear's rubber inkwell, an organ made by the New Haven Organ Company, an original Mysto Magic Erector Set, and a three-story dollhouse with a thousand details of decoration. Along with these displays are historical photographs, maps, ships' models, a wonderful ongoing *Amistad* exhibit that includes Nathaniel Jocelyn's portrait of Joseph Cinque, and changing exhibitions.

114 Whitney Avenue (203–562–4183). Open year-round Tuesday through Friday 10:00 A.M. to 5:00 P.M. and Saturday and Sunday 2:00 to 5:00 P.M. (except closed on Sunday in July and August). Closed major holidays. Adults $2.00; children 6 to 16 $1.00.

Amistad *Memorial and the* Amistad *at Long Wharf Pier*

Lessons of courage, honor, and justice are to be learned at the base of the marvelous bronze sculpture outside New Haven's City Hall and aboard the recreation of the *Amistad* itself at Long Wharf Pier. Created by Kentucky artist Ed Hamilton, the *Amistad* Memorial reminds visitors of the bravery of Joseph Cinque.

ELM CITY FIRSTS

Historians, archivists, and ordinary diehard fans of New Haven have had some fun compiling lists of the city's famous "firsts." Of course, counterclaims have occasionally refuted these assertions, but New Haven buffs aver that the world as we know it would be entirely different if not for these local inventions:

Football The story goes that Yale freshmen and sophomores—en masse—regularly accosted one another in a kind of chaotic romp involving a round ball, a large field, and two goalposts. The older and wiser sophomores eventually decided that perhaps only twenty of each class should meet on the field, and Walter Camp organized the gridiron pattern and created the rules that made the wild rumpus into a new game called American football.

Frisbee Mrs. Frisbie's pies—and their metal tins—were made in Bridgeport, but Yalies who had finished their pies took the tins to the New Haven Green and sent them whirling in a new twist, so to speak, on the game of catch. Soon plastic versions replaced the tins, and now students play Ultimate Frisbee all across the nation.

Hamburgers In 1900 Louis Lassen couldn't bear to throw away the tender meat scraps from his thin-sliced steak sandwiches, so he ground them up, packed them together in a patty, and made history. (Stop in at Louis' Lunch, 263 Crown Street, for the full story.)

Hot Dogs Who's to say who really wrapped the first bun around a plump sausage? Some say it happened here, and the proof rests at least partly in the Yale student newspaper that printed, in about 1900, the first written reference to the immediately popular sandwich.

Pizza Frank Pepe is definitely the father of American pizza and that's all there is to it. (Try a taste test at Pepe's Pizzeria Napoletana, 157 Wooster Street.)

Lollipops The word (and the sweetmeat or candy treat for which it stood) has existed since the late eighteenth century, but New Haven says lollipops as we know them were invented here in 1892 by George Smith of the Smith Candy Company, who was the first fellow to put a stick in it.

The story of the *Amistad* Africans started in the seas off Havana, Cuba, in 1839 when fifty-three Mendi captives seized control of the merchant ship *La Amistad,* which was taking them closer and closer to the unspeakable ordeal of a lifetime of slavery. Eventually apprehended by the U.S. Navy as the ship met the waters of Long Island Sound, the slavers accused their captives of piracy, and the Africans were taken into custody and held in the New Haven jailhouse, formerly on a site just opposite the present City Hall. Here the captives awaited trial, as abolitionists and attorneys and even former President John Quincy Adams joined the battle to restore the freedom of the Africans.

The heroic acts of the group's leader, Sengbe Pieh, also known as Joseph Cinque, are celebrated on the 14-foot, three-sided bronze sculpture that stands near the site of the jailhouse where the illegally kidnapped Mendi Africans were imprisoned. Although the morally laudable and eventually triumphant teamwork of the principal players in this incident did not lead directly or immediately to the release of other captive Africans, it did contribute greatly to the abolitionist movement and inspired the courage of countless other Africans who sought, fought for, and won their own freedom.

The monument reminds all visitors of the importance of pursuing justice, freedom, and equality for all people against all odds. A tour ($5.00 per adult or $3.00 per child) of the re-creation of the schooner itself (usually in port from April through October) is a moving, eye-opening experience that makes the reality of the Mendi ordeal all the clearer. When the schooner is in port, it also does three-hour public sails Monday through Friday from 5:00 to 8:00 P.M. Tickets are $25 for adults and $15 for children under 12. Reservations are necessary.

The Memorial is located in the plaza at 165 Church Street at the New Haven City Hall. Accessible year-round and round the clock at no charge.

The Freedom Schooner Amistad *is berthed, when she is not sailing as an educational ambassador to other ports, at Long Wharf Pier off Long Wharf Drive. For a schedule of* Amistad *homeport tours and voyages, call Amistad America at 203–499–3894 or visit their Web site: www.amistadamerica.org for further information. The Web site is an excellent source of facts about the* Amistad *incident and the construction of this historic replica.*

Creative Arts Workshop

Just a few blocks from the New Haven Green and the university, this three-story workshop houses studios for masters and students of painting, drawing, pottery, jewelry, printmaking, sculpture, photography, and weaving. Children as well as adults can participate in studio tours and classes. Call ahead to find out what artists might be crafting on a particular day. All visitors may also admire the exhibitions in the Hilles Gallery and purchase the works for sale in the shop.

During the workshop's annual holiday exhibition and sale, more than 400 juried artisans from around the country display more than 10,000 pieces of artwork in the gallery. Called the *Celebration of American Crafts*, this exhibition showcases fine art as well as decorative and functional artworks in all media. Shop from mid-November through December 24.

80 Audubon Street (203-562-4927). Open year-round. Gallery and shop open Monday through Friday 9:00 A.M. to 5:00 P.M. and Saturday 9:00 A.M. to noon. Different hours during annual holiday exhibition and annual Sunday open house. Call for dates at these events.

New Haven Symphony Orchestra

The fourth oldest orchestra in the United States, this symphony offers an October to June concert season in beautiful Woolsey Hall at the corner of College and Grove. Under the direction of Jung-Ho Pak, the symphony performs with internationally known artists in the Symphony Series and the Pops Series. Subscriptions and single tickets are available for both series.

The orchestra also plans Sunday matinee concerts of special appeal to families and at budget-conscious prices, usually held at the Lyman Auditorium of Southern Connecticut State University and at Shelton High School. Before each performance, youngsters may meet the musicians and touch and try the orchestral instruments. Tickets for the three-concert SCSU series in 2002 were $60.00 for adults; were $30.00 single tickets; children under 12 paid $5.00 per concert. In addition to these series, the NHSO presents free concerts in New Haven and on nearby town greens in the summertime.

Offices at 33 Whitney Avenue; concert hall at Grove and College. For tickets and information, call the box office (203-776-1444 or 800-292-NHSO).

Shubert Performing Arts Center

This refurbished theater offers comfortable seats and a state-of-the-art sound system for your pleasure in seeing Broadway musicals, ballet, opera, modern dance, comedy, mime, and much more in a full season from September through May. Located just off the green in the heart of downtown, not far from the university, the Shubert has entertained theater-lovers

MORE NEW HAVEN PARKS

Edgerton Park On Whitney Avenue and Cliff Street near the Hamden line; enter observatory area at 75 Cliff Street (203-777-1886). Comprising twenty-two acres on the National Register of Historic Places, this property was originally owned by Eli Whitney and later became the site of the now-demolished Edgerton mansion built at the turn of the twentieth century as a wedding present for the wife of Frederick Brewster. The park's design was planned according to an eighteenth-century English landscape garden to emphasize the importance of open space. Its Crosby Conservatory of tropical plants has a simulated rain forest path and horticultural exhibits such as carnivorous plants, cacti, and succulents; Greenbrier Greenhouse offers culinary herbs and seasonal plants for sale year-round. Seasonal fairs and concerts draw visitors to the flower gardens, walking, biking, and cross-country skiing paths, and picnic areas. The grounds are open daily year-round from dawn to dusk; the conservatory and garden center are open year-round Monday through Friday from 10:00 A.M. to 5:00 P.M. and on weekends until 4:00 P.M.

Edgewood Park 720 Edgewood Avenue between Whalley Avenue and Chapel Street (203-946-8028). One hundred twenty acres with nature walkways, playground, ranger station with wildlife displays and programs, duck pond, tennis and basketball courts, playing fields, Holocaust Memorial, and Spanish-American War monument.

Wooster Square Green On Chapel Street between Academy and Wooster Place. Near New Haven's Little Italy, a restored historic district of some of New Haven's prettiest architecture, designed in the early 1800s around a central square as if it were in fact in the heart of London. Linger a while in this grassy oasis named for New Haven's Revolutionary War hero David Wooster. Have a look at the monument to Christopher Columbus, then get in line behind all the other hungry patrons drawn to the pizzerias, ristorantes, and trattorias on the outer edges of this tiny enclave.

from its opening in 1914. Many legendary successes have premiered here and gone on to Broadway; among these are such musical classics as *My Fair Lady* and *Damn Yankees,* and plays by Neil Simon and Tennessee Williams.

Tickets are available singly or through the preseason Early Bird Buyer program, series subscriptions, or group sales. Some shows are aimed especially at families and are offered at special prices as low as $10 per ticket. A Starter Student Series offers special hour-long daytime performances for children at $5.00 per student. School groups and home-schoolers should call Ruth Feldman (203-624-1825) for further information.

247 College Street. For a calendar of performances or to order tickets, call the box office (203-562-5666 or 800-228-6622). E-mail: shubert@shubert.com. Web site is www.shubert.com.

Long Wharf Theatre

This thirty-something theater won a Tony Award in 1978 for outstanding regional theater, two Pulitzer Prizes for drama, and two Drama Critics Circle awards for best play—but it's not resting on its laurels. Although it remains in its original home in New Haven's Long Wharf district near the Sound, big changes have taken place within. A recent revitalization of the theater's lobby and other interior spaces underscore the energy of the gifted performers who regularly light up the two stages here.

With the guidance of acclaimed directors and the support of nationally known set designers, actors such as Julie Harris, Joanne Woodward, Al Pacino, and John Lithgow have dazzled the audiences who fill the 491 seats of the intimate auditorium of the Newton Schenck Stage. From Tuesday through Sunday in season, the stage sizzles with the works of classic and contemporary playwrights. On other days, Stage II lights up; this 199-seat proscenium theater stages new works. Single tickets and subscriptions for adults and children ages 10 to 17 are available for the October through May season.

22 Sargent Drive (box office 203-787-4282). Tickets generally $15 to $39 for single performances. For subscription information and season calendar, call the box office or write to Long Wharf Theatre, P.O. Box 9507, New Haven CT 06534, or look on the Web at www.longwharf.org.

Yale Repertory Theatre/Yale School of Drama

From Shakespeare to Shaw and Chekhov to Soyinka, from drama to musical, from hilarious comedy to profound philosophy, the Yale Rep never fails to engage its audiences in its full-scale productions from September or October through May. The Rep itself is the professional arm of this award-winning organization. Some productions are projects of the graduate program of the School of Drama, with student apprentices working with a professional director in various roles from actor to set designer to producer.

A WHIRL BY THE SEA

Lighthouse Point Park was once the popular last stop on the New Haven Trolley line. In those days the park had bathhouses, boat rides, amusement rides, and baseball games, with such legends as Babe Ruth and Ty Cobb playing here on Sunday afternoons in the Roaring Twenties. Today only one of its famed rides remains. Housed in a landmark building on the National Register of Historic Places is the Lighthouse Point Carousel, a well-restored treasure. Jumping horses that slide on gleaming brass poles stand four abreast, alternating with the steadfast steeds, which stand shoulder to shoulder in rows of three. Climb aboard for only 50 cents.

The eighty-two-acre park also has the pre–Civil War **Five Mile Point Lighthouse** and a great little nature center at the East Shore Ranger Station. A marine touch tank displays common shore plants and creatures, and a ship's deck provides a great play space for youngsters to pretend on.

The park's beach is clean and safe, with a first aid station, a snack bar, spotless changing rooms and showers, a small wooden playground, swing sets, and a picnic grove. A public boat launch, a fishing pier, volleyball nets, a nature trail, and excellent bird-watching areas in the bird sanctuary are also here. Hawk, falcon, and eagle watching during the annual migration from late August through November brings birders from all over the state.

The park is at 2 Lighthouse Road. Take exit 50, Woodward Avenue, off I-95 northbound, or exit 51, Frontage Road, southbound; follow the signs down Townsend Avenue to Lighthouse Road and the park (park manager 203-946-8005; ranger station 203-946-8790). The park is open daily year-round, 6:00 A.M. to sunset, without charge from Memorial Day to Labor Day when each out-of-town carload pays $6.00 per day. The carousel operates from Memorial Day to Labor Day on Tuesday through Friday from 3:00 to 7:00 P.M. and on Saturday, Sunday, and holidays from 11:00 A.M. to 7:00 P.M.

The season at the Rep/YSD may include intriguing interpretations of classic plays as well as contemporary and world-premiering works. Staged in the marvelous space created in 1970 within the landmark 1868 Calvary Baptist Church, performances are usually Tuesday

A STEP BACK IN TIME

Future visitors will be able to travel back in time to the year 1800 at the beautifully simple 1780 Pardee-Morris House on Morris Cove overlooking New Haven Harbor, owned and operated by the New Haven Colony Historical Society. Originally built in 1750 on land acquired by Thomas Morris in 1671, the first structure on this property was burned to the ground by the British in 1779 when they invaded New Haven during the Revolution. Subsequently rebuilt on the remaining foundation, the current structure is noted for its stone ends and its third-floor ballroom. Currently undergoing restoration, the wonderfully preserved Pardee-Morris House will offer, when it reopens, a peek into the eighteenth century through the story of the well-to-do family who lived here.

Call the Historical Society (203-562-4183) for information on this reopening.

through Saturday at 8:00 P.M. and Monday at 7:00 P.M. Matinees are scheduled for some productions on Wednesday and Saturday at 2:00 P.M. Call for a calendar of the current season.

222 York Street at the corner of Chapel and York in the former Calvary Baptist Church (203-432-1234). Single tickets generally $25 to $30; subscriptions to six- or ten-play series or make-your-own-series of three to five plays are also available.

Fort Nathan Hale and Black Rock Fort

After a visit to Lighthouse Point, you might want to make another pit stop as you travel north again on Townsend Avenue. Take a left on Fort Hale Park Road to visit two of New Haven's oldest historic sites. **Black Rock Fort** was built in 1776 by order of the Connecticut Colony to protect the Port of New Haven from the British. Unfortunately, by the time Major General William Tryon arrived on July 5, 1779, with three thousand British troops, only nineteen defenders remained at the fort; they were swiftly captured by the enemy, which then marched on to New Haven. (Amazingly, the Brits were repelled the next day in the city by a mere several dozen colonial soldiers.)

Fort Nathan Hale was built near the same site in the early 1800s as the British and Americans prepared again to fight. This time, during the War of 1812, the defenders successfully quashed the British invaders right here. Rebuilt in 1863 with new ramparts, bunkers, a drawbridge, and eighteen guns, the fort was prepared for Civil War action, but it never came.

Now you can make a self-guided tour of both sites. The drawbridge, its moat, the ramparts, bunkers, and other fortifications either still exist or have been restored. In addition to the remains of the forts, there is a handsome statue of the young Nathan Hale, a colorful flag display, and some signage and self-guided tour brochures at the information booth at the entrance to the site. A linear walking park called the Pardee Seawall now connects the forts to each other and to nearby Morris Cove and the Forbes Bluff area. It offers beautiful views of the harbor.

Woodward Avenue (203-787-8790). Open daily Memorial Day to Labor Day from 10:00 A.M. to 4:00 P.M. Free.

Boat Excursions and Charters

Schooner, Inc. Cruises. 60 South Water Street, departing from the Long Wharf Pier off I-95 exit 46 (203-865-1737). If you want to see New Haven from the Sound and get a history/ecology lesson and a great boat ride to boot, call this tour operator during the warm months. Weather permitting, they'll take you out on chartered half-day, full-day, and sunset sails aboard the *Quinnipiack*, a beautiful 91-foot gaff-rigged wooden schooner.

Two kinds of public sails are offered from late May through September. The Sea Adventures are educational trips with an onboard naturalist who helps passengers identify and examine specimens caught in the schooner's trawl net. The trips are offered on Wednesday and Friday from 6:00 to 9:00 P.M. and Sunday from 1:00 to 4:00 P.M.

The sunset cruises are purely relaxing, with great storytelling thrown in for entertainment. They are offered on Sundays from 5:00 to 8:00 P.M. Adults $15, children under 12 $10. On both types of cruises, passengers are welcome to bring picnic lunches or dinners and beverages. Wine or beer is permitted aboard for adults. Private charters are also offered from April to November.

Schooner, Inc., also offers weeklong summer day camps for children from kindergarten through high school. Sea Sprites (grades K-4) explore marine habitats; study marine animals; and do arts, crafts, and games. Seafaring Scientists (grades 5-8) make day sails on the *Quinnipiack* for Long Island Sound exploration. Source to Sound (grades 9-12) allows older explorers to canoe from the headwaters of the Quinnipiac River all the way to New Haven Harbor.

Freedom Schooner Amistad (see pages 102 and 104) Tours and public cruises of historic replica.

Places to Eat in New Haven

Louis' Lunch 263 Crown Street (203-562-5507). Louie Lassen opened this landmark luncheon stand in 1895 and claimed responsibility for the first hamburger cooked in America in 1900. Now in its second century, this famed eatery has a place on the National Register. Now Louis's grandson, Ken Lassen, and his great-grandson, Jeff Lassen, are behind the counter, making fresh-daily, hand-formed burgers and cheeseburgers, served on toast. You can also get steak sandwiches or, on weekend nights, a hot dog or two. Tuna salad made by Jeff's mom, Lee, is served year-round on Fridays. Come here for a taste of culinary history. Open Tuesday and Wednesday 11:00 A.M. to 4:00 P.M., Thursday through Saturday from noon to 2:00 A.M. Closed Sunday and sometimes Monday and for the entire month of August. $

Pepe's Pizzeria Napoletana 157 Wooster Street (203-865-5762). Some would argue that no better pizza has ever been made, even in Italy. Most folks claim Frank Pepe's famous white clam pie is the most delicious item on the menu, but those who eschew clams swear on their own favorites. Be ready to wait for pizza this perfect—it won't matter how early you get here, other aficionados will have staked a place before you. $-$$

Sally's Pizzeria 237 Wooster Street (203-624-5271). Anyone who loves this place knows that Sally was the late, great Salvatore A. Consiglio who learned some of the tricks of his trade from his uncle Frank Pepe down the street. His talented descendants still throw the best pies in the neighborhood into the 12-by-12-foot coal-fired brick oven that pushes out twenty pies at once. Order your favorite pie—no matter where else you've asked for a similar combo, you won't have had it so good until you eat it here. Closed Mondays. $-$$

Claire's Corner Copia Cafe 1000 Chapel Street at the corner of College (203-562-3888). Close to the New Haven Green, Yale University, and the Yale Art Gallery and British Art Center, Claire's offers the best soups made in the city, plus other flavorful vegetarian and vegan dishes, from lasagnas to pasta salads, sandwiches, chili, quesadillas, breads, pastries, and cakes. Order takeout or sit at tables that are semi-self-service. Open for breakfast, lunch, and dinner year-round daily from 8:00 A.M. to 10:00 P.M. $

Bentara 76 Orange Street (203-562-2511). This Malaysian restaurant in the Ninth Square district at the edge of downtown and the up-and-coming State Street neighborhood is a chic, sophisticated place to explore Asian cuisine at its best. Delicious curries, satays, rotis, soups, noodles. "Very Good" *New York Times* review—we can vouch for that as well. Open daily for lunch and dinner, except in summer, when there is no lunch on weekends. $$-$$$

Union League Cafe 1032 Chapel Street (203-562-4299). Just across from Yale's Old Campus in an 1860 landmark building once home to the Union League, the elegantly informal cafe presents country French cuisine with a delightful homespun flair. Time, talent, and creativity define the philosophy here. Ask for a table by the fireplace in winter or at the windows overlooking the passersby on Chapel Street in spring and summer. Open for lunch on weekdays and for dinner daily year-round. $$$

Ibiza 39 High Street (203-865-1933). Casual, contemporary setting for lively conversation and the adventure of choosing (and sharing) tapas, delicious and inventive appetizers or appetizer-size portions of Spanish origin. To do this right, order the traditional glass of sherry and make a meal from two or three of these (about $7.00 each), or order a dozen for the table to share. The kitchen closes at 11:00 P.M., so this is a great late-supper place après-theater. $$

Zinc 964 Chapel Street (203-624-0507). Modern American cuisine is their own buzzword, and chef Denise Appel and pastry chef Ken Ayvasian are ensuring that the food matches the buzz about this cutting-edge winner. The sleek, no-frills decor sets a tone: The focus here is what's on the plate. Fresh local produce and top-quality meats and seafood are a prelude to divine desserts. Don't miss this treat. Live jazz on Saturday nights from 10:00 P.M. to 1:00 P.M. Dinner daily; lunch weekdays only. $$$$

Places to Stay in New Haven

New Haven Hotel 229 George Street (203-498-3100). Elegant accommodations in the heart of downtown. The ninety-two units include balcony suites with wet bars, refrigerators, and deluxe amenities. Valet parking, dry cleaning services, fitness center, lap pool and therapeutic pool, access to adjacent Downtown Health and Racquet Club. Designated smoking rooms and nonsmoking floors. Templeton's Restaurant serves American cuisine; lounge open daily. $$$

New Haven / 113

Colony Inn 1157 Chapel Street (203-776-1234). Sophisticated downtown landmark with eighty-six luxury units ranging from standard double rooms to two-bedroom suites. Association with the Downtown Health and Racquet Club; convenient to downtown and university sites. Valet dry cleaning, valet indoor parking, room service, courtesy van to Tweed airport, train, or bus terminal. Steak house on first level. $$$$

Three Chimneys Inn 1201 Chapel Street (203-789-1201). 1870 mansion located near Yale and the College and Chapel dining, shopping, and entertainment district. Ten guest rooms with private baths, canopied or four-poster beds, oriental carpets, and Georgian and Federal-style furnishings, plus cable television, voice mail, and data ports. Front veranda overlooking formal gardens, library, and club room. Complimentary buffet-style full breakfast and afternoon tea. On-site parking. No smoking except on veranda or in gardens. Young guests welcome over the age of 6; no pets allowed. Elevators provide full wheelchair accessibility. $$$$

Omni New Haven Hotel at Yale 155 Temple Street (203-772-6664 or 800-THE-OMNI). Three hundred and six deluxe rooms, including six luxury suites. Galileo's rooftop restaurant, lounge, health club, on-site garage parking. New incarnation of the old Park Plaza Hotel, fully renovated and greatly expanded, with a location right smack in the middle of New Haven's hub. $$$$

Inn at Oyster Point 104 Howard Avenue (203-773-3334). Web site: www.oysterpointinn.com. This Victorian charmer by the sea is gorgeously restored and decorated, and the gracious hosts pamper guests from start to finish. Four of the six guestrooms have private baths; all guests enjoy afternoon sherry and a buffet breakfast in the dining room. Immaculate and restful. Children over 10 are welcome. $$$-$$$$

Hotel Duncan 1151 Chapel Street (203-787-1273). A genteel throwback to low-tech eras, this ninety-room century-old downtown landmark is in the heart of the Yale neighborhood. $$-$$$

Grand Chalet Inn and Suites at Long Wharf 400 Sargent Drive (203-562-1111 or 800-5-CHALET). One hundred fifty-two units including fifty-five suites. Complimentary continental breakfast. Restaurant, lounge, coffee shop, health club, sauna, outdoor pool. Near harbor sites and Long Wharf Theater; convenient to I-95. $$$

OUTDOOR SUMMER FESTIVALS AND PERFORMANCES

New Haven is well known for the variety of outdoor entertainments it offers in the summertime. Most of these performances are free and appropriate for all ages. Here is a list of the best events.

Outdoor Summer Concerts on the Green/New Haven Jazz Festival Presented by the New Haven Office of Cultural Affairs (203-946-7821). These free summer concerts in July and August on selected Saturday evenings feature outstanding jazz artists from around the globe. At about 6:00 the warm-up music starts; the main act may not begin until 8:00. Bring a blanket and picnic or eat at the food booths set up at the edge of the green. Dance in the twilight with music all around you.

International Festival of Arts and Ideas (203-498-1212 or 888-ART-IDEA; Web site is www.artidea.org). Acclaimed performers come from nearly every continent to unify the global community and raise our awareness and our spirits in an outpouring of artistic energy that now spans two weeks in June each year. Of the hundreds of indoor and outdoor performances staged on or near the New Haven Green and on the Yale campus, many are free. See classical and modern dance. Hear opera, folk, salsa, reggae, jazz, and classical artists. Participate in dances and pageants. Listen to engaging discussions of matters of the heart, the mind, music, and other arts.

Greater New Haven Acoustic Music Society (203-468-1000). This contemporary folk music society sponsors acoustic concerts and workshops featuring national and regional artists. Fall and spring performances are generally held at the University of New Haven, but ten summer concerts are given at the Eli Whitney 1816 Barn across from the Eli Whitney Museum in Hamden, on Whitney Avenue. Call for a calendar.

Residence Inn by Marriott 3 Long Wharf Drive (203-777-5337 or 800-331-3131). One hundred twelve suites (studios to two bedrooms), all with fully equipped kitchens and some with fireplaces. Outdoor pool, Jacuzzi, sports court, access to Downtown Health and Racquet Club. Continental breakfast. Long-term rates for stays over five nights. $$$$

Public Boat Launch

Lighthouse Point Park Exit 50 off I-95, south on Townsend Avenue, right on Lighthouse Road to the park. Parking for sixty cars; seasonal weekend and holiday parking fee.

For Further Information

Greater New Haven Convention and Visitors Bureau 59 Elm Street, New Haven 06511 (800-332-7829 or 203-777-8550). Brochures, maps, and information on lodging and restaurants. Ask for a copy of the *Guide to Greater New Haven*. Open Monday through Friday year-round from 8:30 A.M. to 5:00 P.M.

Long Wharf Visitor Information Center 355 Long Wharf Drive, New Haven 06511 (800-332-7829 or 203-777-8550). Booth off I-95; stocked with maps and brochures from Memorial Day through Labor Day. Open Monday through Friday from 10:00 A.M to 7:00 P.M. and on weekends until 5:00 P.M.

Yale University Free Events Hotline (203-432-9100). Information on all Yale events that the public may attend free of charge

Yale University Sports Hotline (203-432-YALE).

Arts Council of Greater New Haven (203-772-2788). Publishes the free monthly publication *Greater New Haven Arts! A Guide to Arts, Entertainment, and Culture* distributed at many locations in town.

East Haven

Even though East Haven was first settled in the mid-1600s in connection with an ironworks that had been established at the southern end of Lake Saltonstall, the real development of the town came much later as an outgrowth of New Haven's sprawl. Industry here centered on the ironworks that processed bog iron from North Haven, and farming and fishing supplemented the town's economic base. Life in East Haven remained relatively quiet for most of its early history, the high point being the British raid on the town during the American Revolution and Lafayette's encampment on the town green.

Today the town is mostly residential with unremarkable supporting commercial establishments seen mostly by travelers passing along I-95 through the shopping areas on Frontage Road. Few travelers slow down along this route to see what the town has to offer. Those who exit the highway in East Haven, however, will find one of Connecticut's most popular family attractions, the Shore Line Trolley Museum.

The Best of East Haven

Shore Line Trolley Museum

The mostly volunteer efforts of the Branford Electric Railway Association have kept alive and well one of Connecticut's oldest tourist attractions—the oldest continually operating suburban trolley line in the United States. The museum still offers the same sense of old-time Connecticut that it did when it was part of the trolley system that carried thousands of visitors along the shoreline in the early years of the twentieth century. Beginning in 1900, this particular stretch ran from the East Haven Green to Branford's Short Beach; today it follows all but a few missing yards of that exact route through the woodlands, marshes, and meadows—and back to yesteryear.

Nearly one hundred classic trolley cars are stored on the grounds along with the first electric freight locomotive, the country's oldest rapid transit car, and a rare parlor car. The car barns house both restored and unrestored trolleys. Admission to the complex, listed on the National Register of Historic Places, buys you unlimited 3-mile round-trip rides on the trolleys, plus a self-guided tour of the car barns and display areas.

The trolley rides are great fun, especially for young children and adults with a nostalgic sense of romance. Some cars are closed and others are open to the air, briny with the tidal odors of the marshes, the East Haven and Farm Rivers, and the sea, which lies just a few hundred yards from the southernmost length of track on the Branford side.

Special events are planned throughout the year: Laurel and Hardy Days in early June, Canada Days in early July, a Trolley Fair in September, and New York Days in early October. Watch out on the "haunted" rides during the last week in October—not all the passengers are as alive and well as you are. If you haven't had the wits frightened out of you, return again on weekends in December for Santa Days, when the jolly saint himself rides the rails with you.

Enjoy the museum's picnic area, open from May through October, and check out the gift shop for souvenirs. You can arrange birthday parties, group picnics, and other special charters at a group discount for fifteen or more if booked in advance. For these special arrangements and charters, call (203) 467-7365. Rest rooms and a soft drink machine are here, but there is no food concession or snack bar.

17 River Street (203–467–6927). Web site: www.bera.org. Open daily from Memorial Day through Labor Day from 11:00 A.M. to 5:00 P.M. Also at the same hours in April on Sundays only, and in May on Saturdays and Sundays. In the fall, the museum is open on Saturdays and Sundays in September and October, plus Columbus Day and in November on Sundays only, prior to Thanksgiving. Call for a special events schedule for December. Adults $5.00, seniors $4.00, ages 2 to 11 $2.00. Trolleys run at least every thirty minutes; last trolley leaves at 5:00 P.M.

Lake Saltonstall

Tucked into a narrow valley between the hills of East Haven and Branford, the crooked finger of Lake Saltonstall is one of nature's gifts, partly used as a regional freshwater supply and partly as a recreation resource for all visitors. Because Lake Saltonstall is split in half by the boundaries of East Haven and Branford, activities on and around Lake Saltonstall seem well placed in this chapter.

One of the largest freshwater bodies near New Haven, Lake Saltonstall is open to anyone who would like to hike its surrounding trails and fish in its waters. Stocked each spring with brown and rainbow trout as well as largemouth bass, the lake is also home to native fish and waterfowl. Hiking the 10 miles of pretty trails of the 1,900 acres of woodland surrounding the lake is possible year-round, either with an annual $35 permit that also allows you to visit other water authority land throughout New Haven County or with a single-use permit ($5.00 per day). The recreation permits allow one adult plus one adult guest and any number of your children under the age of 21 to use the trails. Annual permits for disabled visitors or people over the age of 60 are $20 (and also include their children and an adult guest).

Fishing season is from the third Saturday in April through November 30, and fishing is also allowed with the purchase of that $35 annual permit or with a single-use daily permit, plus a state fishing

A DAY AT THE BEACH

A spin around the East Haven beach neighborhood of Momauguin is a worthwhile shoreline journey. Interestingly enough, conservationists might say that a drive along East Haven beaches provides a great example of improper and unwise building of houses and seawalls along the coast. To be fair, East Haven is far from the only community in which construction close to the water—in fact, well below the flood line of the 1938 hurricane—defies common sense as well as Mother Nature. Nevertheless, here, as in other towns, human attraction to the beauty of the beach often denies recognition of the Sound's power and potential fury.

Take Route 142 south from Route 1, which you can reach from either 51 or 52 off I-95. Follow Route 142 to Coe Avenue, which leads directly south from the point at which Route 142 swings eastwardly toward Branford. At the foot of Coe Avenue is Cosey Beach Avenue, which runs east-west, immediately parallel to the Sound. The **East Haven Town Beach,** with rest rooms, showers, a pavilion, and snack bar concession, is almost exactly at this junction. As with most public beaches, off-season use of the East Haven Town Beach is unmonitored; thus, visitors are welcome to swim, beachcomb, or picnic here anytime from Labor Day through Memorial Day. A town park and playing fields also lie along Cosey Beach Avenue, as do a variety of restaurants and markets. Call the East Haven Town Beach (203-468-3800) or the Recreation Department (203-468-3367) for information on nonresident use of the beaches in season.

license, which can be purchased at any Connecticut town clerk's office or from the state DEP fisheries licensing office (860-424-3105). Anglers are welcome to fish from the shore or from the 70-foot dock, which is wheelchair accessible. You might also enjoy searching for a quiet spot of your own by going out on the lake in a rental rowboat ($10 per day) or small powerboat with electric motors ($25 per day). Only these rental boats are allowed on the lake. Bring your own bait (worms are the only live bait allowed here) and tackle, plus anything you might want to eat or drink.

To reach the trails or the dock house, take Route 1 east from East Haven to a left turn on Hosley Avenue just over the Branford line. Follow Hosley Avenue to the turn-out for the lake. Purchases of annual permits can be made in person at the Water Authority office at 90 Sargent Drive in New Haven or by phone

(203–624–6671). For a daily permit, come to the dock house anytime between 7:00 A.M. and 1:00 P.M. Monday through Friday or 7:00 A.M. to 7:00 P.M. Saturday and Sunday. Lake area open for hiking and fishing from sunrise to sunset.

Places to Eat in East Haven

The Beachhead Restaurant 3 Cosey Beach Avenue (203–469–5450). An East Haven tradition since the 1940s, this popular establishment was resuscitated a few years back by new owners who renewed old favorites with some innovative twists and a healthier spin. Fresh fish, pastas, and veal and chicken dishes with an Italian background form the backbone of the menu. There's a casual ambiance across from the beach with outdoor patio dining in warm weather, but cottages and condos block all but the smallest slice of seascape. Lunch Tuesday through Friday 11:30 A.M. to 2:30 P.M.; dinner Tuesday through Sunday 5:00 to 10:00 P.M. Closed Mondays. $$–$$$

Sandpiper Restaurant 161 Cosey Beach Avenue on the corner across from Momauguin's park and town beach (203–469–7544). Very casual, very clean, very traditional shoreline seafood shack/diner cuisine. Fresh seafood platters with everything from fried clam strips to lobster, plus salads, house-made chowders, pasta specials, and much more. Happy, busy dining room with great views of the water. Open daily year-round from 11:00 A.M. for lunch and dinner. $–$$

Antonio's 672 Main Street (203–469–2386). American and Italian fare that comes highly recommended after a quarter-century in business. Neapolitan favorites year-round at lunch Monday through Friday 11:30 A.M. to 2:30 P.M. and dinner Monday through Saturday 5:00 to 10:00 P.M. and Sunday noon to 9:00 P.M. $$–$$$

Ristorante Faustini 190 East Main Street (203–467–9498). Reservations are required in this smoke-free establishment. Contemporary and traditional Italian dishes, exquisitely seasoned, with a special section of the menu devoted to healthy selections with a low-fat content. Sublime desserts. Open for dinner only, Tuesday through Sunday. $$–$$$

Place to Stay in East Haven

Holiday Inn Express 30 Frontage Road (203–469–5321). Eighty-two units, outdoor pool, shuttle service to New Haven; complimentary continental breakfast; senior citizen rates. Kids stay free. $$$–$$$$

For Further Information

East Haven Chamber of Commerce (203-467-4305). Maps, brochures on restaurants, lodging.

Cultural Arts Council of East Haven 1380 North High Street (203-486-2963). Ask for a calendar of free Friday-night summer concerts on the town green, plus information on other cultural events.

East Haven Historical Society 133 Main Street (203-467-1766). Info on historic sites such as the Old Stone Church at Main and High Streets, but no tours. One-room collection in private 1790 home near the town green, open Wednesdays from 11:00 A.M. to 2:00 P.M.

Irish-American Community Center 9 Venice Place (203-469-3080). The New Haven Gaelic Players stage the works of well-known Irish playwrights; call for information.

Branford

The largest in population of the shoreline towns that lie between New Haven and New London, Branford is a thriving municipality with a history that blends the features of a summer resort, a suburban bedroom community, and a center of commerce and industry. Visitors who leave I-95 to travel only the Route 1 corridor through town will miss most of the pleasures of this dynamic and multifaceted area. Sadly for tourists, Branford's citizens cherish their precious links to the Sound so much that its public beaches are not currently opened in season to out-of-towners, and many stretches of waterfront property are in private hands. Luckily, however, Branford's roads and trails allow visitors ample opportunity to explore the wooded hills, the quiet coves, and the windswept peninsulas for a taste of the charms that have drawn settlers here for 350 years.

The Mattabesec were the first settlers of this land that they called Totoket, or "place of the tidal river." Not surprisingly, when they sold their land to the English for twelve coats, they reserved the Indian Neck peninsula for themselves. In addition to its value as a place of extraordinary beauty, the peninsula had been home to the Mattabesec tribe since at least

2500 B.C. because of its accessibility to the bountiful fish, fowl, and shellfish of the Sound. Archaeological research in Branford reveals that the Mattabesec had a well-developed way of life that relied upon an intimate understanding of the rhythms of the seasons and the fluctuations of natural supplies of food and shelter.

The English took a different approach to the land. Their aim was to subdue and control the environment, including its native inhabitants. Eventually the Mattabesec left the shores of Branford, and the English pursued their own definition of progress in these ancient tribal lands. The seventeenth and eighteenth centuries brought the clearing of Branford's forests for farms and the construction of wharves for shipbuilding and the oystering industry. In the nineteenth and twentieth centuries came the stone quarries and the factories of such products as hardware, iron fittings, and wire.

During the latter two centuries of development, the shore remained a center for recreation, and the stage, the railroad, and the trolley brought thousands of visitors to the Branford coastline for summer fun. In its heyday as a resort, Branford's shore and islands were dotted with twenty commodious hotels catering to the pleasures of folks from New York and Connecticut cities. Today cottage rentals and a handful of motels house the visitors who still come to tour the islands, ride the trolleys, launch their boats, and explore the woodlands.

This chapter focuses attention on Branford's center and its distinct enclaves of Stony Creek, Indian Neck, Pine Orchard, and Short Beach.

The Best of Stony Creek

One of the prettiest and most relaxing excursions on the Connecticut shore centers around Branford's Stony Creek, as quintessential a quaint New England fishing village as can be found this close to the more sophisticated port of New Haven. Only Stonington in New London County transports you more thoroughly to the nautical past.

Like Branford's other unique sections, Stony Creek has a long and lively history, complete with tales of pirate treasure and other romances of the sea and heart. Once home to farmers, fishers, and quarriers, the village is now famed for its quiet Yankee charm and its sprinkling of pink granite islands just offshore—the Thimbles.

In fact, the village's principal industry, if one can call it that, is the Thimble Islands sightseeing tour business. Three enterprising captains have updated the centuries-old trade of ferrying livestock, groceries, visitors, and even the occasional piano from the town dock to the islands. Now tourists are their most valuable cargo.

The largest group of islands on the Sound, the thirty-three Thimbles range in size from twenty acres to less than a quarter of an acre at high tide. Scattered in the waters around these islands are nearly sixty other rocky mounds visible at least at low tide. Although their size seems to provide a clue to their name, the islands are called the Thimbles after the native thimbleberries that once flourished here.

The islands are in private hands, used as summer hideaways for families and friends. High Island and Money Island enjoy the most thrilling reputations among the islands. None other than Captain Kidd took shelter here. Outer Island and Horse Island have the most honorable reputations; the former is part of the Stewart B. McKinney National Wildlife Refuge and is used by Southern Connecticut State University as an environmental research area; the latter is owned by Yale University and used for marine biology research.

Thimble Islands Cruises

Luckily for the touring public, cruises around this pretty archipelago at least allow a glimpse of the islands, a breath of bracing salt air, and a taste of the beauty of the Sound. To reach the Stony Creek Dock from I-95, take exit 56 and travel south on Leetes Island Road for 2 miles. At the first stop sign, go straight on Thimble Islands Road, and follow the signs to the dock. From Branford Center or Indian Neck, simply follow the signs for Route 146 west, taking a right onto Thimble Islands Road and continuing to the dock. For more information, check out the Thimbles Web site at www. thimbleislands.com.

Volsunga IV (203-488-9978 or 203-481-3345). From Captain Kidd to General Tom Thumb, the stories told by Stony Creek native Captain Bob Milne aboard the *Volsunga IV* are exceeded in quality only by his sure navigation of the reefs surrounding the islands. Milne's 40-foot vessel is rated for forty-nine passengers. Cruises every hour on the hour, weather permitting, daily except some Mondays from July 1 to the day before Labor Day, 11:00 A.M. to 4:00 P.M. From mid-May through June and from Labor Day through Columbus Day, the tour times differ somewhat, with fewer cruises daily and no operation on Mondays for several weeks at either end of the season. Adults $8.00, children $4.00. Groups of more than twelve should make reservations. Two-hour evening charters ($300 for thirty people) are also available.

Sea Mist II (203-488-8905). Captain Mike Infantino, Jr., offers stories that are an entertaining mix of myth and fact, along with the views of the sea, the birds, the islands, and the islanders. The 45-foot *Sea Mist II* carries forty-six passengers. Forty-five-minute cruises every hour on the quarter hour, from 10:15 A.M. to 4:15 P.M. daily except Tuesday, from June 1 through Labor Day, and in May and September (after Labor Day) through October on Friday through Sunday at 12:15, 2:15, and 4:15 P.M. Adults $8.00, children $4.00. Two-hour evening charters available ($275 for thirty people). Reservations suggested for large groups.

Islander (203-397-3921). Captain Dave Kusterer's 26-foot port launch carries twenty-five passengers on a fifty-minute tour. The size of his boat allows exploration of a few spots the larger boats can't reach and also allows Captain Dave to be right there in the middle of the more intimately sized deck. His stories reflect his knowledge of the lifestyles and histories of the islanders. He shares a house on Kidd's Island with relatives who have owned the property since 1903. Cruises every hour leaving at twenty minutes before the hour, from 10:40 A.M. to 4:40 P.M. daily from mid-June through Labor Day. Adults $8.00, children $4.00. Reservations suggested for groups of more than twelve.

The Stony Creek Scene

On your ride down to the water, you may notice Stony Creek's other attractions. Just a hundred yards from the gazebo at the dock is **Stony Creek Marine and Tackle and Fish Market** (4 Indian Point Road; 203-488-7061). It masquerades as a quiet shop selling tackle and seafood along with deli sandwiches, but it's really the hoppin' domain of owner Mike McCleery and a Creeker community called the Sand Worms. Most of us would call this group a house band; Mike calls it "an eclectic aggregation of talented individuals." Among them are a former backup musician for Dave Brubeck, a fellow who toured with the Monkees, and a Juilliard grad, and they bring mostly folk, blues, and Irish tunes to Stony Creek as they play here (usually) on weekends, often outside on the bulkhead in warm weather. You won't be hungry while you listen to them. Year-round, the esteemed owner and short-order cook serves breakfast and lunch daily from 6:00 A.M. and dinner, in the warm season only, Thursday through Sunday until 8:00 P.M. In summertime, you can eat lunch and dinner under a tent at the waterside. On the holiday weekends (Memorial Day, July 4, and Labor Day), the tent is the site of the market's famed Lobster Fests—from Thursday through Sunday on those weekends from noon to 8:00 P.M.

STONY CREEK KAYAK

For an intimate experience with the Thimbles and the Sound, call Christopher Hauge, who offers guided sea kayaking trips around the islands for experienced as well as novice kayakers. Half-day trips last three hours and cost $70 per person; full-day trips take about five hours and cost $120 per person. Two-hour sunset tours are $60 per person; three-hour full-moon cruises are $60 per person. Kayakers can be as young as 8 years old, with parental supervision and/or consent; groups of up to about ten paddlers can arrange to go on a single outing. Guided tours can also be arranged for the Connecticut River, Lake Quonnipaug in Guilford, Branford Harbor to East Haven's Farm River (featuring Kelsey Island and the Short Beach area), and Guilford's Lost Lake, Joshua Cove, and East and West Rivers. **Stony Creek Kayak** (203-481-6401; Web site: www.stonycreekkayak.com) also offers sea kayaking instruction, including lessons devoted to safety and rescue.

A bit farther back from the dock, at the curve of the road, is the **Stony Creek Market** (178 Thimble Islands Road; 203-488-0145; closed Monday), which is great for casual, day-tripping meals, soft drinks, and picnic fare. Come for breakfast from 8:00 to 11:00 A.M. For lunch, come between 11:00 A.M and 3:00 P.M. and take the overstuffed sandwiches and fresh salads out on the front deck for a great view of the harbor. For dinner, from 5:00 to 9:00 P.M. Tuesday through Sunday, the market doubles as **Stony Creek Pizza**, serving thin-crust pies with a great reputation. Come early for dinner for a front-row sunset seat.

In the same building as the market is **Stony Creek Antiques** (172 Thimble Islands Road; 203-488-4802), a place to browse for a one-of-a-kind memento. Directly across the street is a small beach with a swimming area, picnic shelter, and benches. Officially, it is open only to Branford residents, but guests are often here as well, especially between Labor Day and Memorial Day. Parking in this area is very limited, so be sure you have left your vehicle in a legal space before settling in your sand chair, in the park, or over your plate of steamers.

A half block north of the beach, the small town park offers picnic spots, swings, and a sand-carpeted playground with slides and such. At the nearest street corner adjacent to the park is a funky clothing/gifts/antiques shop called **Island Tastes** (152 Thimble Islands Road;

203-483-0564). Up the road just another little piece is the **Stony Creek General Store** (124 Thimble Islands Road; 203-488-1892). Along with sundries like film, sunblock, newspapers, and such, it carries deli goods and breads for picnics; its tidy ice cream parlor serves up malteds, shakes, sundaes, splits, and more.

Stony Creek Puppet House Theatre

One of the village's most notable establishments, despite its modest facade, is the Puppet House, site of theater productions and musical performances throughout the summer and sporadically during the year. Built as a silent movie house around 1900, this ninety-seat playhouse was once the home of Orson Welles's Mercury Theater; today, operating as a nonprofit organization called Puppet House Productions, Inc., the theater welcomes community theater groups and local artists to its stage. In recent seasons, jazz, Christian rock, acoustic folk, and bluegrass artists have appeared on the schedule, and in the summer the Shakespeare Youth Theatre usually stages a production. Look here, too, for children's matinees featuring clown, puppet, or magic shows.

Last but not least, check for the remarkable productions of puppet master Jim Weil, Puppet House director Joe Davis, and their amazing Sicilian puppets. Beautifully painted and dressed in armors of hand-embossed brass, the last are 100-year veterans of the stage, which battle each other furiously in the enactment of tales of the Crusades, Charlemagne and his Paladins, and the Sicilian Knights.

128 Thimble Islands Road (203-488-5752 or 203-931-6326). Seasonal children's shows; year-round calendar of productions for teens/adults. Call for calendar or ticket information.

The Best of Pine Orchard and Indian Neck

You won't have seen some of the prettiest parts of the Branford-area coastline unless you make the drive or bicycle ride along Route 146 through Pine Orchard and Indian Neck. These are mostly residential sections with little of the shore accessible to tourists, but the ride is so pretty and the views so striking that a journey past the houses most of us can only dream of owning is still a jaunt worth taking.

Follow Route 146 from its intersection with Thimble Islands Road; from that point, this designated scenic highway is called Stony Creek

Road, but it will soon turn toward the south, and you may notice that it is then called Totoket Road, then Blackstone Road, then Elizabeth Street, then Limewood Avenue, and finally, swinging northward from the shore, Montowese Street. Not to worry—it's all Route 146, so just follow the signs. When you reach the small commercial corner of Indian Neck, where Route 146 swings away from the Sound and Limewood Avenue becomes Montowese Street, take a brief detour to the left on Linden Avenue for some beautiful shoreline vistas. If you are walking or cycling, you are free to stop along the route through Pine Orchard and Indian Neck to rest at whatever pretty view strikes your eye, but motorists will find no public areas and few good pull-outs in which to stop their cars. Even walkers and cyclists should keep in mind that the lawns, beaches, and beach association parks are private areas.

From 1850 and well past the turn of the twentieth century, Pine Orchard and Indian Neck were much more public than they are today. Summer hotels lined the shore, and the trolley brought city emigres by the scores to the clambakes and croquet games and tennis courts overlooking the boating and swimming in the Sound. Bad weather or bad finances led to the demise of these summer playgrounds, and today only one of Branford's famed summer hotels remains in operation.

The Indian Neck Scene

The **Owenego Inn** (203-488-3805) at 40 Linden Avenue in Indian Neck was opened in 1847 and includes an annex built in 1867 and a cottage from 1812. With a broad front lawn and sweeping views of the Sound from its 500-foot waterfront, it is the popular site of wedding receptions and other special parties from late April to early November. Its Thirsty Gull bar and patio is reserved for members of the Owenego Beach and Tennis Club, but the main bar upstairs (it has no name) welcomes the public after 5:00 P.M. Be sure to linger awhile here on the deck before you continue your shore drive. If you can't bear to leave this lovely scene, the Owenego also offers seasonal and overnight lodgings. A half-dozen or more spacious guest rooms in the main inn offer sinks in the room and a community bath—a truly old-fashioned charm that can't be found anywhere else on the Connecticut shoreline.

Retrace your route to Linden Avenue's intersection with Route 146 and stop for a while at this commercial junction. Here you will find **Lenny's Indian Head Inn,** a New England seafood favorite (see Places to Eat), and **Pasta Cosi** (3 Linden Avenue; 203-483-9397), popular for its contemporary Italian cuisine, fresh pasta, and house-made desserts, served in warm weather on a great outside patio or inside year-round. For fabulous take-out seafood, premier lobster bisque, fresh breads, and every other gourmet treat you'd want in a picnic basket, stop at **Bud's Fish Market** (203-488-1019). They fly their lobsters in daily from Nova Scotia, and they'll steam any quantity for you to take home. If you need a crisp chardonnay to accompany your meal, stop at the **Indian Neck Liquor Store;** for other picnic needs, try the **Indian Neck Shore Market.**

The Best of Branford Center

Since early in Branford's history the area surrounding the town green has been a center of activity, and today that is no less true than in 1699 when the green property was bequeathed to the town. Site of free summer concerts, arts and craft festivals, and the like, the green is bordered by such important buildings as the town hall, the 1843 Congregational Church, and the 1851 Trinity Episcopal Church.

Come to Trinity Church for monthly concerts given from September through May by the **Branford Folk Music Society** (203-488-7715), which brings together local, national, and international performers for traditional vocal and instrumental folk music. A small tablet near the southeast corner of the green marks the former site of the Reverend Samuel Russell's house, where ten prominent clergymen met in 1701 to assemble their donated books as the beginning of the library for the newly founded Collegiate School, later known as Yale College and now the famed university. Also surrounding the green are shops, restaurants, and an ice cream parlor. Noteworthy among the restaurants are **Darbar of India** and **Le Petit Cafe.** Among the structures in the center of Branford, the James Blackstone Memorial Library and the Harrison House are especially notable.

James Blackstone Memorial Library

Railroad magnate Timothy Beach Blackstone paid for construction of the library to honor his father, James Blackstone, born in Branford in 1793 and elected its first selectman as well as a member of both the senate and house of representatives of the Connecticut General Assembly. Constructed from 1893 to 1896 from Tennessee marble, the library was modeled after the Erectheum on the Acropolis in Athens. Ionic columns, marvelous bronze doors, and a domed rotunda are among the details that architect Solon Spencer Beman added to the building.

The focal points of the spacious rotunda are the eight murals, painted by Oliver D. Grover, that draw the eye toward the beautiful glass-ceilinged dome 50 feet above the marble floor. Called *The Evolution of the Book*, the 11-by-9-foot paintings depict Egyptians gathering papyrus reeds for the manufacture of paper, scenes from the *Iliad*, monks illuminating medieval manuscripts, and Gutenberg holding the first proof of the Bible printed in his press.

758 Main Street (203–488–1441). Open Monday through Thursday 9:00 A.M. to 8:00 P.M. and Friday and Saturday 9:00 A.M. to 5:00 P.M. Closed major holidays.

Harrison House

Home to the Branford Historical Society, this classic saltbox home was built in 1724 as the home of Nathaniel Harrison. With the typical post-and-beam construction of the time, the house features original paneling and clapboards. Period furnishings, early farm tools, kitchen implements, and historical memorabilia are among the Branford artifacts here. A barn, a privy, and an eighteenth-century flower and herb garden are also on the two-acre property.

124 Main Street (203–488–4828). Open June 1 through October 1, Thursday through Saturday from 2:00 to 5:00 P.M. and by appointment. Free, but donations are welcome.

The Best of Short Beach

The wide ribbon of roadway marked Route 142 curls south from Route 1 invitingly, coaxing the traveler toward the shore, past beautiful Granite Bay, and then westward to East Haven. Also called Short Beach Road and Shore Drive, Route 142 and the smaller avenues that splinter from it encompass the neighborhood called Short Beach. Mostly residential today, Short Beach still retains the summery character that it sported as a resort area in the golden days of the trolley.

Late Branford resident and poet Ella Wheeler Wilcox, most famed for her lines "Laugh, and the world laughs with you; Weep, and you weep alone," called Short Beach her "Earthly Eden"—no exaggeration considering the spectacular view of the Sound she enjoyed from her home at the edge of the bay. No less breathtaking now than it was a century ago, Granite Bay is the focus of the neighborhood, a cozy warren of small streets lined with modest homes and summer cottages, a handful of commercial establishments, and a few pocket-size parks.

The Short Beach Scene

At the East Haven River, Route 142 curves uphill across the East Haven line, so look for a place to park in the neighborhood before you cross that border. In any season, Short Beach is perfect for bicycle and pedestrian traffic, and because parking at the public beaches in this area is closed to out-of-town visitors in the summer season, a tourist's best bet is to explore on foot. Find a place to park on one of the side streets, and lace up your sneakers or unclip your bikes for a tour better than any you could get by car alone. Remember that the off-season from Labor Day to Memorial Day is the time when visitors can use beaches and parks that are reserved for Branford residents in the summer. Parking prohibitions must be respected, all year long.

A nice place to start a long walk or a pleasant bike ride is at the **Harbor Street Market** (312 Harbor Street; 203-483-1612), where you can buy breakfast, lunch, or even dinner picnic fare from 6:00 A.M. to 9:00 P.M. daily. Ask the staff to pack up your treats and beverages, then head down Route 142 and find your way down to the water on one of the side streets.

If you'd like to head inland a tad, walk south on Route 142 from the Harbor Street Market and then north on Court Street. Pass through the gate across the pathway that leads to the Branford end of the **Shore Line Trolley** line that originates in East Haven (203-467-6927). Bring your picnic aboard the trolley and take the 3-mile ride across the meadows to the ticket terminal and museum and then back to the Branford platform, where they'll let you debark. You'll pay the operator $5.00 per adult and $2.00 per child, and he or she will get you a ticket for the museum as well as the return trip when you arrive at the East Haven depot. Keep in mind that the museum opens in East Haven at 11:00 A.M. and the trolleys run every thirty minutes, with the last leaving East Haven at 5:00 P.M. You ought to be at the Branford end at about ten minutes past or twenty minutes before the hour to catch one of the twice-hourly trolleys. You can even call the trolley in advance to let them know you'd like a ride and they'll be sure to pick you up.

To add to your perfect day, continue your tour of Short Beach by walking, cycling, or driving along Clark Avenue back out to Route 142 and following it back around Granite Bay to a right turn on Stannard Avenue. Take another right turn on Harbor Street and go to the town dock and Parker Memorial Park at Branford Point. (The distance from Clark Avenue to Parker Memorial Park is about 2.5 miles.) Parking for this beach park is limited in summer to Branford vehicles but is open during the off-season to out-of-towners. If you are driving in the summer season and are a nonresident, you may find one of the ten or so one-hour public parking spots at the dock and then you can walk into Parker Park for a dip and a picnic. You could also park a small distance away at the town boat launch area, dropping your gear first at the park. Walkers and cyclists can visit here year-round. The park offers a beach, picnic areas, swings, rest rooms, grills, and other amenities for outdoor recreation, and the town dock at Branford Point offers a great place to fish, to watch the maritime traffic, or to enjoy the beautiful views at the Harborview overlook next to the dock.

Places to Eat in Branford

Lenny's Indian Head Inn 205 South Montowese Street in Indian Neck (203-488-1500). If you drive by here without turning in for dinner, you'll be missing a famed menu of New England seafood, epitomized in Lenny's Famous Shore Dinner of clam chowder, cherrystones, sweet corn on the cob, lobster, steamers, and watermelon. The casual ambiance of worn wood floors and wooden booths makes Lenny's a happy, noisy place perfect for families; great specialties like zuppa di clams and house-made seafood bisque, and a wine list and beer on tap make it a fine place for adult tastes. Indoor seating year-round; patio in warm season. Open daily year-round for lunch and dinner. If it's busy here, definitely walk over to **Pasta Cosi** (see page 126). $-$$

Sam's Dockside At Bruce and Johnson's Marina, Block Island Road off South Montowese Avenue (203-488-3007). Views of this spacious marina and beautiful sunsets over the trees on the horizon draw crowds in the summertime, but it's the excellent seafood and grilled specials that cause an hour-long wait here some weekend nights. Indoor and outdoor dining. Grilled chicken, Caesar salads, and other favorites are offered along with fresh seafood fried, broiled, steamed, or sautéed. Great New England clam chowder. Open from 11:30 A.M. for lunch and dinner from March through the end of October. $-$$$.

Le Petit Cafe 225 Montowese Street (203-483-9791). Tiny and charming, this diminutive establishment offers French bistro cuisine—homemade French bread and gourmet meat, fish, and cheese dishes. Open Tuesday through Saturday 10:00 A.M. to 7:00 P.M. Prix fixe dinners; $$$$

Che Tango 130 Shore Drive (203-481-0102). For a lovely meal in one of Branford's prettiest shoreline enclaves, try this charming establishment not far from the harbor. Italian and Argentinian cuisines are the focus here, where one choice is as delicious as the next. Fresh seafood and pastas, seasonal produce, grilled meats, and much more are served graciously by an impeccably trained waitstaff. Be sure to choose one of their housemade desserts—there'll be no disappointments. The ambiance is warm and inviting, but more refined than casual—the perfect place for a quiet romantic dinner. Open daily from 5:00 P.M. $$-$$$

Darbar of India 1070 Main Street (203-481-8994). If you love Indian cuisine or if you would enjoy the adventure of experimenting, come to Darbar, right on the green downtown. Delicious traditional favorites plus a few Nepalese specialties delight the senses and tease the palate. Vegetarians will revel in the abundant and tasty choices perfect for them. Try the best bargain in town for lunch—the buffet special Friday through Sunday from noon to 2:45 P.M. for $7.95 per person. $-$$

Places to Stay in Branford

Days Inn and Conference Center 375 East Main Street (203-488-8314 or 800-329-7466). Seventy-seven units with three suites and two mini-suites, outdoor pool and Jacuzzi, continental breakfast. $$$

Ramada Limited 3 Business Park Drive (203-488-4991 or 800-950-4991). Eighty-five units including one efficiency and thirty suites. Rooms have king or two double beds; suites have a double bed, a convertible sofa/daybed, and a kitchenette with fridge and microwave. Health club includes small indoor pool, spa, weight room, and sauna. Continental breakfast. $$

Owenego Inn 40 Linden Avenue in Indian Neck (203-488-3805). The last of this area's shoreline hotels, overlooking the Sound with 550 feet of beachfront and all the charms of yesteryear paired with modern amenities. Seasonal, monthly, weekly, or nightly accommodations. Open April through early November. $$$

By the Sea Inn and Spa 107 Montowese Street (203-483-3333). Web site: www.bytheseainnspa.com. This restored Victorian mansion offers four comfortably appointed guest rooms, including one four-room suite, and provides spa services such as massage therapy, hand and foot care, body wraps, and aromatherapy. Private baths, antiques-filled common rooms, sundeck, continental breakfast. $$$$

Public Boat Launch

Branford River to Branford Harbor Turn south off Route 1 onto Route 142 (Short Beach Road); take a left on Stannard Avenue to Goodsell Point Road, and a left into the dirt access road and parking area; steep ramp; seasonal weekend and holiday parking fee.

For Further Information

Branford Chamber of Commerce 230 East Main Street (203-488-5500). Lodging and restaurant information, maps, and brochures.

Branford Land Trust (203-483-5263). 246 Pleasant Point Road, P. O. Box 254, Branford CT 06405. Call or write for guides to hiking and cross-country ski trails.

Branford Recreation Department 46 Church Street (203-488-8304). Information on use of town parks and beaches.

Guilford

Guilford's wide, colonial green, crisscrossed by pathways that seem to lead back in time, encourages the visitor to pause a while to savor the town's agreeable setting on the Sound, its tranquil atmosphere, and its beautiful architecture. Busier now than in earlier decades, especially along commercialized sections of Route 1, Guilford is still considered one of the most pleasant places on the Connecticut shore.

Named for the town of Guildford in Surrey, England, Guilford was settled by the English in 1639. Led by the Reverend Henry Whitfield and lawyer William Leete, the mostly young and prosperous Puritan farmers and landowners purchased the land called Menuncatuck from the Menuncatuck people of the Mohegan nation. For a few coats, some hats, a couple of iron kettles, and a handful of hatchets, the Menuncatuck sachem squaw Shaumpishuh gave the English, a parcel at a time, land that includes present-day Guilford and Madison.

Earlier, in the summer of 1637, the Mohegan sachem Uncas and his people had helped the English hunt down the Pequots who had survived the massacre at Mystic only to be murdered in Guilford on the peninsula now called Sachem's Head. In that battle, Uncas took the head of the slain Pequot sachem and placed it in the fork of a prominent oak tree, where it rested for years as a reminder of the Mohegan victory. Perhaps Uncas failed to predict that if the English were anxious to decimate his enemies, the Pequots, they might not be too reluctant to break faith with his people as well.

Surely he didn't predict that the woodlands of Menuncatuck would ring with the sound of axes as the English cleared great swatches of land for their farms and for the four stone houses they built as protection against the Dutch. As more English arrived, the Mohegans were pushed back from the shoreline to the settlements near the Thames River. By 1774 only twenty-three Menuncatuck natives remained within Guilford's boundaries.

Today Guilford has an eclectic flavor that enriches the largely residential community. Charms of the country are still apparent in its orchards, farms, lakes, and nature preserves; the link to the sea is obvious in its scenic shoreline drives and busy marinas. Appealing in all seasons, Guilford is a shoreline gem.

The Best of Guilford

Henry Whitfield State Museum

The Henry Whitfield House is the oldest stone house in New England and the oldest house in Connecticut. Built in 1639 for the Reverend Henry Whitfield, the post-medieval structure has stone walls 3 feet thick and is the last remaining of four such houses strategically placed in Guilford as strongholds for the citizens during threat of attack by the Dutch.

Guilford's founder and first minister, Whitfield lived in the house and conducted community business and religious services here before he left his fellow settlers and returned to England in 1647. Now more a museum than a period house, the restored structure contains an outstanding collection of furniture, housekeeping implements, textiles, weapons, and other important Connecticut pieces. An introductory exhibit explains the history of the area, the house, and the inhabitants of the region in the colonial period. The entire house, including the attic, is open to the public, as are the gardens and lawns. Among the large collection of local artifacts displayed in the attic, you can see the 1726 Ebenezer Parmelee steeple clock, the first wooden works tower clock made in the colonies. In the separate, adjacent visitor center, you will find a tourist information area in the front hallway, stocked with free brochures, maps, and information on other local attractions and accommodations. A reference library, an exhibit gallery with changing displays, and a charming gift shop are also in this building.

248 Old Whitfield Street, south of the green at the corner of Stone House Lane (203–453–2457 or 860–566–3005). Web site: www.guilfordct.com/ community.cfm. Open for mostly self-guided tours Wednesday through Sunday from February 1 to December 14, from 10:00 A.M to 4:30 P.M., and from December 15 through January by appointment. Adults $3.00, children 6 to 17 $1.50.

Hyland House

On Boston Street, northward and around the corner from the stone Henry Whitfield house, is a red overhung saltbox frame house with leaded glass casement windows and hand-split clapboards. Originally the home of George Hyland and his family, it is believed to have been constructed in 1660. The museum's focus is on the fifty to seventy-five years before the Revolution, and everything that the family might have used during that period is displayed.

Here visitors step into the eighteenth century, especially in the wonderful kitchen in the 1720 lean-to addition at the back of the house. Little imagination is necessary to conjure visions of pre-Revolutionary family life in this marvelous space with its boards, bowls, and basins worn smooth by the fingertips and footfalls of generations of early Guilford homemakers. Be sure to have a look at the "gossip wheel"—a double spinning wheel that allowed two women to spin yarn together as they shared news and stories.

The architectural details and the collections in this house are among the finest in the state. Gorgeous paneling, wide-board floors, walk-in fireplaces, rare examples of Delftware, and artifacts of every sort are abundant throughout the house. Outside, the flower and herb garden at the back of the house is especially lovely in summer and fall.

84 Boston Street (203–453–9477). Open from early June to early September daily except Mondays from 10:00 A.M. to 4:30 P.M. and on weekends from Labor Day to Columbus Day. Adults $2.00, children 12 and older $1.50, children under 12 are free.

Thomas Griswold House

Greatly restored by the Guilford Keeping Society, this 1774 saltbox home just a few doors east of the Hyland House has an original Guilford cupboard and a 10-foot-wide fireplace with two beehive ovens. Home to five generations of Griswolds, who changed the house to meet their needs, the house has been returned to its original saltbox shape. Now on the National Register of Historic Places, the home's period rooms are set with furnishings and implements in positions of use. Samplers, coverlets, costumes, dolls and toys, and a whimsical napkin ring collection are among the treasures here.

An antiques festival held annually on the last Saturday in July and an annual Civil War encampment are hosted on the museum's expansive grounds. On these special days the museum's blacksmith shop and barn are also open.

171 Boston Street, at the corner of Lovers Lane (203–453–3176 or 203–453–4666). Open from mid-June until October 1, Tuesday through Sunday, 11:00 A.M. to 4:00 P.M. Adults $2.00, students $1.00.

Guilford Handcraft Center

Notable among the special shops *not* on the green is the outstanding Guilford Handcraft Center. The Handcraft Center, founded by local artists in 1962, comprises a shop, a gallery, and a school. The center has pottery, weaving, painting, and metalsmithing studios, plus a variety of multiuse classrooms for instruction in such other arts as basketry, etching, printmaking, woodcarving, and much more. Visiting artists travel here to offer workshops in their areas of expertise.

The Mill Gallery hosts various small expositions and special events throughout the year. You can purchase the works of as many as 300 artisans, and the school offers classes and workshops for adults and children.

411 Church Street (Route 77), north of Route 1 and approximately 200 yards north of the I–95 overpass (203–453–5947). Studios open year-round for classes and visitors; call for schedule and course catalog. Gallery and shop open year-round Monday through Saturday from 10:00 A.M. to 5:00 P.M. and Sunday from noon to 4:00 P.M. Extended hours for annual Holiday Exhibition and Sale in December. Closed Thanksgiving, Christmas, and New Year's Day. Free.

Westwoods Trails

Henry David Thoreau would have loved these pathways. In 1862 he wrote, "I think that I cannot preserve my health and spirits, unless I spend four hours a day at least . . . sauntering through the woods and over the hills and fields, absolutely free from all worldly engagements." Few of us are afforded the luxury of four-hour daily walks, but each of us should try this once a month on Connecticut's exceptional trails.

Westwoods is a great place to start. Its thousand acres of forest and marshland are laced with 40 miles of trails that lead to waterfalls, rock cliffs, colonial and Indian caves, rock carvings, and vistas of the Sound and lake. The G Trail connects the Westwoods trails to the Stony Creek Quarry Preserve; here you can see the remains of old quarrying operations. A trail map is essential to a safe hike here; pick one up at the Guilford Free Library, the town hall on the green, the community center on Church Street, Bishop's Farm Market on the Boston Post Road, Breakwater Books on Whitfield Street, or from the Guilford Land Conservation Trust, P. O. Box 200, Guilford CT 06437.

To reach Westwoods, take Route 146 west from the Guilford green for less than a mile to Sam Hill Road and park in the small unpaved lot right near that corner. Follow the white-blazed trail from that point and connect with any of several other trails you will note on your map.

Trail entrance on Sam Hill Road near its junction with Route 146 (203–453–8068). Open year-round at no charge from dawn to dusk. **Note:** *The trails have been temporarily closed due to safety issues arising from a tree disease that causes rotting limbs. Call for information on the reopening of the area.*

DOWNTOWN GUILFORD

One of the most exceptional colonial greens in New England is at the core of downtown Guilford. Lying south of the Boston Post Road, its twelve acres are dissected by pathways and dotted with benches that make it a popular site to relax and to play. Once an unkempt and irregular sixteen-acre parcel of ponds, pasture, and gravel pits over-run by sheep and geese, the green is now tidy and rectangular, bordered by three churches and colonial, Federal, and Victorian structures that house restaurants, galleries, and shops.

Placed on the National Register of Historic Places in 1976 along with much of the rest of the town center, the green is the third largest in the Northeast. In summer, come here to listen to an outdoor concert or to browse at one of its frequent fairs or festivals. In winter, enjoy the lighted Christmas tree, the candlelight church services, and the old-fashioned trolley rides that make holiday shopping especially festive.

An excellent guide to the green and its surrounding streets has been published by the Guilford Preservation Alliance. Available at **Breakwater Books** (203-453-4141; 81 Whitfield Street on the green) or through the **Guilford Keeping Society** (203-453-3176), *Guilford: A Walking Guide* by Sarah Brown McCulloch is an informative examination of Guilford's architectural importance. *Around the Green: A Children's Walking Guide,* by Guilford educator Joann Carmody Corlett, is an interpretation of the adult version.

Guilford's green is bounded on the north by Broad Street, on the east by Park Street, on the south by Boston Street, and on the west by Whitfield Street. Church, Fair, and State Streets lead from Broad Street north to the Boston Post Road. Whitfield Street continues south past the green toward Guilford Harbor and the beaches, so if it's a view of the Sound you're hoping to see, head down there.

Also known as Route 146, Water Street is a designated scenic highway. Officially, it begins at the eastern end of Boston Street, but visitors to the green will spot signs for it near its intersection with Whitfield Street. Be sure to include this 12-mile route back toward Branford on a driving or bicycling tour. Along the way, turn off at Mulberry Point Road or Sachem's Head Road for a ride through the scenic neighborhoods at the edge of the Sound. Parking is prohibited on most of the roads in this residential area, and the beaches are private, but the views are free and the roads are public.

NATHANAEL B. GREENE COMMUNITY CENTER

Just yards from the north end of the Guilford Green at 32 Church Street is Guilford's public community center (203-453-8068); open to the public year-round Monday through Friday from 8:30 A.M. to 4:30 P.M. and on weekends seasonally. Upstairs are the offices of the Guilford Parks and Recreation Department (203-453-8068), where visitors may obtain season passes to Lake Quonnipaug. Public rest rooms are located on the center's first floor, and free public parking is available to visitors who would like to leave the car and walk through downtown.

Jacobs Beach

Hikers and bikers may want a refreshing swim or at least a cool wind through their hair after some trail exercise. Head down to the Sound for a rest on the sand at Jacobs Beach. Comb the sand for treasures swept in on the tide, listen to the rustling marsh reeds whisper a seaside serenade. You can swim if the lifeguards are on duty, but you can use the beach and volleyball court even if the guards are off duty. Rest rooms and a pavilion with picnic tables and nearby grills are here. A playscape in a large grassy area makes the space fun for children. The beach itself is relatively small, but it's a pretty spot, and out-of-towners are welcome.

Seaside Avenue off Whitfield Street (Guilford Parks and Recreation, 203–453–8068). Park and playground area open year-round from 8:30 A.M. to 9:00 P.M. Swimming allowed only when lifeguards are present, from Memorial Day to Labor Day, on Monday through Saturday from 9:00 A.M. to 5:00 P.M. and on Sunday from 11:00 A.M. to 5:00 P.M. Out-of-town visitors pay $6.00 per vehicle on weekdays and $8.00 per vehicle on weekends from Memorial Day through Labor Day.

Chaffinch Island Park

To enjoy a view of the water with a bit more privacy, head to Chaffinch Island Park. It's just across the harbor from Jacobs Beach, but you'll need to take Seaside Avenue back out to Whitfield Street. Take a left on Whitfield and return to its intersection with Route 146 near the green. Hang a left onto Route 146, then another left onto Mulberry Point, and another left onto Chaffinch Island Road. At its end, past

Brown's Boatyard, is a pretty park overlooking the Sound and the marshes at the mouth of the West River.

The land practically rolls into the sea at this point, as you'll see if you park the car or your bikes in the gravel lot near the huge boulders in the center of the park's circular drive. Climb the humped back of the grassy knoll that provides great picnicking sites and walk out to the edge of the water. Wave-worn rocks arch gently above the water at the southernmost tip of land; be sure to explore here and enjoy the views of Faulkner Island and its lighthouse. Picnic tables appear late in May and stay until autumn, but besides those the town provides only trash barrels. The gift is that most of the year the only visitors are you and the gulls.

At the foot of Chaffinch Island Road off Mulberry Point Road; open year-round daily, dawn to dusk; no facilities; no charge.

Lake Quonnipaug

Freshwater swimming may be more pleasing to you than swimming in the Sound. If so, head north to Guilford's mile-long Lake Quonnipaug for salt-free water play, boating, fishing, and picnicking. This pretty lake is in a beautifully rural area dotted with barns and pastures, stone walls and fences—the perfect setting for a New England day trip.

GUILFORD HANDCRAFTS EXPOSITION

Surely the most magical of all the events held on the Guilford green, this fabulous three-day festival, from Thursday to Saturday in the middle week of July, celebrates American handcrafts created by juried artists from all corners of the nation. Displayed under huge tents, the pieces demonstrate an astonishing array of talent in every medium. Basketry, woodcraft, weaving, jewelry, toys, clothing, candles, tinsmithing, leather goods, sculpture, pottery, paper crafts, glass, furniture—you name it, it's here.

Thousands of folks converge on the green for this beautiful event, which begins around midday and continues through the evening. Hands-on activities and demonstrations and a small variety of entertainments such as storytellers, face painters, or other performers help make the expo a happy experience for all visitors. Adult admission $5.00; children under 12 free. Call for more information (203-453-5947).

A good-sized beach and grassy area are open to the public there. Lifeguards are on duty whenever the swimming area is open. Rest rooms with outdoor showers are also provided. Small cartop boats such as inflatables, canoes, kayaks, sailboards, or tubes may be launched from the grassy area, but no snorkeling or scuba diving is allowed. A state-owned public boat launch ramp is at the north end of the lake, outside of the Guilford property.

Route 77 in North Guilford, about 3 miles north of Route 80. Open Memorial Day through Labor Day (gated during remainder of year) Monday through Saturday 9:30 A.M. to 7:30 P.M., Sunday 11:00 A.M. to 7:30 P.M. Purchase day tickets at the lake for $6.00 per person on weekdays and $8.00 per person on weekends. Best buy for families is a season pass for $30 per adult 21 to 59 or $50 per household. The pass allows unlimited visits per season and can only be purchased at the Guilford Parks and Recreation Department (203–453–8068) at 32 Church Street.

Dudley Farm

If you're exploring Route 77 (its total length from the Guilford green to its end in Durham is 11.56 miles), you may wish you could stop in at one of its appealing farmsteads—even the one called Insulting Manor has a kind of allure—but you might feel shy unless you're in immediate need of hay or manure. Lucky for you, one of Guilford's historic farms has gone public, hanging out a welcome sign for visitors with an appetite for country pleasures. Settled in the arms of nature, the eight standing buildings and nearly two dozen remnant structures at this peaceful ten-acre farm site are the legacy of the Dudley family, who tilled the soil and tended both crops and animals through two centuries in Guilford.

Under development as both an attraction and an education center, the farm offers guided and self-guided tours, activities, workshops, and demonstrations. Tours of the farm and adjoining mill site feature an 1840s farmhouse with some of its seventeen rooms restored to their turn-of-the-twentieth-century state, an enormous U-shaped barn that evolved through two centuries of farm life, a sugarhouse, a small barn restored for use as a schoolhouse for visiting classes, herb and flower gardens, a vegetable field, and beehives. Long-range plans include restoration of the entire farmhouse and the standing buildings, plus the creation or restoration of other areas in a style circa 1900.

Day-trippers may prefer to visit on Saturdays when the farm is at its busiest. In the morning it offers a farmers' market of its own produce as well as the produce of local farmers and crafters. Depending on the season,

FAULKNER ISLAND LIGHTHOUSE

Slightly more than 3 miles off the coast of Guilford is a small island that rises steeply out of the water. From shore it sometimes resembles a long, flattish ship firmly at anchor, but its ever-changing shape is at the root of its current fame. Formed during the Ice Age when glaciers pushed rock and soil southward and scooped out Long Island Sound, Faulkner Island was well-known by the Menuncatucks. They called it Massancummock, or "place of the great fish hawks," and they frequented it in spring and summer in search of game and shellfish. Colonial farmers, on the philosophy that what's yours is mine, supplanted the Menuncatucks and grew crops and grazed livestock there. In 1802 the island began to serve its most useful purpose; in that year Thomas Jefferson commissioned a lighthouse on it to warn mariners of dangerous shoals.

Today, however, the white octagonal tower is itself at grave risk as erosion of the island's east embankment threatens the lighthouse's stability. In 1991 a committee formed to save the light, which is the second oldest in the state. Faulkner Light still operates as an aid to navigation and orientation, and the Faulkner's Light Brigade can't bear to see it slip into the Sound. Just 35 feet from the bluff face, the light is now protected by an erosion control plan and an initiative to restore both the tower and the island's wharf. The island itself is part of the Stewart B. McKinney National Wildlife Refuge. One of the world's largest breeding colonies of the roseate tern, Faulkner is also second home to more than 150 species of other migratory birds.

The Light Brigade sponsors an annual migration of humans to a sort of island open house. On the first Saturday after Labor Day, visitors can tour the tower and learn about the research on the terns from the biologists who set up house here during nesting season. (For information on visiting the island, call 203-453-8400 or 203-453-1111.)

you may also see the farm staff demonstrating sheep-shearing, beekeeping, twig furniture construction, rag rug weaving, or barn chores and tool repair. On the first Saturday of each month, musicians play acoustic instruments under the trees. On Friday evenings, you may enjoy occasional poetry readings, history talks, or musical entertainment. Special events throughout the warm seasons include an Arbor Day celebration, May Day festivities, and a Farm Day. You might even see or volunteer to help out at a barn raising. The Dudley Farm Foundation produces a newsletter. Call to order a copy and a schedule of events.

2351 Durham Road (Route 77) north of Route 80 (203–457–0770). Open year-round Monday through Saturday from 10:00 A.M. to 2:00 P.M. Farmers' market from June through October on Saturday from 9:00 A.M. to noon. Suggested donation for house tour, $3.00.

Bishop's Orchards

One of the many charms of the coastal towns to the east of New Haven is that farms and orchards still flourish right along Route 1. Established in 1871, Bishop's is perhaps Guilford's best-known and most popular of these, open to the public year-round for fresh-from-the-field shopping in its large market or pick-your-own pleasures in its many fields and orchards. Fresh produce of all kinds, eggs, breads, cheeses, and locally made jams, honey, cookies, pies, and cider help make Bishop's a great place to build either a picnic or a banquet. Look here in the fall for mums, gourds, and cornstalks for autumn decorating; come back in December for wreaths, garlands, and Christmas trees.

Call the infoline for the latest news on picking your own harvest throughout the summer and fall. Come for strawberries in June, blueberries in July, peaches and pears in August, raspberries in September, apples and pumpkins in October.

1355 Boston Post Road (farm market 203–453–2338; pick-your-own infoline 203–453–6424). Open year-round Monday through Saturday from 8:00 A.M. to 6:00 P.M and from 9:00 A.M. on Sunday.

Places to Eat in Guilford

Quattro 1300 Boston Post Road (203–453–6575). Delicious Italian cuisine elegantly presented. Popular with adult diners. Open for lunch and dinner daily. $$–$$$

Som Siam 63R Whitfield Alley (203–458–0228). Authentic and delicious Thai cuisine is beautifully presented and impeccably served in this small restaurant tucked in a historic alley off the green. Lunch and dinner daily. Outside patio in season. $$–$$$

The Stone House 506 Whitfield Street (203–458–3700). Web site: www. stonehouserestaurant.com. Dine with a view of the water, the gulls, and the rigging of the sailboats and fishing boats in Guilford Harbor. Start

THE MONASTERY OF
OUR LADY OF GRACE

You won't come closer to Heaven than this secluded enclave preserved for the glory of God by the most devoted of servants—the Dominican nuns who seek the face of the Lord through their silent contemplation, their study, and their prayer. Within the confines of their beautiful enclosure, the sisters also observe other practices of simplicity and sacrifice, making candles and pottery, sewing liturgical vestments, creating artworks in praise of God, and growing vegetables and flowers.

Although their orchards and gardens are screened from view, their chapel is open daily and guests are welcome. The sisters' voices rise in prayerful song several times daily; those seeking peace and healing will surely find comfort here. Vespers, offered at the close of the afternoon on weekdays and on Saturday evenings, is especially moving. Visitors may also purchase the sisters' handiwork in the monastery gift shop. An area outside the cloister offers visitors a shaded pathway punctuated by the Stations of the Cross; it is accessible year-round at all times. An annual monastic fair is a small but merry celebration of the gifts of the harvest; call the gift shop to inquire as to its date this year.

To reach the monastery, go north from I-95 on Route 77 for about 5 miles; turn right on Race Hill Road, which is the first right after Route 77 crosses Route 80. The monastery is at the corner of Race Hill and Hoop Pole Roads. Daily mass is at 7:00 A.M. on weekdays and 8:00 A.M. on Sunday; vespers is at 4:40 P.M. on weekdays and 8:00 P.M. on Saturday. Additional masses are scheduled on special holy days such as Christmas and Easter. The gift shop (203-457-0599) is open Monday through Saturday from 10:00 to 11:45 A.M. and from 1:00 to 4:00 P.M.; on Sunday it opens at 9:00 A.M. A few guest rooms are available in the sisters' retreat quarters for those who would like to join the sisters for a few days or a week of prayer, silence, and solitude.

with the crab and shrimp dumplings; sample the lobster bisque; enjoy the scallop and herb risotto; and finish with crème brûlée topped with seasonal berries. Excellent at lunch and dinner Tuesday through Sunday. $$$

Esteva 25 Whitfield Street (203-458-1300). Web site: www.estevaamerican cafe.com. This three-star-rated cafe is the sophisticated creation of chef Steve Wilkinson. Right on the green, it is a lovely spot for an elegantly casual lunch or dinner. Bright and airy and delicious, it is a comfortable place in winter and in summer on the back patio. Open for lunch Tuesday through Saturday; dinner daily; Sunday brunch. $$$

The Place 901 Boston Post Road (203-453-9276). Seasonal dining in the rough, at one of Connecticut's most unusual eateries. Outside under tents, sit on rough-hewn seats at picnic tables and eat charcoal-grilled steak, pit-roasted corn on the cob, fresh seafood, and more. Open May through October, depending on the weather, Monday through Thursday from 5:00 to 10:00 P.M., Saturday 1:00 to 11:00 P.M., and on Sunday from noon to 10:00 P.M. $$

Places to Stay in Guilford

Guilford Corners B&B 133 State Street (203-453-4129). Romantic decor in a restored 1732 Georgian colonial near the center of town. Spacious rooms with private baths; a two-room suite great for families has a shared bath. Four-poster queen-size beds, sherry in the afternoon, home-baked treats in the continental-plus breakfast. Hot tub on deck; spacious porch. Open year-round. $$$$

Cottage on Church Street B&B 190 Church Street (203-458-2598). Smack-dab in the center of everything, but a world away from the bustle of suburbia. A sunny soul-soother with charm to spare. A private cottage with a king-size bed, sitting and dining area, full bath, and garden patio. Full breakfast of baked goodies and fruit delivered to your door in the morning. Smoke-free. $$$$

Sound Reach B&B 50 Christmas Hill Road (203-457-0415). The owners of this lovely secluded property with distant glimpses of the sound offer three rooms, including one two-room suite, and continental breakfast. No smoking and no pets. $$$.

Guilford Suites Hotel 2300 Boston Post Road (203-453-0123 or 800-626-8604). Thirty-two suites with bedrooms, sitting rooms, baths, and kitchenettes; continental breakfast; open year-round. $$$-$$$$

Public Boat Launch

Guilford Town Marina At the town dock at foot of Whitfield Street (203-453-8092). One transient slip; boat launch ramp (nonresident day use $20). Phone, rest rooms. **Guilford Mooring** (203-458-2921) restaurant for seafood and family fare (boaters welcome at the Mooring's dock). Also, just steps away, is the **Bait House** (203-458-2554), which offers a full line of marine supplies, bait and tackle, take-out burgers, sandwiches, drinks, and snacks, plus kayak rentals (children under 18 must be accompanied by an adult; renters must have a driver's license and credit card).

For Further Information

Guilford Chamber of Commerce 741 Boston Post Road, Suite 101 (203-453-9677). Maps, brochures, general information.

Guilford Web site: www.guilfordct.com.

Madison

Once called East Guilford and connected geographically and politically to the town of Guilford, Madison seemed at one time typical of the small English settlements along the coast. Farmers and fishermen kept Madison well-stocked with onions and potatoes and oysters; sawmills and shipyards used the natural resources of both forest and harbor to build Madison's reputation as manufacturer of oceangoing wooden vessels. Incorporated as a separate town in 1826 and renamed in tribute to President James Madison, the village eventually took a different course from that of other rapidly developing coastal towns.

The railroad and the steamship brought an end to the era of great wooden sailboats, and, by the late nineteenth century, the clamor and activity at Madison's shipbuilding wharves changed to a different kind of clatter. The shipyards closed, and the hotels opened, welcoming train passengers who fell in love with the natural beauty and healthy atmosphere of Madison's beaches. By 1904 Madison was an established seaside resort area, with more than 300 cottages dotting the shoreline.

Today Madison is primarily a residential suburb populated by descendants of its original settlers, happy heirs of those pretty Victorian cottages, and families of professionals and executives who work in more developed towns within commuting distance. Early each June, Madison's population swells by several thousand as the "summer people" return to the shore and tourists double the sidewalk traffic past Madison's shops, galleries, and restaurants. Hammonasset State Park draws more visitors than any other park in the state, and Madison merchants, restaurateurs, and cultural arts folks work hard to coax travelers to linger. Pack a bicycle, a bathing suit, and a beach blanket, and come to enjoy the halcyon time warp that bewitches pretty Madison.

The Best of Madison

Deacon John Grave House

Close to four centuries have elapsed since European settlers brought new models of housing to the summer campgrounds of the native population. Concerned more with surviving the harsh New England winters than with adapting to the nomadic lifeways of the Algonkians, the colonists built sturdy shelters guaranteed by massive posts and beams to withstand the assault of severe weather. Have a look at the colossal central fireplace of Madison's Deacon John Grave House, and you'll be unsurprised that the house has stood on this spot since the settlement's earliest days.

Just a block east of the Madison green on a pretty two-acre parcel known in the past as Tuxis Farm, the Grave House was occupied for more than 300 years by descendants of its original owner, Deacon John Grave. Adapted for use in the past as an ordinary, a school, a wartime infirmary and weapons depot, and even a courtroom, the house also was home to ten children at one time—and that was before its eighteenth-century additions were added! Come here to imagine the life of a farming family in pre-Revolutionary days, see the secret staircase that led to a room used for storing arms during the French and Indian War, hear the ghost stories associated with the house, and admire the pretty dooryard garden.

Call to inquire about special days when tours include demonstrations or costumed interpreters, often in association with other special events such as the Civil War reenactment and encampment that takes place in April or May at Hammonasset State Park. In some years during late October, the ghosts of the house are enlisted to help out with some haunted Halloween shenanigans. This dramatic event is very realistically staged and promises to send shivers up the spines of those brave enough to enter.

581 Boston Post Road (203–245–4798). Open in summer Wednesday through Friday from noon to 3:00 P.M., Saturday from 10:00 A.M. to 4:30 P.M. and Sunday from noon to 4:30 P.M. After Labor Day through Columbus Day, open Saturday and Sunday noon to 3:00 P.M.; in winter by appointment. Adults $2.00, children $1.00. Call for information on special events.

Allis-Bushnell House

In Madison, large numbers of vintage homes still rest right along the Boston Post Road (Route 1). Along this thoroughfare are homes that belonged to Madison's earliest families. Markers on the houses note their original owners—Scranton, Dudley, Wilcox, Bradley, Chittenden, Meigs—but travelers can admire only their exteriors. The stewardship of Madison residents with a respect for history has kept these homes in private hands that minister lovingly to their preservation.

To see an eighteenth-century interior that is open to the public, drive to the center of the village. Built exactly a century after Madison's Deacon John Grave House, the 1785 Allis-Bushnell House is headquarters of the Madison Historical Society. The house is notable for its unusual corner fireplaces and cupboards, its beautifully stenciled floors, the exceptional collection of tools and fishing and farming equipment and artifacts in its annex, and its pretty formation of eighteenth-century herbs in its lovely rear garden. Home of Cornelius Bushnell, a founder of the Union Pacific Railway and chief financier of the Civil War ironclad ship USS *Monitor,* it also has a collection of fascinating memorabilia regarding the famed vessel.

If you are lucky, you may be greeted by costumed junior docents who add a charming and authentic touch as they perform tasks throughout the house. Senior docents lead the one-hour tours that are willingly tailored to your interests and schedule. Children may particularly enjoy the museum's small collection of toys, dolls, period costumes, and interesting medical implements. Many of these items have been relocated to the historic Lee Academy on the Madison green, where a children's museum has been established. Inquire at the main house for its hours of operation.

853 Boston Post Road (203–245–4567). Open Memorial Day to October 1 on Wednesday, Friday, and Saturday, 1:00 to 4:00 P.M. Donations requested.

DOWNTOWN MADISON

Madison's centerpiece is its tree-shaded green surrounded by homes from three centuries. The stately, white First Congregational Church is a Greek Revival beauty capped with a gilded dome that once served as a landmark to guide returning seamen into Madison's harbors. Today the church seems to preside over the happy activity of weekend art festivals, antiques shows, and concerts that blossom on the green from April through October.

From late May through November 1, the Madison Visitors Information Center (6 Meetinghouse Lane; 203-245-5659) operates in a tiny yellow brick building called the Powder House, immediately to the east of the larger yellow-brick Memorial Hall at the east end of the green. Hours vary, but on weekends from 9:00 A.M. to 6:00 P.M. you can usually stop for brochures and a calendar of events or to obtain directions to local points of interest.

The relatively small area of downtown Madison makes it especially conducive to strolling. The business hub of Madison centers on the intersection of the Boston Post Road and Wall Street. Springtime brings a flourish of cherry blossoms; in winter the center esplanade is adorned with lighted Christmas trees in whitewashed half-barrels that in summer overflow with colorful flowers.

If the scenery is not enough to urge visitors to slow their pace, Madison's shops provide a marvelous alternative to chain stores and impersonal outlets. Many of the boutiques, galleries, antiques stores, cafes, and restaurants of Madison are located in vintage homes and historic commercial buildings. Be sure to stop for coffee or cappuccino at the **Madison Gourmet Beanery** or have lunch at **Perfect Parties,** then browse a while at **R. J. Julia Booksellers** (voted the best independent bookstore in the entire nation) or one of the score and more eclectic establishments offering clothes, jewelry, clothing, toys, handcrafts, and home furnishings. A restorative cup of tea at the incomparable **British Shoppe** and its **Front Parlour Tea Room** may be just the right end to an afternoon in Madison. Don't skip town without stopping at **Marie's Sweet Shop**. This little mint-green storefront with the park bench out front has terrific homemade ice cream, great chocolates, and all the fountain treats you'd expect from an independent ice cream emporium.

Madison Town Beaches

While Madison extends northward nearly 15 miles from the shore of the Sound to the border of Durham, it is primarily rural and nearly strictly residential north of I-95. A driving tour of the area south of the Boston Post Road gives the visitor a sense of the coastal flavor of Madison and also takes a route past or near its beautiful beaches. Open a map of Madison and discover the roads that lead to the shore. Along the route you choose, stop at Madison's wonderful beaches and historic wharves.

The Surf Club is the largest town beach, with playing fields; a nature trail; bocce, basketball, volleyball, and horseshoes courts; a large picnic grove with barbecue grills; and a pavilion with a first aid station, rest rooms and showers, a game room, and a snack bar.

The tiny crescent of **West Wharf Beach** lies at the left side of the stone wharf at the foot of West Wharf Road. Stop at this point for a great view of Tuxis Island to the east near the shore and Faulkner's Island in the distance to the southwest. Anglers, photographers, and barefooted tidepool explorers are drawn to the area's famed rock outcroppings, once called Reuben's Rocks. Beautiful from dawn to sunset, this popular destination was the site of Madison's busiest and most profitable shipbuilding wharf in the nineteenth century.

At **East Wharf Beach**, tucked neatly in the heart of Madison's private beach community, a large wooden gazebo shelters visitors in all seasons; rest rooms, a water fountain, and an outdoor shower add to the comfort of summer travelers. A public landing place since 1765, this site was home to Minor's Shipyard until 1890, when the yard and all of the tall ships in it burned to the ground.

Just yards from Hammonasset State Park at the place where tranquil Tom's Creek enters the Sound, **Webster Point Beach** presents a secluded alternative for folks who walk or bike in from the center of town. In exchange for its lack of parking, lifeguards, and facilities, visitors enjoy a wide sandbar, good snorkeling places, and lots of privacy.

Webster Point Beach at the foot of Pent Road off Webster Point Road (walk-in only; no street parking, even in the off-season), East Wharf Beach on Middle Beach Road, West Wharf Beach at the foot of West Wharf Road, and Surf Club Beach on Surf Club Road. From Memorial Day through Labor Day, day-use fees ($10 per vehicle per day; plus $10 for each driver and passenger) are charged for nonresident visitors. There is no charge in the off season For further information, call the Madison Beach and Recreation Department (203–245–5623).

Hammonasset State Park and Meigs Point Nature Center

If you wander east from the center of Madison on the Boston Post Road, you will soon reach Hammonasset State Park. Enormously popular, this park offers nearly one thousand acres and 2 miles of shorefront—Connecticut's longest stretch of public beach. Provided for your comfort and pleasure are pavilions and picnic shelters, a 550-site campground, playing fields, a nature center with walking trails, a bike path, a wide, wooden boardwalk, and sun, sand, rocks, and salty spray in abundance.

Come here to camp, swim, fish off the jetty, scuba dive, picnic, play ball, hike, sailboard, or boat on Long Island Sound. Day visitors and campers alike should stop at the **Meigs Point Nature Center.** An excellent small facility, it has fresh- and saltwater aquariums, a marine touch tank, dioramas, and a good variety of live amphibians and reptiles of the area. Outside is the Willard's Island walking trail that rambles through the salt meadow and onto Willard's Island, once farmed in colonial times and now home to the small mammals and birds of the marshlands.

The nature center rangers provide free bird walks, slide presentations, canoe trips, bike hikes, and nature workshops for all ages throughout the summer. Special activities such as the Junior Naturalist program and the Outdoor Explorer program are scheduled for children. Held midweek in July and August, the children's programs are open to drop-in visitors.

The parking lot immediately to the east of the nature center is a good place to stow the car if you'd like to set yourself up on the beach for a few hours to catch a few rays or watch the ospreys that nest here. Across the road from the lot is a long wooden walkway to one of the park's smaller, quieter pavilions. If you travel eastward from the nature center toward the boat launch site at Meigs Point, you'll stop at a dead-end parking area just before the lane to the beach reserved for boaters. Be sure to park and walk to the top of the rocky hill at the point; its sandy paths lead to beautiful views of the Sound and shore. An expansive wooden deck at the summit provides a place to enjoy the broad sweep of seascape and the songs of the gulls and warblers.

For those unsatisfied by a mere few hours at the shore, Hammonasset's windswept campground is a great seaside vacation spot. Well-run and very clean, it is extremely popular in the summertime. The sites are almost all open, so if you like the hills and woods, you're in the wrong park. Bring a metal tub or fire ring if you want to sit or sing around a campfire; pack a grill or hibachi if you want to cook over a flame; the state provides no grills or firepits at this park, and campfires are permitted only in metal containers. Campfire programs, bingo, an occasional dance and a children's playground with swings and a great wooden ship ensure fun for all ages. A camp store rents fire rings and stocks firewood, a moderate variety of groceries, and essentials like marshmallows and chocolate.

Bring bikes and in-line skates—the campground has excellent lanes for both sports. Biking and in-line skating are possible year-round, even though the campground closes; just park your vehicle outside the gate and enter the lanes with bikes or blades.

Off the Boston Post Road at exit 62 of I–95. Park (203–245–2785) open daily year-round, 8:00 A.M. to sunset. Campground (203–245–1817) open mid-May to September 30. Nature Center (203–245–8743) open late April to September 30, Tuesday through Sunday, 10:00 A.M. to 5:00 P.M. Per-vehicle admission charge $5.00 for in-state license plates and $8.00 for out-of-state plates on weekdays from Memorial Day to Labor Day; $7.00 and $12.00, respectively, on weekends. Also $5.00 and $7.00 on weekends only from mid-April to Memorial Day and from Labor Day through mid-October; weekdays free to all during those weeks. No charge off-season. Campsites $12.00 nightly. Alcohol-free.

CHESTNUT HILL CONCERTS

A summer day spent in Madison can stretch well into the evening if you stay for one of the concerts of the acclaimed Chestnut Hill chamber music series. Produced for thirty summers, the series drew its early performers from the Yale Music School. Now the concerts, performed at Madison's First Congregational Church on the green, feature world-class performers from New York, Boston, and Europe. The acoustics in this spacious yet intimate setting are superb for the purpose. Classical chamber music with an emphasis on the Romantic period is the focus of the series, but the program may yield equally pleasant surprises.

Four concerts are offered each season on the first four Fridays in August at 8:00 P.M. Subscriptions are $40 to $70; individual tickets are $12 to $22; children attend for free. For further information, call the box office (203-245-5736).

Many concertgoers picnic before the performances. Boxed picnic suppers can be ordered in advance ($15 per person) and picked up at the church after 6:00 P.M.

Places to Eat in Madison

Cafe Allegre 725 Boston Post Road (203-245-7773). By day, sunlit rooms and front-porch seating; at evening, an air of elegance in a vintage inn at the heart of downtown. In the main dining rooms, enjoy Italian cuisine with a gourmet flair, charming table lamps, and an atmosphere of elegance. Seafood, pastas, freshly made sauces, tasty house-made soups. Open Tuesday through Sunday for dinner; lunch Tuesday through Friday. $$$-$$$$

The Wharf Restaurant at the Madison Beach Hotel; 94 West Wharf Road (203-245-0005). The only restaurant on the Sound in Madison. Seafood, steaks, and pasta for lunch and dinner in the main dining rooms. Upstairs at the Crow's Nest lounge are sandwiches, chowders, and other light fare. Live music in the Crow's Nest on weekends after about 9:30 P.M. If you want to enjoy a quiet, leisurely dinner downstairs, make reservations for 7:00, not 8:00. Open late March through December. $$

Zhang's 44 Boston Post Road (203-245-3300). This sit-down restaurant with an alluring tropical ambiance has a Far Eastern flair, offering Chinese and Japanese fare at moderate prices. All dishes are spiced to your tastes, and dozens of choices are on the menu. Take-out available, too. Sushi and sashimi bar. Open daily year-round for lunch and dinner. $-$$

Lynch and Malone's Restaurant 56A Academy Street (203-245-1145). Smartly dressed salads and sandwiches, grilled seafood and steaks, terrific salads, innovative pasta dishes. Open year-round daily for lunch and dinner and Sunday brunch. $-$$

Friends and Company 11 Boston Post Road (203-245-0462). A busy local favorite on the banks of the East River. Casual and reasonable with good pastas, fresh fish, crisp salads, excellent herb bread. Best of all, smoke-free. Open year-round for dinner daily; lunch Wednesday through Saturday; Sunday brunch. $-$$

Lenny and Joe's Fish Tale 1301 Boston Post Road (203-245-7289). A busy favorite on the Hammonasset end of town. Casual eat-in or take-out atmosphere with indoor, porch, or outdoor picnic-table seating. Heaping plates of fresh fish, corn on the cob, salt potatoes, good rings, lobster, chowder, and much more. Open year-round for lunch and dinner daily. $

Red Tomato Pizzeria 37 Boston Post Road (203-245-6948). Order out or eat in at this cheery eatery that makes excellent thin-crust New

Haven-style pizza baked right on the bricks. Fresh vegetable and meat toppings make it easy to design your own tasty creation—even the clams are freshly shucked. Calzones, a house salad, and antipasto are also on the menu. Closed Monday. Call for hours. $-$$

The Clam Castle 1324 Boston Post Road (203-245-4911). Serving the shoreline since 1967, this classic seafood shack is owned by two amiable brothers who take pride in upholding the tradition of fresh fish, famed New England and Rhode Island clam chowder, lobster rolls, soft-shell crabs, clams nearly any way you can eat 'em (including clam fritters); and much more—all served cheerfully in a laid-back and casual but immaculate setting. Eat inside or out. Open daily for lunch and dinner, from March through Thanksgiving. $

The Front Parlour Tea Room at the British Shoppe; 45 Wall Street (203-245-4521). Enter the 1690 Meigs Bishop House and enter another world—one you'll want to linger in well past teatime. Perfect crumpets and scones, delicate finger sandwiches, delicious pot pies and homemade soups, and, of course, the finest of teas and tea cakes, served exquisitely in the most romantic of settings by the most gracious of hosts. It's hard to leave the table, but be sure to save time to shop for teapots, bone china, English toiletries, and other British treasures in the marvelous store. Luncheon Monday through Saturday 11:30 A.M. to 1:30 P.M.; afternoon tea Monday through Saturday 2:00 to 4:00 P.M. and Sunday 12:30 to 4:00 P.M. $

Places to Stay in Madison

The **Madison Beach Hotel** 94 West Wharf Road (203-245-1404). Directly on the beach, this restored 1800 hotel offers a taste of Madison's history as a Victorian seaside resort. Add to that charm the best possible views of Madison's beautiful shoreline. Thirty-five rooms, including six suites; some units have balconies overlooking the Sound. Continental breakfast served on the porch, in the Victorian lobby, or on your balcony. Beach chairs and towels provided. Open March 1 to January 1. $$$

Dolly Madison Inn 73 West Wharf Road (203-245-7377). In total, thirteen rooms in a traditional New England inn and the "Tiltin' Hilton" out back. Several of these are large enough for families. Just a block from the beach. Restaurant. $$-$$$

The Inn at Lafayette 725 Boston Post Road (203-245-7773). Includes five elegant, comfortable guest rooms with private marbled baths,

THE LEGEND OF TUXIS ISLAND

The small island just offshore Madison is Tuxis Island. Algonkian legend says that a great giant scooped up a handful of rocks and soil and flung it into the Sound, creating in one action the island and Tuxis Pond, which formed in the hollow left in the earth by the giant's hand. Today the island is uninhabited; it once was the site of a YMCA camp and has had at least one cottage on it. A nesting platform has recently been raised on the island to attract ospreys. As for the pond, it lies behind the firehouse in the center of town. A wooden boardwalk traces its western edge, and a small park with benches overlooking the pond's aeration fountain is accessible from the public parking area off Wall Street behind the post office.

gracious antique furnishings, and attention to detail apparent in every corner. Continental breakfast, fruit, and champagne. Open year-round. $$$$

Tidewater Inn 949 Boston Post Road (203-245-8457). Elegant non-smoking inn with pretty gardens and a romantic ambiance. Total of nine guest rooms with private baths; full breakfast; complimentary wine in late afternoon; beach passes, beach chairs, and beach towels in summer. Children over the age of 7 only. $$$$

Madison Post Road Bed and Breakfast 318 Boston Post Road (203-245-2866). You'll feel like you've lived here forever in this nineteenth-century treasure with twentieth-century comforts. There are three rooms with private baths, two with shared baths, and a welcoming common room. Full breakfast; deeded beach rights in walking distance; beach chairs and towels. Families welcome; children under 12 stay free. $10 extra for porta-crib or rollaway bed. Nonsmoking. Open year-round; rates lower from January 1 to May 15. $$$-$$$$

Morning Glory Bed and Breakfast 395 Boston Post Road (203-245-9196). Offers three beautifully decorated guest rooms with private baths, country antiques, and a private entrance to this lovely Federal home. Separate studio with king-size bed, sitting area, full bath, and fridge. Air conditioning. Flowered patios and magnificent perennial beds. Full breakfast. Beach passes. Nonsmoking. Families with children over the age of 12 are welcome. Open year-round. $$$-$$$$

Beech Tree Cottages 1187 Boston Post Road (203-245-2676). Nightly

OSPREY!

The cry of the female osprey and the spiraling air ballet of her mate during the courting season have to be among the most dramatic events to occur on the Connecticut shoreline each year. With the support of the public and the work of the biologists involved with the Long Island Sound Program of the Connecticut Department of Environmental Protection, the osprey population on the eastern shore has risen to new heights. Decimated in past decades by the effects of the pesticide DDT on the shells of their young, the ospreys have experienced such a hopeful comeback in recent years that they have been removed from the category of Special Concerns on the Connecticut endangered species list. In the summer of 1999, more than 139 nesting pairs fledged nearly 315 youngsters from the nesting platforms and natural nesting cavities along the coast. Now Connecticut residents and visitors look forward each spring to the return of the ospreys from their winter digs in South America. Still protected under the U.S. Migratory Bird Act, the ospreys have no rivals as the most majestic residents of the Connecticut shore. Hammonasset State Park in Madison is home to several pairs of nesting ospreys.

and weekly rentals are available in summertime at this three-acre enclave just steps from Hammonasset Beach. Each clean but simply furnished cottage has a bath and kitchen facilities; some are perfect for couples; others large enough for a small family. Friendly hosts. Lovely grounds with rope swing, volleyball net, walkways. Weekly rate in 2002 was $575; nightly $$$$.

Public Boat Launches

Hammonasset State Park at Meigs Point. One mile south of exit 62 from I-95. Cartop or carry-in access only. Launching over sandy beach; shallow at low tide. No docking or anchoring. No launch fee; parking fee on weekends and holidays in season.

East River State Boat Launch. On the east bank of the East River. From Boston Post Road, travel south for approximately 2 miles on Neck Road, Ridgewood Avenue, and Circle Beach Road to a right turn on a gravel drive to the riverbank. No fees. Ramp only; no slips or moorings, no fuel or services; portable toilet in season only.

For Further Information

Madison Chamber of Commerce 22 Scotland Avenue (203-245-7394 or 888-342-7394). Maps and brochures.

Madison Web site: madisonct.com.

Madison Land Trust P.O. Box 561, Madison CT 06443. Trail guide to thirteen hiking trails on conservation trust land.

Clinton

Any traveler approaching Clinton along the Boston Post Road at its western boundary with Madison will get an instant sense of the town's close connection with the Sound. The Hammonasset River cuts a swath through golden salt marshes; twisted junipers along the road bend permanently from the effect of the sea breeze; marine supply stores and boatyards advertise the latest deals for sailboarders and yachters alike. Heavy with salt and the briny mud smells of the sea and shore and marsh, the air also carries the sounds of screeching gulls, slapping rigging, and bellowing foghorns.

Halfway between New York and Boston, halfway between New Haven and New London, and situated on the land that in colonial days lay between the colony of Guilford and the colony of Saybrook, Clinton enjoys a central location that adds to its appeal to travelers. Once called Homonoscitt, Clinton's colonial settlement began in 1633 when Hartford Colony appointed a committee to lay out the Homonoscitt land as a plantation.

As was true in most settlements along the Sound, Clinton's early economy focused on farming, fishing, and shipbuilding. Its earliest claim to fame is that the first classes of what later became Yale College were held in the parsonage of its minister, the Reverend Abraham Pierson, also appointed first rector of the school. Later the town became known for its manufacture of Pond's Extract, distilled from native witch hazel cut from the Clinton woodlands. The Chesebrough-Pond's factory is still a noticeable presence along Route 1. By the end of the nineteenth century Clinton, like her shoreline sisters, had developed a summer colony as steamships, the railroad, and improved highways encouraged the influx of visitors from the city. Today Clinton maintains its centered position between the busy cities to its east and west, still offering residents and travelers a respite from the hubbub and a link to the sea.

Very, very low in true tourist attractions, Clinton is a perfect town for skipping stones off the jetty, hitching a ride on a fishing charter, combing antiques stores for some old-fashioned treasures, and topping off the day with a shore dinner and an ice cream cone.

The Best of Clinton

Adam Stanton House and Store

Every Connecticut town has a noteworthy house open to the public, and Clinton is no exception. Owned and maintained as a museum of American antiquities by Connecticut National Bank, this house was built in 1789 by Adam Stanton, a Rhode Islander who came to Connecticut during the Revolutionary War. Stanton operated a general store and a salt distillery on the property. Preserved with both store and home portions, the house contains almost all original furnishings. Along with an excellent collection of china and furniture, the house has some interesting features such as hinged wall paneling that allows the panels to be fastened to hooks in the ceiling so as to expand two rooms into one.

Stanton's store has been restored to its earliest condition, with its original counter, shelves, accountant's desk, and even labeled drawers. Behind the house is the original well of the Reverend Abraham Pierson, who owned an earlier house built on the site in 1694. It was in that first house that Pierson, from 1701 to 1707, taught the first classes of the new collegiate school later known as Yale.

63 East Main Street (860–669–2132). Open June 1 to September 30, Tuesday through Sunday from 2:00 to 5:00 P.M. Free; donations welcome. Ages 6 and older.

Captain Elisha White House

More commonly known as the Old Brick House, this 1850 home is owned by the Clinton Historical Society. The oldest brick house on the

DOWNTOWN CLINTON, ANTIQUES CAPITAL OF THE SHORE

The center of downtown Clinton stretches along Route 1 for quite a distance, with the highest concentration of commercial buildings starting somewhat west of Route 81 and ending somewhat east of Route 145. The strip immediately east of Route 81 is where visitors will find the Andrews Memorial Town Hall, the information center, the Vece Gazebo, and most of Clinton's historic sites. Along this thoroughfare visitors will also find one of Connecticut's highest concentrations of antiques shops. Here's a partial list:

The Loft at Cramer's Corner 57 West Main Street (860-669-4583). Open daily 11:00 A.M. to 5:00 P.M. This landmark shop has a congenial owner and an eclectic collection; great lamps, bottles, household tools, writing implements.

Clinton Antique Center 78 East Main Street (860-669-3839). Open daily 10:00 A.M. to 5:00 P.M. except New Year's Day, Easter, Thanksgiving, and Christmas. Eighty-five dealers in an enormous group shop.

Miriam Green Antiquarian Bookshop and Gallery 88 East Main Street (860-664-4200). This shop is lined with books and tables and bronzes and cabinets full of distracting curiosities. Located in a 1920s garage in the heart of the antiques district, this incredible shop is crowded with a constantly changing inventory of the elegant, the odd, and the compelling bits of flotsam from the last three centuries. Along with fine and period decorative arts, proprietor Susan Alon offers reference information and appraisals for old books and just about anything else. Open year-round, seven days regularly and by chance.

As Time Goes By 14 West Main Street (860-669-2231). In another of Clinton's historic homes are seven rooms of vintage clothing and antique furniture lovingly preserved and available for sale. From funky to fabulously elegant, this collection is must-see quality. Usually open Wednesday through Sunday 11:00 A.M. to 6:00 P.M. Best to call ahead.

M. Sarba Fine Arts Café 95 East Main Street (860-669-5062). This charming art gallery-cum-cafe located in one of Clinton's historic homes offers paintings, glassware, and sculpture as well as fine European gourmet coffees, cappuccinos, lattés, pastries, hot and cold soups, and more. Utterly gracious and welcoming. Outdoor deck in season. Open daily 10:00 A.M. to 8:00 P.M. $

Waterside Antiques 109 East Main Street (860-669-0809). Open Thursday through Sunday 11:00 A.M. to 4:00 P.M. Primitive furniture, textiles, woodenware, redware, folk art and lighting reproductions, baskets, glassware.

shoreline from New Haven to New London, as well as the only brick house in Clinton, the house was built from handmade English brick brought to America as ballast in the ship of prosperous sea captain Elisha White. Today the property includes eighteenth- and nineteenth-century furnishings, portraits, and landscapes as well as a genealogical library inside and a colonial garden outside.

The Clinton Historical Society also maintains a local history room in the Andrews Memorial Town Hall (room 107). Its collections include dolls, china, silver, clothing, household implements, pressed glass and tin, and nautical items. The room is open on weekdays in July and August from 2:00 to 4:00 P.M., on Wednesdays only from September through June, or by appointment.

Elisha White House, 103 East Main Street (860–669–6059). Open on Wednesday year-round from 9:00 to 11:00 A.M. and in July and August on weekends from 2:00 to 4:00 P.M. or by appointment. Free.

Clinton Town Beach

If it is the sea that has beckoned you here, then you must be sure to sink your toes in the sand at Clinton's pretty town beach. Out-of-town visitors can use this crescent-shaped parcel for a reasonable day fee. From the center of town, turn south off the Boston Post Road onto charming

1630 HOUSE VISITOR'S INFORMATION CENTER

In front of the firehouse at 49 East Main Street is a small brown cabin that houses Clinton's Visitor's Information Center. From its hand-hewn boards to its wooden pegs, the structure is an exact reproduction of a typical 1630 house of the New England colonies. Staffed in the warm seasons by helpful volunteers, the center is stocked with maps, brochures, and other information to aid the traveler's enjoyment of the town. Hours are seasonal, but generally they are weekends from 9:00 A.M. to 3:00 P.M. from late May though Labor Day and on weekdays from 12:30 to 5:00 P.M. from late June through late August. Should the cabin be closed, stop by the Chamber of Commerce, directly across the street, on weekdays from 9:00 A.M. to 3:00 P.M.

Waterside Lane. This narrow avenue leads past lovely old houses and crosses a wooden bridge at the edge of the shore. Within the beach area are a children's playground, rest rooms and an outside shower, volleyball courts, barbecue grills, and a snack bar that provides simple summer fare. This small, quiet beach is perfect for families with very young children and couples in search of some solitude.

At the foot of Waterside Lane off Route 1. Open year-round. Concession and rest rooms in season only. Day-use fee, $7.00 per car.

Chamard Vineyard

Established in 1983 on a sun-kissed forty-acre property just 2 miles from the shore, Chamard has twenty acres of vines used to make premium table wines from such classic European grapes as chardonnay, cabernet sauvignon, pinot noir, merlot, and cabernet Franc. Wine maker Larry McCulloch and owner William Chaney credit Clinton's moderate microclimate and rich, stony soil for the success of the vineyard. Surely their own expertise and dedicated hard labor have something to do with the growing reputation of the beautiful wine-making operation here.

Even the brief distance through the vineyard from the gate to the winery reveals the painstaking work of pruning, trellising, and hedging the vines. A visit to the magnificent winery includes a walk through the underground wine cellar and barrel aging rooms. Throughout the tour, the wine-making process and its technology are clearly explained. In crisp weather a cheerful fire adds to the relaxing ambiance of the tasting room; in spring and summer the doors to its spacious deck overlooking the pond and vineyards are swung open so visitors can savor the wine samples in the open air.

The tours and tastings are complimentary, but you may be tempted to purchase a bottle or two. The purchase of a case buys you an invitation to return to the vineyard for special events such as barrel tastings. Be sure to buy a bottle of Chamard's prize-winning chardonnay for your picnic dinner or a spicy cabernet Franc to accompany Thai or Cajun dishes. Superb!

115 Cow Hill Road (860–664–0299 or 800–371–1609). Tastings and tours Wednesday through Saturday 11:00 A.M. to 4:00 P.M. Call ahead to confirm hours, especially during winter or on holiday weekends.

Boat Excursions and Charters

Early Bird Charters Captain Tony Barone; Clinton Town Dock, Riverside Drive (860–664–4540). The 34-foot twin diesel takes up to six passengers on sportfishing cruises (all bait and tackle supplied) or Long Island Sound cruises; half- or full-day trips.

Bluefin **Charters** Captain Ray Zabulis; Cedar Island Marina (860–659–9920). Forty-foot twin diesel offers full-day, half-day, and night fishing trips inshore; and offshore to Montauk and Block Island. Overnight tuna fishing trips to the Canyons.

Places to Eat in Clinton

Aqua Restaurant 34 Riverside Drive (860–664–3788). Near Cedar Island Marina with great views and a friendly ambiance for families as well as adult diners, this is the place for seafood a cut well above that of the typical shoreline fish house. Traditional favorites like fish and chips are also on the menu for shore dinner diehards or hungry children. There's no better place to watch the sailboats return to the marina. Open nearly year-round for lunch and dinner. $–$$$

The Log Cabin Restaurant 232 Boston Post Road (860–669–6253). In a real log cabin with lace at the windows, choose from a large menu of steaks, chicken, seafood, salads, and much more, all served in very generous

PRETTY AS A PICTURE

A visit to the **Clinton Town Dock** could be the perfect close to your day. Take Grove Street south from Route 1 at the weathered blue sign that lists the harbor sites. This quiet, residential avenue reaches the water about a half-mile down, then turns onto Riverside Drive, where you will find marinas, restaurants, a great old lobster shack, a public boat ramp, and tiny Esposito Beach.

Strolling the dock area on foot is the best way to see the sights. Park in the large public lot between the boat launch and the Cedar Island Marina and order an ice cream at the dockside snack shack. Sit a spell at Esposito Beach. No lifeguard supervises here, and only a few benches on a pretty brick patio provide a resting spot on this diminutive pier-side patch of sand. But it's a great place to watch the boats go by, and the view just before sunset across the boats and water to Cedar Island is the sort that artists come to paint.

portions with a huge bowl of steaming pasta for the whole table. Open year-round daily for lunch and dinner. $$

Chip's Pub III 24 West Main Street (860-669-3463). Casual pub fare. Burgers, sandwiches, salads, soups, ribs, steaks, pasta; children's menu. Open year-round daily for lunch, dinner, Sunday brunch. $-$$

Taste of China 233 East Main Street (860-664-4454). Open for lunch and dinner daily year-round, this sit-down restaurant has a growing reputation as the best Chinese establishment on the shoreline. Fabulous extensive menu served in a pleasant ambiance in an otherwise unremarkable building at the edge of the salt marshes on Route 1. $$-$$$

BB&G Lobster 152 Commerce Street (203-669-2005). Fresh live lobster for those with a pot to cook it in, or steamed lobsters for a small extra fee. Bait, ice. Open late spring to early fall, Tuesday through Saturday from 9:00 A.M. to 5:00 P.M. and Sunday until 3:00 P.M. In early spring, Wednesday through Sunday at the same hours. $

For breakfasts and beach and picnic fare, try any of these Clinton favorites; just ask the locals: **Aunt Shirley's Pizza & Deli** (68 West Main Street; 860-669-3354); **Saldamarco's Market** (86 East Main Street; 860-669-3469); **The Coffee Break** (27 East Main Street; 860-664-0808; or **Malone's** (51 West Main Street; 860-664-0607).

Places to Stay in Clinton

A Victorian Village-Marina Cottages 345 East Main Street (860-669-3009). This complex of cottages and chalets offers weekly rates for vacationers. The owners have furnished the cottages and embellished them with fretwork and windowboxes, but many are rented to "in-betweeners" and other longer-term guests. The best bet for travelers are the two-story chalets. Each has a full bath, whirlpool tub, gas fireplace, two sleeping areas, fully equipped kitchenette, private phone, and cable TV. Nonsmoking. Landscaped common area. Available year-round by the week only. Call for rates.

Clinton Motel 163 East Main Street (860-669-8850). Clean, basic lodging; air-conditioned double rooms with refrigerators, phones, televisions, baths; outdoor swimming pool. Open year-round. $$

Riverdale Farm Campground 111 River Road (860-669-5388). At the edge of the Hammonasset River on a twisting country road are 250 wooded or riverfront sites. Spring-fed pond for swimming, fishing, canoeing. Rest rooms, showers, launderette, camp store. RV hookups. Recreation hall; tennis, horseshoes, shuffleboard, basketball, and softball. Open April 15 to October 1. AAA-approved; Woodall-rated. Daily, weekly, and monthly rates. $

Public Boat Launch

Clinton Town Dock and Ramp Riverside Drive (860-669-2611). Transient berths; boat ramp (day use $15, seasonal nonresident $70); fuel.

For Further Information

Clinton Chamber of Commerce 50 East Main Street (860-669-3889). E-mail: chamber@clintonct.com

Clinton Web site: www.clintonct.com.

Clinton Park and Recreation Department Killingworth Turnpike (Route 81) (860-669-6901). Information on the Ethel C. Peters Recreation Complex (bocce courts, horseshoes pits, picnic area, concession stand, kiddie park, and fields and courts for softball, soccer, football, tennis, and basketball), the Indian River Recreational Complex (nature trail, in-line skating area, pond and river fishing, ballfields, and pavilion), and Deane Haag Nature Trail.

Westbrook

Anchored to the sea by its twin rivers, the Menunketesuck to the west and the Patchogue to the east, Westbrook makes the most of its 4 miles of shorefront. A good stretch of this prime real estate is publicly owned and/or protected, so human as well as furred and feathered creatures can enjoy a taste of the sea in this quiet community.

Settled in 1638 as the Pochaug, or Patchogue, section of Saybrook

Plantation, Westbrook was renamed in 1810 and incorporated as a separate town in 1840. Shipbuilding was the primary industry here until the age of the steamship and the railroad, and the manufacture of staves and heads for use in hogshead barrels made sure that colonial goods bound for the West Indies arrived safely.

It was through the genius of one of her native sons that Westbrook contributed most to maritime history. David Bushnell, born in Westbrook about 1742, set aside his wages until he had saved enough to enroll in Yale College at the age of 31. During his last year as a student there, he invented the submarine and brought it back to Saybrook to test it. Completed in 1776, Bushnell's wood-and-steel *American Turtle* was a hand-powered one-man ship that submerged when its ballast tanks were filled with water. Used in an unsuccessful attempt to attach a torpedo mine to the belly of the sixty-four-gun British man-of-war *Eagle* in New York Harbor during the Revolution, the submersible vessel was the forerunner of the modern-day submarine.

Today the United States center of submarine production has moved eastward to Groton, and the vessels plying the waters of Westbrook are mostly pleasure craft and fishing boats. The ripple of sails and the chatter of lines teasing at spars are the sounds to steer by if you want to find the best parts of Westbrook.

The Best of Westbrook

Westbrook Town Beach

Even if you are not a sun worshipper, a drive along Westbrook's beaches may do wonders for your soul. From the Boston Post Road, turn south onto Seaview Avenue. Highlighted by one of the prettiest views of the water and the offshore islands, this drive also takes you to what might very well be the best public beach from Clinton to Old Saybrook. For a small day fee that nonresidents pay only in summer, you can spend the day on the sand or stroll the long walk past the cottages that line the roadway across from the shoreline.

Officially called West Beach, this town-owned property is clean and well maintained. In the summer, lifeguards help to ensure public safety, and the rest rooms, showers, and concessions make the beach a good destination for a daylong visit to the seaside. Perfect for young children and reluctant swimmers, its swimming area has an extraordinarily sandy bottom that slopes very gradually toward deeper water.

A small playground provides entertainment for the young and the young at heart.

Seaview Avenue. Open 8:00 A.M to 10:00 P.M. Day-use vehicle fee from Memorial Day through Labor Day. Rest rooms, concession, and outdoor showers in summer only; lifeguards in summer only. Call the Westbrook Park and Recreation Department (860–399–3095).

Salt Island and Middle Beach

Diminutive Middle Beach is located at the southern end of Salt Island Road off Route 1, a short distance east of Route 153. The road turns toward the left as you reach its end, and the beach lies across the road from private cottages. Limited parking is available here, and there are no facilities such as changing areas or rest rooms. The swimming area is not lifeguarded, and signs state that no fires, dogs, flotation devices, or ball-playing are allowed. All of these factors conspire to make Middle Beach a perfect spot for a peaceful swim or a quiet picnic. The larger of the two small islands directly opposite the beach is Salt Island, the site of early saltworks, oil works, and warehouses where fishing and trading ships once loaded their cargoes.

Open all year; no fee; no facilities .

Salt Meadow National Wildlife Refuge

This beautiful spot comprising salt marsh, grassland, and forest habitats, is the headquarters for the Stewart B. McKinney National Wildlife Refuge, which also includes seven other Connecticut shore sanctuaries (including Chimon, Sheffield, and Goose Islands in Norwalk and Faulkner Island in Guilford). Sliced into northern and southern parcels by railroad tracks, Salt Meadow begins, at its southernmost tip, at the confluence of the Menunketesuck and Patchogue Rivers, just yards before the two rivers meet the Sound. This southern parcel is still mostly inaccessible; the best way to enjoy the southern parcel is over a plate of whole clams at Bill's Seafood Restaurant (see Places to Eat), which affords great views of the marsh and its osprey platform.

The northern portion of the 192-acre refuge has nearly 3 miles of public trails through all three habitats, from the salt marsh at the rim of the Sound, through shrubs and grassland, and upward to the woodland as much as 110 feet above sea level. Bring binoculars; more than 200 species of birds have been observed at Salt Meadow. Migrating warblers stop to

WESTBROOK FIFE AND DRUM MUSTER

When the Ancient Mariners march down the Boston Post Road with their fifes trilling and their cannon booming, you'll swear you've awakened in an earlier century. Colonial flags wave, and the boots of the drummers in tricornered hats hit the pavement in exact unison. Songs of the Revolution pierce the thick salt air of late summer, drowning out the usual cries of the gulls over Westbrook center. An annual event since 1959, the Westbrook Fife and Drum Muster brings thousands of visitors to town the fourth weekend of every August. Approximately fifty fife and drum corps from the East Coast meet for a two-day encampment that includes an opening tattoo on Friday evening, a Saturday parade, a muster that lasts throughout Saturday afternoon, and informal jam sessions on both evenings.

The tattoo, beginning on Friday at 7:00 P.M. in the Ted Lane Field behind the Westbrook Town Hall, features just a half dozen corps; the jam session following the formal portion is a casual affair open to musicians from any corps. On Saturday the two-hour parade begins at 11:00 A.M. on Route 1 in the center of town and ends at the encampment in Ted Lane Field, where the muster, in which the corps perform separately, lasts until about 6:00 P.M.

The whole event is free unless you buy a trinket or two on Saturday at the flea market where vendors display wares related to the music and culture of the corps. Here's the place to find a tricornered hat or a handcrafted fife. A food concession at the field offers burgers and dogs and the like, or you can pack in a picnic. Parking is available at the back of the Town Hall or in the back lot of the Wilcox Fuel Company; be here by 9:30 A.M. on Saturday to be sure of a spot. This popular event is a shoreline classic.

vacation here in springtime. Be sure to wear long pants and socks and/or tick repellent, and please leave bicycles and pets at home.

A trail map is posted on a kiosk near the main entrance headquarters building. If you are packing snacks or sandwiches, be a thoughtful guest. Garbage of all kinds endangers the lives of the migratory and resident birds and mammals who are sharing their space with you. Your attention to proper trash disposal assures that you and other humans will be invited back. An area especially for picnicking has been created near the main office building, which has rest rooms.

Old Clinton Road. From I–95 exit 64, go south on Route 145 to the blinking red light at the first intersection, then left on Old Clinton Road to the refuge entrance and trailhead 1 mile on the right. Or, from Route 1, head north on Old Clinton Road, which lies just west of the town green; refuge will be on your left. Open year-round daily, half an hour before dawn to half an hour past dusk. Call for more information (860–399–2513).

Military Historians Museum

The Company of Military Historians Museum on the town green houses the nation's largest collection of American military uniforms. Completely restored and operable military vehicles from World War II and other late twentieth-century conflicts, plus other memorabilia such as army crests and books and videos about American military involvements, are also a part of the collection.

Westbrook Place on North Main Street (860–399–0460). Open year-round Tuesday through Friday 8:00 A.M. to 3:30 P.M. and by appointment on evenings and weekends. Free.

The Pink Sleigh

Head north, appropriately, from exit 65 off I-95 to see a little bit of magic. Best seen in the twilight when the air is crisp, this spot is a haven of peace and beauty for anyone who delights in the wonder of Christmas. Housed in an old barn, this store is breathtakingly beautiful—a place where every small child (and not a few adults) will suck in his or her breath in awe of its glitter and gold. Dazzling displays of every color and material fill the two-story 1830s rustic barn, which is in itself lovely.

Stepping into this place is like stepping into an elfin workshop hidden in the hills. Tucked into every corner and hung from the highest rafters are thousands of ornaments recalling the spirit of Christmas and the loving message of one Jolly Old Elf. Whether you prefer designs made in America or imported from the finest manufacturers in Europe, you will find treasures here for every taste and style.

For the crafter, the store stocks materials for autumn and Thanksgiving wreaths and centerpieces: candles, silk and other everlasting flowers and greenery, and an extensive stock of tassels, garlands, and ribbons. As far as Christmas is concerned, the Pink Sleigh can't go wrong.

512 Essex Road (Route 153), half a mile north of I–95 (860–399–6926). Open from early July until Christmas Eve, Tuesday through Saturday from 10:00 A.M. to 5:00 P.M. and Sunday from noon to 5:00 P.M. Also open 10:00 A.M. to 5:00 P.M. on Mondays from Columbus Day to December 24, and until 8:00 P.M. on Thursday, Friday, and Saturday in December.

Boat Excursions and Charters

Catch 'Em Charters Captain Richard Siedzik; Pilot's Point Marina, North Yard (860–223–1876 or 860–399–5853). Five-hour sportfishing cruises for one to six passengers. Bait and tackle provided; mate will clean and fillet your catch. Bring your own lunch and soft drinks.

Places to Eat in Westbrook

Westbrook Lobster Restaurant and Market 346 East Main Street (860–664–9464). On the Clinton/Westbrook line, this spic-and-span eatery has served up broiled, grilled, and fried seafood for forty years. Steamers, steamed lobsters, quarter-pound lobster rolls, crab cakes, New England clam chowder, lobster bisque, famous clam chili, and much more. Open daily for lunch and dinner year-round. Smoke-free. Fish market. $–$$

Boom! Seaside Avenue, in the Brewers' Pilot's Point Marina (860–399–2322). In the midst of the boatyard is this newcomer in 2002; the service, one hopes, will have worked out its kinks by the time of this publication, but the food is good, the room is warm and airy all at the same time, and the sunsets are divine. Outdoor deck in season. Open for lunch and dinner. Call for seasonal schedule. $$$

The Whole Enchilada 1121 Boston Post Road (860–399–1221). For a quick, casual meal, try this excellent eatery. Healthy Mexican cuisine is the fare; try the gazpacho, chili, burritos, soups, quesadillas. Take-out or eat in at the small bar. Open year-round daily from 11:30 A.M. $

Bill's Seafood Restaurant 548 Boston Post Road at the Singing Bridge (860–399–7224). Coming from the Westbrook Green, cross the Patchogue River on the metal deck of the newly restored 1925 steel bridge that has its name on the National Register of Historic Places. Listen carefully for the happy hum of your car wheels as you turn right into the dusty parking lot of Bill's. This local favorite has good food, reasonable prices, and a setting that couldn't be more picturesque. Watch the swallows swoop and chatter;

look for the ospreys nesting above the tidal marsh. The moon rises nicely over the boats in the marina, and the clientele is much more colorful and interesting than in fancier places. If you're going to eat chowder, steamers, and clam strips, you might as well do it in a place that hums most nights with live jazz, Dixieland, and rock 'n' roll, played by locally famed combos. $–$$

Edd's 478 Boston Post Road (860–399–9498). For quick and delicious breakfast, lunch, and early, casual dinner or take-out, Edd's is terrific for soups, panini, spaghetti pie, lasagna, incredible pies and muffins, and much more, at the riverside; open daily year-round. Eat *en plein air* at the picnic tables or in the gazebo. $–$$

Cafe Routier 1353 Boston Post Road (860–399–8700). New in this location in 2002 and with a new menu to celebrate the move, Cafe Routier has changed for the better. Chef Jeffrey Renkl has expanded the original French bistro fare to include new American innovations in two lovely dining rooms. Open for lunch Tuesday through Saturday; dinner daily; Sunday brunch. $$$

Water's Edge 1525 Boston Post Road (860–399–5901). In the luxury resort of the same name, have an elegant breakfast, lunch, dinner, or Sunday brunch overlooking the shore. The *New York Times* gave the restaurant a "Very Good" rating; the *Hartford Courant* gives it three stars. Reservations are a must for Sunday brunch, voted the best brunch in the state by readers of *Connecticut* magazine. Offered year-round, this sold-out affair begins at 10:00 A.M., last seating at 2:30 P.M. $$$–$$$$

Places to Stay in Westbrook

Welcome Inn B&B 433 Essex Road (Route 153) (860–399–2500). Web site: www.welcomeinnbandb.com. Built in the 1890s, this comfortable homestead is a relaxing oasis that inspires restful dreams. Lovingly and beautifully decorated and furnished, this smoke-free home offers guests three equally charming rooms, plus extras like complimentary sherry in the afternoon and a delicious home-cooked full breakfast. Inviting deck and parklike grounds. Though best suited to adults, the inn welcomes family groups that may want to share the house for a small reunion or special event. Open year-round. $$$–$$$$

Westbrook Inn B&B 976 Boston Post Road (860–399–4777). This 1878 Victorian home is often booked solid in summer and fall. Restored to its original colors and decor, it has nine rooms, plus one suite and a two-bedroom cottage perfect for families or couples looking for extra privacy and some elbow room. Air-conditioning, color televisions, and refrigerators in all rooms. On the river with a dock and fishing; three minutes to beach. Continental breakfast daily; full breakfast on Sundays, on the wrap-around porch in fair weather. Gear available for boating, biking, and fishing. $$$$

Angel's Watch Inn 902 Boston Post Road (860–399–8846). Web site: www.angelswatchinn.com. This establishment aims to give its guests their own private heaven in an 1880 Federal home just a block and a half from West Beach. Its five air-conditioned guest rooms evoke the Victorian or Art Deco periods. Three have private baths; two share a bath or can be booked as a private suite or single. Full gourmet breakfasts fuel guests until dinnertime. Beach blankets and towels are in every guest room; barbecue grills are in the backyard if you'd like to make a dinner here. Strawberries dipped in chocolate may tease you to relax in the afternoon with a complimentary glass of wine or iced tea. The house sleeps fifteen; reunions and wedding parties are welcome. $$$–$$$$

Captain Stannard House 138 South Main Street (860–399–4634). Web site: www.stannardhouse.com. The worst complaint about this establishment is that it's closed to guests from December through March. In season, the eight spacious guest rooms in this enormous nineteenth-century sea-captain's mansion offer visitors the comfort of private baths and the charm of pretty, antique furnishings. Close to the beach and the center of the village, the house and its eclectic additions total an amazing 10,000 square feet. Not surprisingly, the gracious host says he's never had an unpleasant guest—the pleasing accommodations and delicious breakfasts can't fail to keep moodiness at bay. Should you be tempted to frown host Vern Mettin may even sing to you. $$$$

Talcott House 161 Seaside Avenue (860–399–5020). With an unobstructed view of the Sound and a private bath in each of its four waterfront guest rooms, this expansive cottage is a summer dreamhouse. A hearty continental breakfast is served in the fresh and sunny common room each morning, perfect for energizing guests for a walk on the beach or an invigorating swim. One first-floor room has its own private porch overlooking the water. Open most of the year, except for a month or so in winter when repairs and alterations are done. $$$–$$$$

Water's Edge Inn and Resort 1525 Boston Post Road (860–399–5901 or 800–222–5901). If you have the budget and a desire for something bigger, this resort offers fifteen acres on the Sound, and more than 165 rooms, including thirty-three plush rooms in the main inn and sixty-eight luxury two-bedroom villa units in time-share buildings. A private beach, terraced gardens, tennis courts, indoor and outdoor pools, health spa and fitness center, and a public restaurant with water views are all part of the package. Nightly entertainment and planned activities for all ages are on the resort's active schedule. Have fun on the Sound in a paddleboat, relax in the Jacuzzi, have a massage and a facial, and then dine overlooking the sea. Open year-round. $$$$

Beach Plum Inn 1935 Boston Post Road (860–399–9345). Offers eighteen immaculate, air-conditioned, and nicely decorated motel-type units, including some efficiencies and seven separate cottages. Play area, heated outdoor pool, picnic area with grills, five-minute walk to private Chapman Beach, beach passes to public town beach. Refrigerators, color cable TVs, and modern baths in every unit. Nightly and weekly rentals. Owned and operated by the congenial Fortier family. Continental breakfast and guest lounge. Van transportation to trains and local attractions. Open year-round. Two-diamond AAA rating. $$–$$$$

For Further Information

Westbrook Chamber of Commerce P. O. Box 267, Westbrook CT 06498 (860–395–0445).

Westbrook Web site: www.westbrookct.com.

Westbrook Parks and Recreation: 860–399–3095.

Westbrook State Welcome Center on I-95 northbound between exits 65 and 66. Staffed Memorial Day to Labor Day daily from 8:00 A.M. to 6:00 P.M. and on some spring and fall weekends. Maps, brochures, information on lodgings, restaurants, attractions. Rest rooms, picnic area. Closed in midwinter.

Old Saybrook

Nowhere else on Connecticut's 253–mile coastline has human progress been more obviously outwitted by the sea than in Old Saybrook. In this case, however, the supremacy of the sea against human interference has, ironically, been a gift to the 410-mile Connecticut River. At the shallow mouth of New England's longest waterway, nature provided the Connecticut River Valley with its first big break: a big old sandbar. Located right near Fort Saybrook at Saybrook Point, the sandbar impeded colonial navigation, prevented large oceangoing vessels from entering the river, and thus arrested the development of a deepwater port. Thanks to the tides and currents that create the shoals and sandbars, the Connecticut is the largest river in America without a port. Consequently, despite pollution that entered the waterway from upriver factory waste, the river has stayed healthier than many others and its towns have retained many of their oldtime characteristics. While much more developed commercially than its peaceful sister, Old Lyme, across the river, Old Saybrook has managed to protect its prettiest parts.

Founded by a group of high-falutin' Englishmen of Puritan descent, Saybrook Colony was first reported seen in 1614 by Dutchman Adriaen Block, who explored and charted the river past what is now Hartford. Long after Block had sailed away from the pesky Saybrook Bar, the English arrived in 1635, to ready the place for the building of their fort. Viscount Saye and Lord Brooke were among the fifteen lords who were granted this land by the Earl of Warwick, and they gave their names to the colony. Surprisingly, however, neither of these two ever lived in the settlement. John Winthrop was the gentleman actually responsible for the establishment of the town, and Lion Gardiner was its first engineer.

In its early years, the Saybrook Colony also included the settlements of Chester, Deep River, Essex, Lyme, Old Lyme, and Westbrook. Today it is the most populated and most commercially developed of these now-separate towns, but its location on the river, its providential sandbar, and its 16 miles of shoreline ensure that it remains a popular recreational destination.

Begin a driving tour of Old Saybrook by taking Route 154 south from I-95, bearing left on Main Street and continuing basically straight on College Street (both of which are Route 154) toward the water. Stop to see the following sites along the way, and wander the side roads, too, especially North and South Cove Roads, where you will have views of marsh and sea and historic homes. Cyclists may want to rent a bicycle to explore these sights. Call Saybrook Point Inn (860–395–2000) or Saybrook Cycle Works (860–388–1534) for rental information.

The Best of Old Saybrook

General William Hart House

Today the home of the Old Saybrook Historical Society, this structure was originally the home of General William Hart, who retired here after leading Patriot troops against the British in the American Revolution. Many members of the Hart family lived in town for many years, and the house still contains Hart family furnishings. Built in 1767, it bears the marks of an affluent owner; besides being a general, William Hart owned a fleet of trade ships. Fine wood paneling covers many first-floor walls, and Staffordshire tiles with scenes from Aesop's Fables decorate the library fireplace. Docents give guided tours of the fully restored house. Outdoors, visitors are free to explore a beautiful and extensive eighteenth-century herb garden and award-winning rose garden. Call for a calendar of events and activities or special tours.

350 Main Street (860–388–2622). Usually open from May through mid-September, Friday to Sunday, 1:00 to 4:00 P.M. Free; donation suggested.

James Gallery and Soda Fountain

Not far from the Hart House as you drive out of the main business area toward the section of Route 154 called College Street, your eye may be caught by a sign marking a curious combination of enterprises. True to its label, the large white house on the right is both old-fashioned ice cream parlor and marine art gallery.

Built in 1790 as the general store for the Humphrey Pratt Tavern, this clapboard building with the red and white awnings operated as a pharmacy (and later also as a soda fountain) from 1877 to 1994. Originally owned by Peter Lane, the business was turned over to Miss Anna Louise James in 1917. The first black woman pharmacist in Connecticut, the well-loved Miss James ran the store for fifty years, and it is due to her maintenance of the house and her own historical importance that the house was added to the National Register of Historic Places in 1994.

When the pharmacy closed in 1994, marine artist Yves Parent added a twist to the historic business. Retaining the original wooden display cases and the 1896 soda fountain, complete with a gray marble bar, oak Coke tables and chairs, and its old black-and-white floor tiles, Parent modified the pharmacy space to display top quality marine art by painters from all over the country.

Current owner Shelley Nobile, also owner/innkeeper of the Deacon Timothy Pratt House B&B next door, has breathed new life into both soda fountain and gallery. The gallery has been set in the back two rooms to give browsers a quiet spot to shop. Among the artworks are oils, watercolors, photography, and prints, plus local crafts and gifts.

The new design has created a spacious "front parlor" that gives visitors more room in which to linger over floats, frappes, sundaes, milkshakes, and specialty teas and coffees. Baked goods, jars of old-fashioned candies, and creative fountain treats are served in a spotless setting.

Making matters even better is the occasional live music offered at no extra charge on Friday or Saturday evenings from 7:30 to 9:30 P.M. In the next year or two, look for a full-fledged coffeehouse ambiance in the evenings and perhaps a tearoom/cafe for lunches et cetera. Three additional bed-and-breakfast rooms of the Timothy Pratt B&B next door are also in this building.

2 Pennywise Lane, right at the edge of Route 154 (860–395–1406). Open daily from Memorial Day through Labor Day, noon to 10:00 P.M.; weekends only from Labor Day to Memorial Day, Friday and Saturday from noon to 10:00 P.M., Sunday from noon to 6:00 P.M.

Saybrook Point Park and Fort Saybrook Monument Park

Proceed down Route 154 to its end to enjoy the pleasures of **Saybrook Point Park.** Stop for a while in the big parking lot to your left as you approach the dead end in the roadway here and walk to the seawall along the Connecticut River. You'll find great fishing spots on the seawall, long-range binoculars to help you get a better view of the boats and lighthouse, and benches and picnic tables.

You can play eighteen holes at the **Saybrook Point Mini-Golf Course** (203–388–2407); it's affordable and well maintained with traditional designs that hark back to simpler times. Be sure to flip a coin into the Wishing Pond near the Brooklyn Bridge. Picnic tables add to your comfort. The course is open daily from Memorial Day through Labor Day.

You can also have lunch or dinner inside the **Dock & Dine** restaurant overlooking the river or outside on its patio. Outside, you can choose from the full menu or from the lighter fare on the Quick Bites menu. However long you dally over the table, leave time to see the artwork of the

SAYBROOK VISITOR INFORMATION

At the south end of the town green near the Old Saybrook Town Hall is a visitor information booth that operates in the summertime. Volunteers can help you find your way to beaches, attractions, restaurants, and lodgings, and they can give you a walking tour pamphlet to nearly forty nearby historic sites and structures. Stop here from Memorial Day to Labor Day, Monday through Friday from 9:00 A.M. to 2:00 P.M. Throughout the year, you can visit the Chamber of Commerce offices at 146 Main Street, Monday through Friday from 9:00 A.M. to 3:00 P.M.

wonderful **Saybrook Colony Artists** (noon to 5:00 P.M. Tuesday through Sunday; summer evenings 6:00 P.M. to darkness) at their gallery in the Connecticut River Room at the restaurant. Steven Cryan, famed for his amazing model trains and his fine paintings of the history of Saybrook and its lighthouses, boats, and trains, exhibits here along with his wife, painter and portraitist Lauren Cryan.

Just a few yards back up Route 154, **Fort Saybrook Monument Park** covers eighteen acres. Along its pathways are storyboards that depict the history of Saybrook Colony and the fort that Lion Gardiner built here in 1635. Originally the site of a Nehantic Indian village before the Dutch and English arrived, today the site is a great place for enjoying the views of the marshes and the shorebirds that inhabit the area. In or near the site are other historic points of interest such as a statue of Lion Gardiner, the Cypress Cemetery with its tomb of Lady Fenwick (wife of Saybrook Colony governor George Fenwick) and other Saybrook notables, and a stone monument marking the location of Yale College in its early years. The park and these ancillary exhibits are open daily year-round at no charge.

When you've soaked up the sights, follow Route 154 across the causeway and all the way around the peninsula. Enjoy the water views as you drive along this wide-open-to-the-Sound coast road, usually called Maple Avenue along this stretch. Cyclists may rest along the way to enjoy the sights, but motorists won't find too many places to stop along this route. It's a mostly residential neighborhood with private beach associations, but a town beach awaits you if you follow Route 154 toward the left onto Indianola Road, which becomes Great Hammock Road after the coast turns northward at Cornfield Point.

THE WINDMILL OF SAYBROOK

Lion Gardiner, the first architect of Old Saybrook, built a windmill at Fort Saybrook in 1636. Similar to Dutch designs, the windmill was perfectly functional as a grinding mill, but its principal purpose was as a lookout tower from which sentries could detect raiding Pequots during the war that terrorized the settlers in 1636–1637. Before the Pequots attacked, Lion Gardiner barricaded the windmill site with a sort of old-fangled land mine system: long, sharp nails driven into long pieces of wood that were left on the ground in front of the advancing natives. As the Pequots landed at Saybrook Point, they stepped onto the boards and screamed as the nails pierced their feet. Alerted by their cries to the direction of their approach, the colonists successfully defended the fort from attack. The windmill as well as the settlers survived the war, but the windmill finally burned to the ground 175 years later. Its millstones can be seen near the shore on the left side of College Street, past the Hart House and the James Gallery and Soda Fountain, but a good distance before you reach Fort Saybrook Monument Park. Right in front of a private home, the stones are surrounded by a low iron fence with a sign.

Follow College Street (Route 154) to its end at Saybrook Point Park (860–395–3123). Open sunrise to sunset daily year-round. Free.

Harvey's Beach

One hundred yards of sandy shore greet the feet at Harvey's Beach, a town-owned property tucked between the picturesque marshes and rows of cottages along Route 154. Available throughout the year for diehard beachcombers, it officially opens on Memorial Day weekend for summer activities. A bathhouse with rest room facilities, outdoor showers, and a concession is the only structure here, at least outside of the tiny entrance booth that collects a daily fee from nonresidents in season only. A swing set provides simple entertainment for the youngsters.

Lifeguards are on duty on weekends only from Memorial Day through June, then daily through Labor Day. Check to be sure that a food vendor has been given the contract for the snack bar/concession before you decide *not* to bring a picnic or refreshments from home or market. Lifeguards leave at 4:30 P.M., but beach-lovers may stay on the sand until sundown. Swimming after lifeguards leave for the day is at your own risk.

Great Hammock Road, Route 154 (Parks and Recreation, 860–395–3152). Free to residents; nonresidents pay daily charge from Memorial Day to Labor Day only: $8.00 per vehicle and driver, 50 cents per additional passenger, walk-ins $1.00 each. Seasonal passes $85 (available from Parks and Recreation).

Boat Excursions and Charters

Deep River Navigation Company (860–526–4954). The M/V *Aunt Polly* departs Saybrook Point near the Dock and Dine restaurant and sails downriver for a two-hour cruise of Long Island Sound. Daily, mid-June to Labor Day; $12 per person. Also cruise options to Essex Harbor (two hours, $12) or late afternoon lighthouse cruise (one hour, $8). Lively narration about flora, fauna, and local history and lore on every cruise. Children 3 to 11 half price, children under 3 free; senior discounts. No reservations necessary; free parking. Rest rooms, snack bar on board.

Captain John's Sport Fishing Center (860–443–7259). Departs Saybrook Point for winter wildlife cruises to see bald eagles upriver; February and March. Naturalist on board.

Eden **Charters** Captain Paul Retano (860–388–5897). Customized sportfishing cruises for one to six passengers on a 31-foot twin-engine sportfisher for "less time travelin', more time fishin'." Inshore bottom fishing, offshore fishing, and deep-sea fishing off Montauk, from flounder to tuna. Bait and tackle provided. Ferry Point Marina.

Sea Sprite Captain Peter Wheeler (860–669–9613). Saybrook Point Marina. Twenty-two years doing deep-sea charters; all kinds of fish in their respective seasons, May 1 to December 1. Plum Gut, the Race, Block Island Sound, Montauk; $525 full day/$425 half day, by reservation only, on a 42-foot Hatteras Sportfisherman; up to six passengers. Bait and tackle provided.

North Cove Outfitters 75 Main Street (860–388–6585). Call for information on special trips planned by naturalists from this great outfitters store: hawk-watching, bird walks, meteor-watching, kayaking clinics, paddle sport rally, slide lectures, and more. Ask for a copy of the wonderful *Explorer* newsletter.

Places to Eat in Old Saybrook

Saybrook Fish House 99 Essex Road (860-388-4836). A classic tucked away from the main drag, this establishment is a sure bet for dozens of traditional favorites like clams casino, shrimp scampi, and crab cakes, plus plenty of innovative daily specials featuring the freshest of fin and shellfish. Open year-round, lunch Monday through Saturday; dinner Monday through Sunday. $$-$$$

Rosemary & Sage 1080 Boston Post Road (860-388-1166). Occupying the former home of Cafe Routier, this newcomer has a small but ambitious menu of pastas, chops, steaks, chicken, and seafood. Try the Tortelloni Bolognese and the peppercorn lamb. Very nice. Open for lunch on weekdays and dinner Monday through Saturday. $$$

Terra Mar Grille at Saybrook Point Inn; 2 Bridge Street (860-388-1111). Overlooking the inn's marina, enjoy American and Northern Italian cuisine with views of Long Island Sound at the mouth of the Connecticut River. Elegant ambiance for special occasions; fresh seafood, creative pastas, exquisite house-made desserts. Open year-round daily for breakfast, lunch, and dinner and Sunday brunch. $$$-$$$$

Saigon City 1355 Boston Post Road (860-388-6888). Beautifully presented and graciously served Vietnamese cuisine in, surprisingly, an eighteenth-century farmhouse setting. It works—and it's delicious! Open year-round for lunch and dinner. $-$$

TAKE A TROLLEY

Summer visitors may enjoy a tour of Old Saybrook on its seasonal trolley. It runs on the hour from 9:00 A.M. to 10:00 P.M. on weekends in June and September and daily throughout July and August. Among the points of interest are historic landmarks like Fort Saybrook Monument Park at Saybrook Point, the private area called Fenwick (home of Katharine Hepburn), the marinas, the railroad station, and downtown commercial areas. Stay on for the full one-hour loop tour and listen to the commentary from the driver, which makes the ride of interest to tourists. Rides are $1.00, or $3.00 for a full-day pass.

Gateway of India 1333 Boston Post Road (860-388-9627). An unpretentious setting in a modest shopping area, but a fine dining experience, say aficionados of Indian cuisine. Vegetarian, chicken, seafood, and lamb specialties, curries, tandoori, and biryani, wonderfully seasoned and fun to share. The all-you-can-eat lunch buffet is a best buy from noon to 3:00 P.M. on Friday, Saturday, and Sunday. Open year-round for lunch and dinner daily. $-$$

The Cuckoo's Nest 1712 Boston Post Road (860-399-9060). Voted Connecticut's best Mexican restaurant, this definitively casual eatery offers tasty Mexican, Cajun, and Creole cuisine. Live music on weekends and outside patio seating in summer. Open daily year-round for lunch and dinner, plus southwestern Sunday brunch buffet from 11:30 A.M. to 2:30 P.M. $-$$

Dock & Dine at Saybrook Point (860-388-4665 or 800-362-DOCK). Right on the Connecticut River, grab a picture-window seat for good, fresh seafood, chicken, pastas, and surf and turf. In the warm season, eat outside on the patio near the river; choose full or Quick Bites menu. Open year-round daily for lunch and dinner. $$

Aleia's 1687 Boston Post Road (860-399-5050). Aleia's offers a contemporary twist on Mediterranean cuisine. Freshly prepared, light sauces, vegetarian choices, and tempting house-made desserts draw the dinner crowd indoors. Bakery open Wednesday through Friday 9:00 A.M. to 5:00 P.M. and Saturday 9:00 A.M. to 4:00 P.M. Dinner served Tuesday through Sunday from 5:30 to 10:00 P.M. $$-$$$

Pat's Kountry Kitchen 70 Mill Rock Road East (Route 154) (860-388-4784). Pat's has a reputation as the best place for families in the whole darned state. She's not resting on those laurels, though; daily specials are always added to the already extensive menu that pleases everyone from infancy to grandparenthood. Decorated from top to bottom with toys and dolls and bears galore, the large dining room is a casual and friendly place. Open Monday, Tuesday, and Thursday through Sunday year-round from 7:00 A.M. $

Johnny Ad's 910 Boston Post Road (860-388-4032). You can't do Saybrook without a visit to Johnny Ad's. Forty years of incomparable drive-in seafood. Have the perfect fish sandwich, an order of rings, and a real milkshake. Open all year in case you need a midwinter fix. $

Places to Stay in Old Saybrook

Saybrook Point Inn and Spa 2 Bridge Street (860–395–2000 or 800–243–0212). Put yourselves in the lap of luxury and wait for the pampering to begin; sixty-two elegant rooms decorated in English country style and overlooking river, Sound, and marina; seven suites in the inn and one lighthouse room with kitchenette. Spa, steam room, and fitness room; indoor and outdoor pools, bicycles, restaurant and lounge. $$$$

Deacon Timothy Pratt B&B 325 Main Street (860–395–1229). Web site: http://connecticut-bed-and-breakfast.com/. Offers two rooms with private bath and fireplace and one two-room suite with private bath in a restored 1746 center-chimney colonial on the National Register. Four-poster beds; air-conditioning; cable television; phone and modem lines; lovely common rooms and pretty property with a tree swing, hammock, and gardens. Full homestyle breakfasts with treats like Belgian waffles or heart shaped blueberry pancakes served by candlelight in the dining room on fine china. In historic district on gaslit Main Street; walk to everything. Open year-round; lovely in all seasons. $$$$

Days Inn 1430 Boston Post Road (860–388–3453 or 800–329–7466).

SUMMER ARTS ON THE GREEN

Old Saybrook offers two more ways you can linger downtown in the summertime. On Wednesdays from late June through late August a series of outdoor concerts is held at the gazebo on the town green on Main Street. Bring chairs or a blanket and a picnic or dessert and soak up the sounds of a different group each week from 7:00 to 8:00 P.M. All concerts are free of charge.

You won't be able to leave the Annual Old Saybrook Art and Craft Show quite so inexpensively. The arts here are sure to lure your checkbook right from your pocket. Held on the last weekend in July, the show brings more than 200 artisans to the green from 10:00 A.M. to 5:00 P.M. on Saturday and Sunday. Painters, photographers, potters, metalsmiths, jewelry-makers, sculptors, and doll-makers are among the artists exhibiting here. Admission is free.

LYNDE POINT LIGHTHOUSE

The Old Saybrook Inner Light at Lynde Point was honored by the State of Connecticut when it chose the image of the lighthouse by local artist J. H. Torrance Downs for its commemorative Long Island Sound license plates. Originally built in 1803, the first lighthouse here was only 35 feet high and constructed from wood. The present 71-foot structure is the second incarnation, completed in 1839. Painted white and made from brownstone blocks, it was first fueled by whale oil but later received a 500-watt electric lightbulb, visible as far as 13 miles away. Beginning in 1852 one of its keepers, James Rankin, kept meticulous logbooks, recording not only the maritime traffic but also the weather and the migration of birds. Today his records are in the Smithsonian Institution.

Fifty units (four have whirlpool or sauna); in-room fridge and microwave. Rooftop indoor pool, continental breakfast. $$$

Comfort Inn 100 Essex Road (860-395-1414). One hundred twenty suites and double rooms, indoor pool, sauna, exercise room, laundry, restaurant. $$$-$$$$

Sandpiper Inn 1750 Boston Post Road (860-399-7973 or 800-323-7973). Forty-five units, outdoor pool, beach passes. Basic, but nicely kept and popular with families. $$-$$$

Public Boat Launch

Baldwin Bridge I-95 to Route 9 North; take either exit 1 or 2, turn right and follow Ferry Road to the launch area under the Baldwin Bridge. Daily fee; room for seventy-five cars.

For Further Information

Old Saybrook Chamber of Commerce 146 Main Street (860-388-3266). Information, brochures, walking tour map. Open Monday through Friday 9:00 A.M. to 5:00 P.M. Tourist information booth on the town green open from Memorial Day to Labor Day 9:00 A.M. to 2:00 P.M.

Old Saybrook Web site: www.oldsaybrookct.com or www.oldsay
brook.com

Old Saybrook Parks and Recreation 308 Main Street; actually in the
small white modular building at the rear of the main street school building behind Old Saybrook Town Hall (860-395-3152). Purchase seasonal
beach passes here, Monday through Friday 9:00 A.M. to 5:00 P.M.

Old Lyme

A curious mix of authors, painters, and mariners inhabits Old Lyme, a
lovely village that revels in its artsy reputation as well as its nautical one.
It's no surprise that Old Lyme can employ the word *colony* to describe
itself—it has long attracted residents who fall neatly into one or more of
these three categories.

One of the earliest and most permanent of these groups were the
artists who gathered at the home of Miss Florence Griswold from 1899
until nearly four decades past the turn of the century. Known as the Lyme
Art Colony, the folks who lived at Miss Florence's beautiful late-Georgian
mansion played with light, color, and texture until they successfully settled upon characteristics which later became known as American
Impressionism.

Long before Old Lyme caught the attention of artists, it had been an
enclave of mariners. Back in 1665, when the town's first thirty families
split off from the colony at Saybrook to form their own union, many
citizens were farmers and a few were merchants. The water and the
rivers bordering their land caught their attention, but for more practical reasons than light and shadow. Maritime trade and shipbuilding
became the principal industries of the village during the eighteenth and
nineteenth centuries.

At the end of the clipper ship era, the wharves went silent, and the
docks were filled with passengers from the steamships. Outsiders, like the
artists, came from the cities to the shore, and the character of the still very
small town shifted toward tamer adventures. Summer cottages sprang up
along the Sound, and a resort atmosphere settled upon the village. Life in
Old Lyme (population 6,500) is fairly quiet these days. The population

nearly doubles in summer when the cottagers return, and the principal industry seems to be getting the family boat in the water.

The Best of Old Lyme

Florence Griswold Museum

Located on eleven beautifully landscaped acres next to the lovely Lieutenant River, this National Historic Landmark built in 1817 holds a magnificent collection of the works of the first American Impressionist artists. Beginning in 1899, these creative spirits brought their paints and brushes to Old Lyme and accepted the gracious hospitality of Florence Griswold, sea captain's daughter and owner of the house. Setting their easels on the sand, at the edges of marshes, and on the banks of the rivers, they endeavored to capture the marvelous summer lights and shadows, the colors and movements of the sea, sky, and shore.

As much a history museum as an art museum, the house features period rooms as well as galleries of Impressionist works, contemporary works, and changing exhibitions that celebrate other artistry throughout the year. You may wander the upper gallery rooms of the museum unescorted, but a guided tour of the downstairs period rooms is given first. Visitors of all ages will enjoy the tales of Miss Florence and the talented houseguests who came to re-create the beauty of Old Lyme. Especially wonderful are the original paintings these artists left directly on the wall panels in the dining room.

Outside of the main house is the restored studio of William Chadwick, re-created to represent its appearance during his lifetime. Recently acquired acreage and a handsome Colonial revival house that was part of Miss Florence's original estate now includes restored gardens showcasing perennial herbs and flowers, extensive new galleries on the riverbank, a wonderful arts education center, a new museum shop, and period rooms with furniture and Griswold's personal effects. Visitors are encouraged to stroll and relax on the adjoining properties. Be sure to paint en plein air while you are here; call ahead regarding painting workshops.

Every December the mansion is decorated with trees for the Holiday Tree Festival. Story readings and special tours of interest to children are offered to families who visit during this time, but this festival has appeal to guests of all ages. Call for the exact dates of this year's fete, then plan to do some holiday shopping at the wonderful gift shop offering books, prints,

OLD LYME TREASURES

The influence of the American Impressionists on Old Lyme culture is clearly seen in its art school and in the galleries and shops that pepper the village center. Most notable among these is the **Lyme Academy of Fine Arts** (84 Lyme Street; 860-434-5232). This nationally accredited school offers a bachelor's degree program in fine arts plus part-time study in drawing, painting, and sculpture. The school's gallery features the work of its renowned faculty and students. Visitors are asked for a small donation and are welcome to stop by Tuesday through Saturday from 10:00 A.M. to 4:00 P.M. or Sunday from 1:00 to 4:00 P.M.

The **Lyme Art Association** (90 Lyme Street; 860-434-7802) also has a gallery displaying the work of regional artists. Five major shows are hung each year, and demonstrations, workshops, and lectures may also be of interest to visitors. The association's hours are roughly the same as the academy's. A suggested donation of $3.00 is appreciated at the gallery. Call for schedules and hours.

Other shops and small galleries on Lyme Street allow visitors to see and purchase the work of talented local contemporary artists as well as past masters. The best of these is the **Cooley Gallery** (25 Lyme Street (860-434-8807), which offers fine American paintings of the nineteenth and twentieth centuries. Excellent, too, is the **Shippee Gallery** (Mile Creek Road; 860-434-5108); it is open by appointment only. The **Old Lyme Frame Shop** (91 Halls Road; 860-434-1004) offers antique maps, old and new etchings, nautical art, and new posters. **Morelock Antiques** (860-434-6333) at the Village Shops on Lyme Street offers eighteenth- and nineteenth-century furniture and home furnishings plus other decorative objects, drawings, and prints. English, European, and American fine collectibles are among the eclectic selection in this shop.

posters, stationery, and other items related to American art, architecture, and regional history and culture.

96 Lyme Street (860-434-5542). Web site: www.flogris.org. Open year-round June through December, Tuesday through Saturday from 10:00 A.M. to 5:00 P.M. and Sunday from 1:00 to 5:00 P.M.; January through May, Wednesday through Sunday from 1:00 to 5:00 P.M. Adults $5.00; seniors and students $4.00; children under 12 free. Only the first floor of the main house is wheelchair accessible. Guided tours are generally offered on the half hour.

I SCREAM, YOU SCREAM

Summer on the shore screams for ice cream, and the **Old Lyme Ice Cream Shoppe** delivers the goods. Lou Mae Albert and her son Steve make perhaps the best dairy confections on the whole Connecticut shore. Made right on-site with best-you-can-buy natural ingredients, the rich treats come in thirty-four delicious flavors like chocolate raspberry truffle, toasted coconut, and black cherry swirl. Italian ices and sorbets are also made fresh daily. You have to try this; they're working for you every day from at least 11:00 A.M. to 9:00 P.M. You'll find them at 34 Lyme Street; 860-434-6942.

First Congregational Church of Old Lyme

Considered one of the most beautiful churches in all of New England, the First Congregational Church was designed by Samuel Belcher, also the architect of the Florence Griswold mansion. Built in 1817, the original building burned to the ground in 1907, but the congregation agreed to replace the church with a new structure that would be an exact replica of the first. The builders achieved their goal in 1910. The church's graceful Ionic columns lead the eye upward to its soaring steeple, and its simple but elegant interior is a tribute to Belcher's artistry. Walking tours featuring this church and other Lyme Street landmarks are scheduled from time to time; call the Lyme Historical Society (860-434-5542) for information. The church is also the setting for one of the region's finest chamber music series; for information on the current season of Musical Masterworks, call (860) 434-2252

The church is at 2 Ferry Road (860-434-8686) in the center of Old Lyme. Visitors are welcome; call for information.

McCulloch Farm

One of Connecticut's hidden treasures is the oldest continually operating and largest Morgan horse breeding farm in the state. Visitors are more than welcome, but a call ahead is required to ensure that someone here will be able to give you a tour. Half a dozen or more foals are born here each spring, and you can see them and their elegant parents nearly any day year-round. The farm itself is a Connecticut pearl—400 acres are yours to explore. While it's not at all laid out as a tourist attraction, its bridle paths lead through its quiet corners, where you may enjoy the wildlife of the eastern woodlands. The owners kindly ask that you enjoy the property respectfully. They prefer no pets and no picnicking, and there is no hand-feeding of their magnificent Whippoorwill Morgans.

Come in the spring for Open Barn Day, when visitors are welcomed into the barns for a close-up look at the newborn animals and how the farm operates. Come in early fall (sometimes the first weekend in September) for Versatility Day, which is a daylong demonstration of the talents and tasks performed by the horses. Morgans from all over the country arrive for this eye-opening show. Both events are free.

100 Whippoorwill Road (860–434–7355). Open daily from 10:00 A.M. to 4:00 P.M. but advance calls are required. Call for dates of twice-yearly special events.

Griswold Point and Great Island
Roger Tory Peterson Wildlife Area

A walk to Griswold Point will be a highlight of anyone's exploration of the Connecticut shore. This area is accessible by canoe and car, by foot and bicycle. In the off-season, when White Sands Beach is not restricted to Old Lyme residents only, nonresidents may park at the beach. From its parking lot, walk westward below the high-tide mark for about a half-mile to Griswold Point. Motorists may also enjoy views of the area by following the route the canoeists would take to the boat launch ramp. To reach that point, take Route 156 south for three-tenths of a mile from exit 70 on I-95 and take a right on Smith's Neck Road.

This beautiful twisting road, lined with stone walls and the stunted flora of the shoreline, leads to a parking area near the state-owned landing at the end of the road. No foot trails provide access to the area at this point, but a large observation deck with wonderful signage provides a sense of the area's diversity and prepares visitors for bird-watching opportunities. Recently renamed the **Roger Tory Peterson Wildlife Area,** Great Island is one of Connecticut's natural treasures. From this vantage point, the island spreads before visitors like a floating emerald blanket. Crowds of snowy egrets decorate the gently shifting grasses of the salt marsh. Herons rise gracefully from the mudflats, and ospreys draw the eyes skyward. Come near sunset for a magnificent display of light in this pristine environment.

The hike around the perimeter of Griswold Point is about 2 miles; should you decide to *cross* the spit, do so only on one of the two trails

LORDS COVE AND HAMBURG COVE

To fully immerse yourself in the beauty of Old Lyme it seems necessary to gain at least a modest understanding of the relationship between the sea and the river, the salt marshes and the tides that influence the ecology within them. Quiet waters and softly rustling cordgrasses and phragmites belie the steady miracle constantly at work in the salt marsh. As the fresh river waters rush to the Sound at each low tide and the salty sediments sweep upriver with each high tide, a rich and unique ecosystem is created. Even the black muck that impedes human foot traffic and threatens boat props is alive with microorganisms and redolent with the aroma of the plant nutrients chopped and whisked and stirred into a fine stew by the moving waters. Feeding on that stew are the snails and the frogs, the mud worms and the fiddler crabs—even the mosquitoes and their microscopic larvae—and feeding on them are the sandpipers and the mummichogs and the marsh hawks, and on and on upward through the estuarine food web—to the raccoons and the muskrats, the meadow mice and the minks, the white-tailed deer and their loathsome passengers—the ticks that made Lyme a household word.

A good route for contemplation of the salt marsh begins at the edge of the Sound at **Griswold Point,** either at **White Sands Beach** off Route 156 or Smith's Neck Road off Route 156. Then leave the marsh at Griswold Point and travel north on Route 156. Stop at Ferry Road (*left* turn) and follow it to the state-owned park near the DEP Marine station (860-434-6148). A riverside boardwalk provides beautiful views and breezes. Return to your vehicle and to Route 156 north, under the I-95 overpass and past Route 1. By car or bicycle, travel to the ends of any of the small roads at the left of Route 156 (Binney Road, Pilgrim's Landing, Tantummaheag Road) for views of **Calves Island, Goose Island, Lords Cove,** and **Nott Island.** Return to Route 156 and drive north through the pretty countryside bordering the Nehantic State Forest until you reach the village of Hamburg, which lies at the edge of Hamburg Cove at the mouth of the tiny **Eight-Mile River.** Take the left fork in the road after you pass the Congregational Church and follow Old Hamburg Road to the river's edge. Picnic here if you'd like to rest and refuel as you process the amazing impact of the sea and the river.

across the protected dunes. Pets should be left at home or at least kept out of this area, because the point is a nesting site of piping plovers and least terns. The Nature Conservancy usually fences areas where nests have been noted; please respect these boundaries should you come in the nesting season, between mid-May and early July. Connecticut's largest colony of ospreys can be observed from late March through the fall.

Access to Griswold Point is from White Sands Beach or Smith's Neck Road, both off Route 156. Open year-round, dawn to dusk; no overnight camping; no charge. Access from White Sands Beach is limited; from Memorial Day to Labor Day, parking at the beach is reserved exclusively for Old Lyme residents with windshield beach stickers. Walkers and bicyclists may enter the beach at any time. Be aware that White Sands Beach has two parts, a public town beach and a private beach association. If you are on foot or bicycling, do not cross private property to gain access to the beach. At the public beach, rest rooms are open in season only; there are no concessions or other facilities.

Sound View Beach

A wide, popular beach in the midst of a busy beach colony that looks like a throwback to earlier decades is great for playing or relaxing on a summer day or for strolling in autumn or winter. No coolers are allowed on the beach, there are no changing facilities and no lifeguards, and the only rest rooms are nearby portable toilets. Even so, tons of sunbathers come here, and on warm weekends the joint is hopping as the delightfully summery and slightly seedy arcades, amusements, and snack bars along Hartford Avenue are crowded with visitors.

The Carousel Shop, loaded with beach needs from ice cream to sunscreen, also rents and sells inflatable boats, sand chairs, and beach toys. (The boats and floats are allowed in the water at Sound View Beach—unlike in other lifeguarded public swimming areas where the lifeguards forbid such equipment.) **The Carousel Shop** (860-434-3908) also operates a brightly painted 1925 carousel, which runs nightly from 7:00 to 9:00 all summer. One ride is $1.00, twelve rides are $10.00, and so on up to one hundred rides for $65.00 for parties or merry-go-round fanatics. This small, carnival-style ride offers every young rider a chance to grab the brass ring.

For food, try the limited but beachy fare at whatever restaurants and snack bars may be open along the beach and on Hartford Avenue. Be sure to have an Italian ice from **Vecchitto's** or an old-fashioned bakery treat from the famed **Beach Doughnut Shop** (860-434-9387). Keep in mind

ISLAND IN THE STREAM

Accessible by water only, Selden Neck State Park offers one of the best opportunities in the state to develop an appreciation for the power and impact of the mighty Connecticut River. The largest island in the Connecticut River, Selden Neck was sold to Joseph Selden of Hadley, Massachusetts, in 1695, thus giving it its name. Originally part of the mainland, the island is believed to have been separated in the 1850s by a high spring freshet that cut a shallow channel across the low meadows at the island's northern end. To this day, especially at low tide, little water covers the bar that remains at the north side of the island.

Visitors with canoes or kayaks can paddle to the island on their own, or they can contact **North American Canoe Tours** (860-739-0791), which offers guided overnight canoe/camping trips to this interesting site from July through October. Primitive campsites are available at Selden Neck State Park from May 1 through September 30, for one-night stays only. The park provides tent ground sites, outhouses, fireplaces, drinking water, and hiking trails, but no concessions, lodgings, or mooring or docking facilities. Open fires aren't allowed. For a permit to camp at Selden Neck ($4.00 per person), write at least two weeks ahead to Manager, Gillette Castle State Park, 67 River Road, East Haddam CT 06423, or call (860-526-2336).

that most of these businesses are seasonal, often opening in late June after the school year is over.

Hartford Avenue off Shore Road (Route 156) (860-434-2760, Parks and Recreation, in summer only). Open 8:00 A.M. to 9:00 P.M. Free street parking or parking fee ($4.00 to $8.00 at public and private off-street lots). No coolers, no pets, and no alcohol allowed on beach.

Places to Eat in Old Lyme

Old Lyme Inn 85 Lyme Street (860-434-2600). In an 1865 farmhouse converted to an inn, the restaurant here serves some of the best meals in the state. The Tap Room and Library Bar evoke the clubby atmosphere of a tavern and offer live entertainment on weekend evenings. The Empire Room's candlelight and sparkling tableware are the perfect backdrop for a marriage proposal or anniversary celebration. A sunny luncheon room just off the front porch is a lovely spot for a casual midday meal. The chef's specialty is probably the outstanding seafood. Veal, chicken, and prime rib are also reliably superb. Open daily year-round except for December 24. Dinner is served from 5:00 P.M. every day. Sunday brings dinner-all-day from noon. Families are welcome; children's plates and prices are on the menu. $$$

Bee and Thistle Inn 100 Lyme Street (860-434-1667 or 800-622-4946). Dine in airy, flower-filled sunporches or a candlelit parlor with a flickering fireplace on a delicious ever-changing menu of award-winning American and continental cuisine. Stenciled walls, warm wooden floors, and an eclectic array of well-loved antiques are among the many alluring features of this beautiful inn. *Connecticut* magazine readers consistently vote this restaurant the most romantic place to dine in the state and aver that its gourmet cuisine is outstanding among its peers. Innkeepers Philip and Marie Abraham uphold this fine tradition. Every dish is finished to perfection and beautifully presented. A harpist on Saturday evenings and the soft touch of other musicians on other weekend evenings add to an idyllic setting. Open for lunch, afternoon tea, dinner, and Sunday brunch, year-round, except for the first three weeks in January, Christmas Eve, and Christmas Day. $$$$

Anne's Bistro Route 1 (Halls Road) at the Old Lyme Marketplace (860-434-9837). Comfortable for both adults dining alone and families hoping to have a tasty meal in a place without golden arches, Anne's is a friendly establishment with a perfect menu for seafood lovers and vegetarians as well as meat-eaters. Delicious house-baked breads, breakfast treats, pastries, and desserts. Open year-round Monday through Saturday for breakfast and lunch and Wednesday through Saturday for dinner. Walk through the interior French doors of the bistro to the **Happy Carrot Bookshop** (860-434-0380)—a cheerful pairing for folks who like to read and eat at the same time. $-$$

Hideaway Restaurant and Pub Halls Road (Route 1) in the Old Lyme Shopping Center (860-434-3335). Similar in focus to Anne's, this casual American restaurant in a village shopping area provides a family-friendly ambiance that is still refined enough for a quiet meal for adults alone. With a few ethnic dishes—a little Italian, a little Tex-Mex—and tasty desserts, patrons should find plenty to satisfy cravings. Open daily for lunch and dinner. $-$$.

Places to Stay in Old Lyme

Old Lyme Inn 85 Lyme Street (860–434–2600 or 800–434–5352). Known for its fine dining as well as its genteel accommodations, this charming inn has thirteen antiques-filled guest rooms as comfortable as an old quilt, as exquisite as the flowers that scent every room in the house. Rest on the front porch in white wicker chairs or explore the gardens in summer; in winter, enjoy the fireplace in the grill room or go for a bracing walk on pretty Lyme Street. Sink into down pillows under a lacy canopy when you close your eyes at night; rise for a continental breakfast of home-cooked goodness in the morning. All rooms have private baths; all are air-conditioned and have telephones, queen- or king-size beds, and televisions. Open year-round except December 24. $$$$

Bee and Thistle Inn 100 Lyme Street (860–434–1667 or 800–622–4946). On five-plus acres bordering the Lieutenant River, this 1756 homestead is both gracious hostelry and award-winning restaurant. The eleven guest rooms (and ten private baths) provide an old-fashioned and cozy ambiance perfect for romance and restful relaxation. Lovely gardens surround the house, six fireplaces add to the homey colonial atmosphere, and the standard of discreetly attentive service is unsurpassed. The inn also offers a cottage with a bedroom, kitchen, sitting room with fireplace, bath, and deck. Breakfast is not included in the price of the guest rooms, but it is absolutely worth every extra penny. Closed during the first three weeks in January. $$$–$$$$

Bayberry Motor Inn 436 Shore Road (Route 156) (860–434–3024). Not far from Rocky Neck State Park is this spotless motel with ten spacious rooms perfect for families and wonderful for couples and seniors seeking quiet relaxation near the shore. Each room has two double beds and a kitchenette complete with fridge, stove, sink, microwave, toaster, and cookware. Although not directly on the water, the Bayberry can still provide a beachy getaway; passes to nearby private beach associations can be arranged, and for a small day fee, guests can enjoy the beautiful state park. Children under 12 stay free. $$–$$$

Public Boat Launches

Four Mile River Boat Launch Access on the west side of the river. Take Route 156 to Oak Ridge Drive, then the first right to the launch area.

Shallow launch conditions at low tide; clearance a problem at high tide. Parking for fifty-five cars. No fee.

Great Island Route 156 south to Smith Neck Road and Great Island Wildlife Area. Sand ramp; shallow at low tide. Parking for thirty-five cars. Seasonal fee.

Lieutenant River Route 156, west side, south of Ferry Road. Carry-in or cartop access only. Parking for three cars. No fee.

East Lyme / Niantic

No matter how the traveler enters East Lyme—from the east along Route 156, from the west along Route 1 or Route 156, or from the north on Route 161—he or she can quickly sense that East Lyme is one of Connecticut's shore playgrounds. Motels provide more than 500 rooms for vacationers, restaurants advertise shore dinners and homemade ice cream, bait and tackle shops sit shoulder to shoulder with boatyards, and fishermen share the Sound with yachters and sunburned kids in Sunfish. Modestly suburban and even downright rural in parts, this town is *the* place in Connecticut to sit on a seaside patio and savor some native broiled scallops while you watch the boats and listen to the gulls.

Originally settled by Europeans in the 1640s, East Lyme was at first a village of just a few hundred people living between Lyme and New London. Primarily a farming community, East Lyme gained some fame for its cottage textile industry (hence the name Flanders for one of its hamlets, after its similarities to Belgian villages and their homemade textiles) and later for its superior fishing grounds.

Today Flanders centers on Route 1 where it bumps north of I-95. While a nice reminder of how the Boston Post Road looked before mile upon mile of gas stations and fast-food joints overtook most sections of it, Flanders itself offers limited activities and attractions for visitors—a few antiques shops, an art gallery, and its outstanding fish market and seafood restaurant. North of the village are Pattagansett Lake, Powers

Lake, and the Nehantic State Forest, which offer real but little-publicized opportunities for outdoor recreation.

Niantic, East Lyme's second village, south of both Route 1 and the interstate, is the center of East Lyme activity. Take Route 161 south and explore it and the east-west Route 156 to gain a perspective on this shoreline gem of private homes and beaches, marinas and fishing piers, and small shops and restaurants. Like most of the smaller shore towns, Niantic is most alive in summer, when concerts on the green, arts and crafts shows, farmer's markets, and festivals celebrating strawberries and lobsters add to the simple pleasures of the sand and the sun and the sky.

Niantic is undoubtedly a summer paradise of the New England variety. The air is so salty it stiffens your hair, the water so clear you won't think it could possibly be the same Sound you swam in nearer to New York. Gulls and ospreys circle over the marshes, boaters circle among the bell buoys and lobster pots, tourists circle for parking spots closest to the seafood shacks and ice cream vendors. Don't neglect East Lyme in the fall, however; that's when it's at its finest. The crowds leave, the rates go down, and the water's still warm.

The Best of East Lyme/Niantic

Rocky Neck State Park

Few better places exist for beachcombing and shore camping than Rocky Neck State Park. Its full mile of sandy beach frontage on Long Island Sound provides swimming, saltwater fishing, and scuba diving opportunities; its 150-plus campsites provide a home away from home for professional beach bums, amateur naturalists, and the children thereof.

Like other state parks, Rocky Neck is safe and clean, but its windswept bluffs and gorgeous views of the Sound and offshore islands clearly create a special attraction. Its crescent-shaped beach has exceptionally clean, fine sand, and the extremely gentle slope of the shore creates an unusually safe swimming area for young children. A magnificent fieldstone pavilion, play areas, picnic tables, benches, and dressing rooms add to visitor comfort and convenience.

Some campers say Rocky Neck's facility is the best campground in the state. Interpretive programs, junior naturalist activities, and a full summer calendar of nature lectures, walks, and slide shows are offered for campers as well as day visitors. The state provides picnic shelters, bathhouses, food concessions, lifeguards, first aid, and telephones for the use

PATTAGANSETT LAKE AND POWERS LAKE

Some native East Lymers say they've never heard of Powers Lake and have never been to Pattagansett. That's great news for folks who would love nothing better than slipping their canoes into quiet waters for a day of serene paddling with the mergansers and mallards. Surrounded by the beauty of the New England woodlands, both lakes are owned and managed by the state, and both offer public boat launches at no charge.

Pattagansett is in general the busier of the two lakes and is stocked with largemouth and smallmouth bass, rainbow trout, and perch. Water-skiing is allowed only between June 15 and the Sunday after Labor Day and is restricted to 11:00 A.M. to 6:00 P.M. To reach 123-acre Pattagansett Lake, take Route 1 in Flanders 1 mile west of its junction with Route 161. The launch is on the north side of Route 1, and a parking area provides room for about fifteen cars. No concessions or other facilities are here, but the lake is close to the stores and delis in Flanders. Be sure to bring sunscreen, drinking water, and bug repellent out on the lake with you; be sure, too, to pack out whatever you bring in.

At 152-acre Powers Lake, which lies within the boundaries of the Nehantic State Forest, you are likely to be entirely alone on any given day. Pristine and beautiful in all seasons, it is a great fishing spot for largemouth bass, yellow perch, pickerel, and sunfish. No water-skiing or surfboard towing is allowed. For access to the state dock at Powers, take Upper Pattagansett Road north from Route 1 in Flanders to a right on Whistletown Road, and a left at about the half-mile point to the gravel ramp at the lakeside. No facilities, except for a parking area for about twenty cars. For more information, call the State Department of Environmental Protection, Boating Division (860–434–8638).

of all visitors. Campers have drinking water and bathrooms with showers and toilets. Most of the campsites are in wooded areas and will accommodate RVs (but no hookups) as well as tents. Other campsites are designated for tents only and have pit toilets.

A wooden observation deck provides a wonderful view of the salt marsh bordering the beach, and recent improvements have resulted in wheelchair access to a great little deck across Bride's Brook, perfect for fishing and crabbing. Fishing for winter flounder and striped bass is popular from the stone jetty that abuts the beach. Elsewhere in the park an interpretive nature trail points out shore flora and fauna.

The park is open year-round. From dawn to dusk in winter, the park's trails and open spaces can be used for cross-country skiing. In the fall, there is simply no better place to enjoy a crisp afternoon.

Route 156 or exit 72 from I–95 (860–739–5471). Open year-round 8:00 A.M. to 8:30 P.M. From Memorial Day to Labor Day, the weekday parking fee is $5.00 per Connecticut vehicle, $8.00 per out-of-state vehicle; weekend rates are $7.00 and $12.00, respectively. Off-season visitors pay a weekends-only fee or no fee at all. Campground open from April through September 30; $12. No pets; campfires are restricted; call for information on cooking fires.

Camp Niantic by the Atlantic

Recommended by *Connecticut* magazine as one of the top twenty campgrounds in the state, this friendly, clean, family vacation spot is actually about a twenty-minute walk from the beach. The family that owns this property has created such a happy environment right here, however, that you may never leave to find the source of the salt breezes that stir the trees in this merry glade. Diehard beach-lovers will be glad to know that their campsite fee includes a pass to the beach at McCook Point Park and a map of the pathways that lead to the shore. At the beach, a great playground, picnic spots, and rest rooms with showers will help you spend a comfortable day in the sand.

Back at camp, the mostly shady sites are temporary homes for 125 RVs, pop-up campers, and tents. Some folks love this place so much they rent for the season, but monthly, weekly, and daily accommodations can also be arranged. Hot showers, rest rooms, a laundry room, a playground, a camp store, and a game room are just some of the amenities here.

A full program of activities is planned to keep youngsters entertained; among the special events are a Christmas in July celebration when Santa himself arrives. On at least four weekends each summer the owners bring in a 100-foot water slide for wet and wacky fun for all ages. Notable among all the events are the totally free dinners planned for all campers on several weekends during the season. On Sunday mornings the owners start the fresh coffee, then head out early to get complimentary doughnuts from the famed Flanders Bake Shop. These generous gestures are

PATTAGANSETT MARSHES

Boaters may want to explore the diversity of the Long Island Sound shore with an up-close look at the marsh habitats at the mouth of the Pattagansett River. Richly productive from an ecological perspective, the marshes of Watts Island and Long Ledge are protected both through the efforts of the Nature Conservancy and by a primary sand dune that is safeguarded from erosion by the rocky outcroppings of Black Point. This environment supports a wide variety of plant and marine life that attracts an equally diverse population of birds and animals. Ospreys, herons, terns, migratory warblers, and many other bird species are easily observed.

The marshes are accessible only by boat, preferably motorized since boaters must enter the Sound to reach the marshes at Watts Island. Neither Watts Island or nearby Griswold Island to its southwest or Huntley Island to its west are open to the public, so your exploration is limited to the waterways that lace through these areas. The nearest public boat launch is at the Four Mile River, opposite Rocky Neck State Park. From I-95, take exit 71 and head south on Four Mile River Road. Take a left on Route 156 and go seven-tenths of a mile. Take a left to the boat launch. Motor south to the Sound, then eastward toward Black Point. Be sure to bring drinking water, snacks, sunscreen, bug repellent, and a tide chart, and pack out all trash and disposable supplies.

the owners' gifts to all the guests who contribute to the wholesome atmosphere apparent here.

271 West Main Street (Route 156) (860–739–9308). Open April through October. Campsites are $20 per night at the beginning and end of the season; $27 per night from late June through Labor Day. Pets are allowed if they are kept on leashes, cats included.

Smith-Harris House

Built around 1845, this white clapboard Greek Revival home has a sort of whimsical personal history that stands out from other more famous Connecticut historic homes. It was once owned by a farmer named Herman Smith and his nephew Francis Harris, who married two sisters named Florence and Lula Munger. The four lived together in the house for sixty years, the husbands farming the property and the wives selling eggs from their chickens and sweet-cream home-churned butter.

A tour here is an oddly charming introduction to mid-nineteenth-century life. The imagination is certainly sparked by the idea of the industrious foursome who lived here. Throughout the house are their personal effects, domestic utensils, textiles, a lovely collection of yellowware pottery, and many original furnishings and items on local history. Outside are a barn with a two-seater outhouse and pretty plantings in the yard.

33 Society Road (860–739–0761). Open April through June and September through December on Saturday and Sunday from 1:00 to 4:00 P.M. Open in July and August, Thursday through Sunday from 1:00 to 4:00 P.M. Open January through March by appointment. Donation.

Thomas Lee House and Little Boston School

The 1660 Thomas Lee House has been touted as one of the best preserved seventeenth-century houses in the region, and its condition is indeed striking. Almost completely unaltered since late in the eighteenth century when a lean-to addition was built, the two-story, four-room house boasts one of the few remaining medieval-style casement window frames in the state. Docents point out the house's finest English furnishings and colonial artifacts and tell a bit about its early history. Right next door is a 1734 schoolhouse that was the first district school to be built in the colonies between New York and Boston; it is curated to represent a turn-of-the-twentieth-century classroom.

230 West Main Street (Route 156) (860–739–6070). Open Memorial Day to Labor Day, Tuesday through Sunday 1:00 to 4:00 P.M. and by appointment. Adults $2.00, children 6 to 15 $1.00.

Children's Museum of Southeastern Connecticut

More a play area and experience center than a traditional museum, this very popular attraction provides a fantastic opportunity to develop young imaginations. In the hands-on area called Kidsville, youngsters can role-play in a kid-size hospital, fire station, grocery store, and three other businesses. Toddlers can be set free among the slides and building toys in the Nursery Rhyme Land play area. Outdoor explorers can go to the garden area and dig for fossils, play with the wondrous bubble table, or scale the climbing wall. Parents may even be tempted to push a button and make the trains go in a model railroad exhibit that depicts the real sights of the Connecticut shoreline and countryside.

Activities and exhibits explore the sciences, the arts, safety and health, and culture and history in various centers such as an arts and crafts area, a computer lab, and a Discovery Room with a live bee colony, a glow-in-the-dark room, an ant farm, and many other features. Changing exhibitions help to keep folks coming to see what's new.

409 Main Street (860–691–1111). Open year-round, Tuesday through Saturday, plus Monday in the summer or when school is closed, from 9:30 A.M. to 4:30 P.M., and on Sunday from noon to 4:00 P.M. Admission is $4.00 for each person 2 and up. Ages 1 to 10. **Note:** The Museum will be moving to Riverside Park in New London in October 2004. Call for further information.

Millstone Discovery Center

At this science center in downtown Niantic, not far from the Millstone Nuclear Power Plant in Waterford, hands-on and interactive exhibits explain nuclear science and energy, show how reactors and power plants operate, and demonstrate the production of electrical energy. Exhibits on conservation and the marine environment of Long Island Sound include aquariums and touch tanks. You can enjoy all of these by yourself or request a guided tour.

SHOPPING IN NIANTIC

The shops and galleries of Niantic provide a nice relief from the summer sun or winter wind. Some favorites are the **Silver Skate Christmas Shop** (488 Main Street; 860-739-8913), **Main Street Antiques** (413 Main Street; 860-739-9101), and the **Made to Be Loved Doll Shop and Hospital** (Route 156; 860-739-7756). Book lovers should plan at least half a day at the 4,000-square-foot **Book Barn** (41 West Main Street; 860-739-5715), which has 75,000-plus used books shelved in several buildings linked by pretty pathways and gardens.

Folks who love the sun and the shore breezes may prefer to spend some time at **Mackey's Bait and Tackle** (Route 156; 860-739-2677), picking out gear for crabbing or for fresh- and saltwater fishing, or at **Scott's Yankee Farmer** (436 Boston Post Road; 860-739-5209), picking strawberries, blueberries, peaches, or apples right from the fields and pies, cider, jams, milk, and produce from the farm stand, open seven days a week all year-round.

A 1-mile self-guided nature trail is on the grounds of the power plant itself, which is located in neighboring Waterford on Millstone Access Road; park in the lot outside the protected power-plant area and look for osprey, herons, foxes, and more. Pick up one of the excellent trail guides at the science center before you go out to hike.

278 Main Street, East Lyme (860–691–4670 or 800–428–4234). Open September through June Monday through Friday 10:00 A.M. *to 4:00* P.M. *Summer hours are Tuesday through Friday 9:00* A.M. *to 5:00* P.M. *and on Saturday until 1:00* P.M.*; closed Sunday and holidays.*

Boat Excursions and Charters

Black Hawk II East Main Street (exit 72, left at Route 156, go about 7 miles, drive under the bridge, turn into parking lot) at Niantic Beach Marina (860–443–3662 or 800–382–2824). Fishing trips out on the Sound are the specialty of this boat, which caters to adult anglers as well as to families. *Black Hawk II*'s crew and captain handle the driving, supply bait and setup, rent rods and reels at $5.00 each if you don't bring your own gear, and turn burgers and dogs at the snack bar if you don't bring your own picnic. Free instruction is available for beginners. They stay out five to six hours in the sun and wind and even in light rain. It's first come, first served; arrive forty-five minutes before sail time on weekends and thirty-five minutes before on weekdays. From June through October, daily sails are at 6:00 A.M. and 1:00 P.M. Fare is $28, children under 12 half price; no reservations necessary.

All of the following chartered fishing boats hold up to six passengers and have captains licensed by the U. S. Coast Guard and registered by the State of Connecticut. **Atlantic Flyway:** Captain Dan Wood (860–442–6343), Port Niantic. **Dot-E-Dee:** Captain Jack Douton (860–739–7419 or 860–739–0156); **Fly Guy:** Captain Kerry Douton (860–739–7419 or 860–739–0156); **Osprey:** Captain Joseph Wysocki (860–739–4129), all at the Niantic Sportfishing Dock, Waterford side of the river.

Ask at **Mackey's Bait and Tackle** (860–739–2677), **Hillyer's Tackle Shop** (860–443–7615), or **J & B Bait and Tackle** (860–739–7419) about local scuba diving and shellfishing opportunities and tips for great fishing spots. These fisherfolk are the ones closest to the latest seasonal news. No license is needed for shore fishing, but freshwater angling requires a license for anyone 16 or older.

THE LEGEND OF BRIDE'S BROOK

As the name implies, modest Bride's Brook is associated with a bit of East Lyme romance. It seems that in the depths of winter back in 1646, a young couple wishing to be wed were desperately disappointed when a bitter snowstorm prevented the usual magistrate from reaching them at the agreed-upon site. Standing together instead beside the icy waters of the swollen brook that then separated their colony of Old Saybrook in Connecticut from the next colony of New London (which was then part of Massachusetts), they called upon the services of the other colony's magistrate. This cooperative fellow was apparently Governor Winthrop himself, and, with all the grace and dignity that could be mustered under the difficult circumstances, he supposedly shouted the vows across the raging torrent. The relieved couple called back their pledges, and the happy pair and the governor parted company at the riverbank. Thereafter, the estuary—which you can visit today at Rocky Neck State Park—was known as Bride's Brook.

Places to Eat in East Lyme/Niantic

Flanders Fish Market and Restaurant 22 Chesterfield Road (Route 161) in Flanders (860–739–8866). This establishment serves the best fish in town. Fried, broiled, baked, steamed, blackened, or raw, the fish are so fresh they're nearly jumping from the water to your table, inside or out. Bring your own wine if you plan to eat here; you can also take out anything on the menu. The sweet potato fries are a must, no matter what else you order. Open year-round Sunday through Thursday 8:00 A.M. to 9:00 P.M. and Friday and Saturday until 10:00 P.M. $–$$

Constantine's 252 Main Street (860–739–2848). Specializing in tasty American cuisine since 1929, this clean, friendly eatery has fresh seafood, steaks and chops, pasta and salads, homemade soups, chicken and veal dishes, great overstuffed sandwiches and platters, and a children's menu. Open for lunch and dinner Tuesday through Sunday. $$–$$$

Dad's Restaurant 147 Main Street (Route 156) (860–739–2113). Overlooking Niantic Bay, this place has been doing seafood right since 1963.

It's ultra-friendly, ultra-casual, and very tasty and has eleven flavors of gourmet soft-serve ice cream for dessert. Open daily for lunch and dinner. $

Village Bake House 289 Pennsylvania Avenue (860-739-9638). Perfect for beach picnic foods or a quick bite at the small tables inside or outside on the wide sidewalk of this shopping center storefront. Baked goods, crusty rolls, excellent soups, chowders, chili, inventive sandwiches, teas, coffees, and gourmet food gifts. Open Monday and Tuesday 7:00 A.M. to 3:00 P.M.; Wednesday through Saturday till 5:30 P.M. $

Places to Stay in East Lyme/Niantic

Best Western Hilltop Inn 239 Flanders Road (860-739-3951). Ninety recently renovated units with televisions and in-room fridges. Outdoor pool, beach passes, continental breakfast. Senior citizen rates. $$$

Niantic Inn 345 Main Street (860-739-5451). Twenty-four roomy studios with dining and living areas and in-room televisions, fridges, microwaves, and coffeepots. Complimentary continental breakfast. Air-conditioned. Beach practically out the door. $$$$

Rocky Neck Motor Inn 237 West Main Street (860-739-6268). Offers thirty-plus rooms, including twenty-six efficiencies, with passes to the state park, televisions, and air-conditioning. $$-$$$.

Elms Hotel 27-37 Ocean Avenue (860-739-5545 or 888-437-1117). Web site: www.elmshotel.com. Just a stone's throw from Crescent Beach, this 1898 waterfront classic offers totally renovated, spotless rooms with private and shared baths, continental breakfast, picnic area with outdoor games, and private beach association passes. $$$

The Island 20 Islanda Court (P.O. Box 2) on Lake Pattagansett (860-739-8316). Provides four large cottages with kitchenettes. Weekly rentals only: $400. Boating, fishing, and swimming in the lake. Also campsites at $25 nightly.

The Inn at Harbor Hill Marina 60 Grand Street (860-739-0331). Web site: www.innharborhill.com. This waterside bed-and-breakfast offers eight guest rooms with private baths, queen-size or twin beds, and water views from every room and every wicker rocker. Enjoy their deluxe continental breakfast on the wraparound porch overlooking the marina or linger instead on your private balcony with views of the Niantic River. Also accessible by boat. Smoke-free. Open year-round. $$$$

Fourteen Lincoln Street B&B 14 Lincoln Street (860-739-6327). Web site: www.14lincolnstreet.com. Chef Cheryl Jean is the innkeeper at this unique bed-and-breakfast inn inside a restored nineteenth-century church. Scrumptious gourmet breakfasts and afternoon teas. Private baths, enchanting grounds, cooking classes and culinary retreats. Exquisite. $$$$

Public Boat Launches

East Lyme Town Ramp On Niantic River at Grand Street, one block north of and parallel to Main Street (Route 156). Ramp for trailered or cartop boats; transient boaters are welcome to pull ashore here with small boats or dinghies.

Niantic River State Boat Launch Located approximately a quarter-mile northeast of the Route 156 bridge across the Niantic River. From the Waterford side of the bridge, take the first left-hand turn onto West Street; take another left at the stop sign and then a quick right, which will lead you down to Mago Point Park. Parking for one hundred cars is at the river's edge straight ahead. Fee in summer. Access to both the Sound and the Niantic River and Bay.

For Further Information

East Lyme Tourism Information Center I-95 exit 74 (860-739-0208). On the right side of Route 161 near the Connecticut Yankee Motor Inn. Open daily July 1 to Labor Day from 9:00 A.M. to 6:00 P.M.; spring and fall hours daily 10:00 A.M. to 4:00 P.M. Maps, brochures, and guidance to restaurants and lodgings are offered here.

East Lyme Parks and Recreation (860-739-5828). Information on in-season use of the beaches and parks. Free use of the town beach at McCook Point Park on Columbus Avenue and Hole in the Wall on Baptist Lane is limited to residents, renters, and overnight guests at local lodgings, plus walk-ins and bicyclists. Nonresidents cannot park at these beaches unless they first purchase a day pass ($15) at the Parks and Recreation Department on Society Road. Amtrak Beach near the Niantic River at the bascule railroad bridge is on Amtrak property and usable on an at-your-own-risk basis (which many folks do). It has no parking lot.

Waterford

Across the Niantic River from East Lyme is the town of Waterford—a community of citizens whose livelihoods are often earned from the Millstone Nuclear Power Plant, Electric Boat in nearby Groton, the naval submarine base in New London, or the Sound itself, as commercial fishermen or sportfishing captains. In any case, their lives are often as closely linked to the sea as those of earlier citizens who built ships, sailed ships, and fished in the nearby waters.

Originally home to the Nehantic people, who also lived in what is now East Lyme, Waterford was settled by the English in about 1651 and was once most important for its rope ferry that took travelers across the Niantic River. Massachusetts governor John Winthrop and his family lived out on the small peninsula now called Millstone Point, operating a 600-acre farm that remained in the Winthrop family for three generations. In 1723 part of the Millstone property was sold to Peter Buor, who quarried millstones there. The property changed hands several times during the next century, but the quarrying operation continued, and by 1910 some 800 men were employed as quarriers.

Quarrying stopped in 1963, and construction of the power plant began in 1966. Today the plant is a prominent sight on the Waterford shore. Lots of folks feel uncomfortable about the looming presence of the vast complex that dominates the point, but the plant is undergoing thorough scrutiny, and the area surrounding the plant provides important osprey nesting sites and other protected areas for wildlife. In fact, conservation and water and soil monitoring at the Waterford shore is probably stricter than at any other point along the Connecticut coastline. Come here to explore the flora and fauna and enjoy the shoreline scenery. Though not as widely known as other shoreline maritime centers, Waterford is one of the best places in Connecticut for recreational boating and fishing. And it is also one of the best places for theater and musical performances. Let Waterford surprise you.

The Best of Waterford

Harkness Memorial State Park

On the gorgeous seaside site of a former private estate, 234-acre Harkness

SUMMER MUSIC AT HARKNESS

If Harkness Memorial State Park is a feast for the eyes, the summer concert series held there in July and August is food for the soul. Internationally and nationally known performing artists, from B. B. King to Itzhak Perlman, entertain crowds of music lovers seated or sprawled on the lawn overlooking the sea. There couldn't be a better way to spend a summer night at the shore in Connecticut than to enjoy one of these Summer Music at Harkness performances (860-442-9199; office at 300 State Street, Suite 400, in New London). Concerts are Saturday evenings at 8:00 P.M., rain or shine; concertgoers are welcome to enter the grounds at 275 Great Neck Road (Route 213) any time after 6:00 P.M. without paying the usual day-use fee for the park.

Subscriptions are available to the whole nine-concert series, or, depending on the performer, you can choose lawn seats for $15 (bring your own chairs or blankets) or tent seats for $28 to $33 (900 white wooden folding chairs are provided). Children's lawn tickets are half-price. If you bring your own dinner, you might want to go all out to try to win the prize for most elegant picnic. The only items prohibited are beer kegs and open grills or hibachis. You can purchase sandwiches from the specially catered concession or desserts and beverages from the vendors who arrive at about 6:00 P.M. Call the office for a calendar of this year's lineup.

State Park is a feast for the eyes, drawing thousands of visitors each year. Bring a picnic to the lovely grounds surrounding Eolia, a forty-two-room Italianate mansion built in 1906 by Jessie Stillman Taylor, who sold the house and its property to her sister Mary Stillman Harkness for a cool $8 million in 1908. This summer home of Mary and her husband (oil tycoon and philanthropist Edward S. Harkness) had grass and clay tennis courts, extensive gardens and greenhouses, an eleven-hole golf course, a bowling alley, and squash courts among its many outstanding features, but it was also a working farm where prize-winning Guernsey cattle were raised.

Bequeathed to the State of Connecticut in 1952, the house has recently undergone a magnificent restoration as a museum and is now open to the public from May 1 through Columbus Day. Visitors can explore the mansion at no extra charge beyond the park entrance fee.

Take a self-guided tour on any day or come for a guided tour given on weekends only. Outside the mansion, beautiful gardens are delightful places to wander on a spring or summer day.

Plenty of picnic tables and charcoal grills help to make meals by the shore comfortable for folks who enjoy leisurely pursuits like watching the sailboats. Visitors who enjoy more active recreation may appreciate the opportunity to fish from the beach or the promontory for the winter flounder, bluefish, and sea bass that make Waterford a mecca for anglers. Swimming and boating are not allowed from the fine white fringe of beach at Harkness, but picnicking and beachcombing are encouraged. The beach is not guarded, however, and waders should be especially cautious if temptation overcomes discretion: The lovely tidal inlet that connects Goshen Cove with the Sound at the park boundary has a powerful current that is of real danger even to strong swimmers.

Harkness Memorial State Park, 275 Great Neck Road (Route 213). Call for park information (860–443–5725) or for concert information (800–969–3400). Open daily year-round from 8:00 A.M. to sunset. Daily parking fee from Memorial Day to Labor Day: weekdays $4.00 for Connecticut license plates and $5.00 for out-of-state plates; weekends $5.00 and $8.00, respectively; free after Labor Day until Memorial Day weekend. Mansion open from May 1 through Columbus Day, 10:00 A.M. to 3:00 P.M. on weekends only in May, June, September, and October and daily in July and August. No swimming; no campfires; no glass or kegs on the beach; all pets must be leashed.

Eugene O'Neill Theater Center

One of the most exciting places in the nation to see live dramatic performances is this theater center overlooking the Sound, not terribly far from the cottage where its Nobel and Pulitzer Prize–winning namesake playwright spent the summers of his youth. Every summer for the past forty or so, students and masters of theater have met in Waterford for intensive workshops that lead to the development of some of the brightest new talents in the field. Nine distinct programs attract writers, actors, directors, musicians, and even puppeteers each season, offering these artists an opportunity to sharpen their skills under the tutelage of an outstanding faculty and with the support of their peers.

The **National Theater Institute,** the National Puppetry Conference, the National Music Theater Conference, and the Cabaret Symposium provide an opportunity to be in the audience when the embryonic works of the artists are brought to the stage for the first time. The evening performances held either inside or out of doors may be finished or nearly finished works honed over several weeks of intense evolution; others may be readings of works still in process with minimal staging or costuming. Ticket prices vary from $8.00 to $25.00. Call for a schedule of the public performances of the current season. Ask about picnicking and/or boxed suppers that can be ordered for preshow dining.

305 Great Neck Road (information and schedule 860–443–5378; box office 860–443–1238). Public performances are planned for each program of study. The Puppetry Conference begins the season in June; National Playwrights Conference performances usually begin in July and run nearly nightly, plus Saturday matinees; Cabaret programs are generally two weekends in August; Music Theater programs are two to three weeks in August; the National Theater Institute has performances during its September to December and January through April sessions.

Colonial Village at Historic Jordan Green

Close to the docks and water is the Jordan Green and its replica colonial village with the 1740 Jordan schoolhouse, the 1840 Beebe-Phillips farm-house, a blacksmith shop with a working forge and smithing tools, a corn crib, and a barn with farm implements, equipment such as horse-drawn farm vehicles, and other historical artifacts. Two small apple orchards and an authentic colonial herb garden complete the historical exhibits; a few other buildings house offices and an education center. Tours include details of home, hearth, agriculture, and local history.

The Sheep to Shawl festival is held for one day each May, focusing on the shearing of sheep, the processing of their fleece, and activities related to creating the finished woolen thread and cloth. Traditional arts and crafts are demonstrated. Hearth cooking, food preservation, candle-dipping, carpentry, and blacksmithing are among the activities you might see.

Rope Ferry Road and Avery Lane (off Route 156) (860–442–2707). Open June 30 through September 30, Wednesday through Friday from 1:00 to 4:00 P.M. or by appointment, plus one festival day in May. Free.

Waterford Speedbowl

Your attention will be a million miles from the sea at the exciting stock-car races that may appeal to travelers weary of boat rides and seafood shacks. The one-third-mile oval track offers Saturday evening races in many categories, including strictly stocks, late models, mini-stocks, and modifieds. Special events such as national championships, ladies' races, and stunt shows are also scheduled throughout the season. Call for a schedule of events and ticket prices. Regular Saturday races begin at 6:00 P.M. A concession offers simple American fast-food fare and snacks.

1080 Hartford Road (Route 85) (860–442–1585). Mid-April through mid-October. Adult tickets range from $9.00 to $13.00, depending on the event. Children 6 to 12 pay $2.00 (or are admitted free with a paying adult); children 5 and under are free. Parking is free.

Boat Excursions and Charters

Sunbeam Express *Nature Cruise Center*

Down at the docks on the Niantic River between Niantic and Waterford at Captain John's Sportfishing Center, you can catch Captain John Wadsworth's nature cruises.

From mid-March to mid-May, Captain John offers **seal-watching trips.** The boat cruises Fishers Island Sound and other areas of eastern Long Island Sound in search of harbor seals and harp seals as well as waterfowl and other wildlife. On Sundays from February through mid-March, the boat leaves for **bald eagle cruises** from the Dock & Dine Restaurant in Old Saybrook and heads up the Connecticut River. The naturalist-guided seal and eagle cruises depart at 9:00 A.M. and return around noon. Throughout the summer are twelve **lighthouse cruises,** on Wednesdays, Saturdays, and Sundays. Crossing the Sound through Plum Gut and across the Race, the five-hour cruise that highlights eleven lighthouses departs Waterford at 10:00 A.M. and 3:00 P.M.

On every cruise, the crew brings lunch food, snacks, and soft drinks aboard for sale in the galley, or you can pack a lunch (no alcoholic beverages). Dress appropriately for the weather. Wear sunblock and a hat and bring a sweatshirt even in summer. Winter gear will be necessary at other times. The heated cabin of this 100-foot boat helps to keep you toasty, but despite the large windows the best viewing is still outside at the rail, so be prepared.

The Sunbeam fleet also includes charter and party boats for **deep-sea fishing cruises** in the eastern end of Long Island Sound. Trips for bass and blues depart at 6:00 A.M. and 1:00 P.M. daily except Wednesday from July 1 through Labor Day and Friday through Sunday in June. Other trips for other fish and in other seasons are also on the schedule, as are night bass fishing and fluke fishing. Adults pay $33.00 plus $5.00 for rod rental; children cost $17.00 plus $5.00 for rod rental. Captain John's boats hold 6 to 149 passengers.

Captain John's Sportfishing Center, 15 First Street (860–443–7259). *Web site: www.sunbeamfleet.com. Seal and eagle watch: adults $30, children $15. Lighthouse cruise: adults $40, children $20. Children under 4 ride for free. Seniors and groups of ten or more get a discount. Reservations recommended. Boats leave promptly; plan to arrive thirty to forty-five minutes prior to departure.* **Note:** Private whale watch charters can also be arranged.

Dot-E-Dee Captain Jack Douton, Niantic Sportfishing Dock (J & B Tackle Shop), 15 First Street (860–739–7419). Fishing charters for up to six people. Reservations required.

Good Company II Captain Joe Garafano, Jr., Waddy's Dock (860–443–0269 or 860–443–0581). Fishing charters for up to six passengers. Reservations required.

Osprey Captain Joseph Wysocki, Niantic Sportfishing Dock, 15 First Street (860–739–4129). Fishing charters for up to six passengers. Reservations required.

Hillyer's Bait and Tackle Shop 371 Rope Ferry Road (860–443–7615). Offers the largest and best selection in the area, if not in the whole state. Located near the Niantic River Bridge at Mago Point, convenient to the Sunbeam fleet and other charters as well as the state boat launch. Come here for expert advice and good to superior equipment for saltwater and freshwater fishing. Huge selection of live bait, from Arkansas shiners to sand worms. Open Monday through Thursday 6:00 A.M. to 7:00 P.M. and on Friday until 8:00 P.M.; on Saturday and Sunday, they open at 5:00 A.M. and close at 7:00 and 5:00 P.M., respectively.

Places to Eat in Waterford

Unk's on the Bay 361 Rope Ferry Road (Route 156) (860–443–2717). Close to the banks of the Niantic River just north of the bridge, Unk's offers good food at fair prices. Nearly anyone around here will direct you to Unk's if you ask for the best casual place for a seafood dinner. It's also well recommended for steak, pasta dinners, and other basic American fare. Children's menu. Outside seating in warm weather. Open daily year-round for lunch and dinner. $–$$$

Sunset Rib Company 378 Rope Ferry Road (860–443–7427). As you might guess, this also-casual place is great for meaty ribs plus sunset views of the Sound and river. Plenty of other choices like chicken, pastas, salads, burgers, and much more. Full bar. Indoor and outdoor seating on upper and lower decks. Small dock for transient boaters looking for a lunch or dinner place. Open daily for lunch and dinner. Closed from late October to early March. $$

Illiano's Pizzeria 709 Broad Street Extension (860-437-1999). Like its sister *ristorante* in Old Lyme (163 Boston Post Road; 860-434-1110), this authentic pizzeria offers delicious thin-crust pizza seven days a week. It also makes Italian-American favorites like spaghetti, ravioli, manicotti, calzones, antipasti, and grinders. Open daily 10:30 A.M. to 10:30 P.M. $-$$

Riverside Grocery Deli Bait and Tackle 150 Shore Road (860-444-0681). If you need beach or boat ride treats, picnic goods, breakfast to go, grinders, homemade breads, or food (or hooks) for the little fishies, they've got it here. Just a block from the Pleasure Beach boat launch at Jordan Cove. Open daily from 8:00 A.M. to 8:00 P.M., except on Sunday and Monday when they close at 1:00 P.M. $

Village Stop Restaurant 97 Rope Ferry Road (860-443-1177). Located in historic Jordan Village, this little place is perfect for breakfast or lunch, eat in or take out. Daily breakfast favorites like Belgian waffles and special omelets; lunch specials; homemade desserts. Open Wednesday through Friday 5:30 A.M. to 2:00 P.M. and on weekends from 6:00 A.M. to 1:00 P.M. $

Places to Stay in Waterford

Camp View Motor Court 334 Rope Ferry Road (Route 156), off I-95 exit 74 (860-442-1047). Twenty cottages with kitchenettes and a beautiful view overlooking Long Island Sound and the Niantic River. Old-fashioned cabins meticulously kept by the same owner for many years. It's not the Harkness mansion, but it's a clean place to rest your head. Play-ground and beach passes. May to November. $$

Blue Anchor Motel 563 Boston Post Road, off I-95 exit 75 (860-442-2072). Fifteen efficiencies, each with one double bed, small fridge, gas stove, basic kitchen furnishings, cable TV, private bath with shower. Close to the Niantic River. Friendly owner—always a plus. $$-$$$

Lamplighter Motel 211 Parkway North, off I-95 exit 81 (860-442-7227). Thirty-eight units, including twenty recently renovated efficiencies with kitchenettes, cable TV, and phones; exercise equipment and outdoor pool. Pets welcome. Continental breakfast. Senior citizen rates. $$$

Oakdell Motel 983 Hartford Turnpike (Route 85), off I–95 exit 82 (860–442–9446 or 800–676–REST). Owned by the same family for nearly three decades, this immaculate motel seems more like a bed-and-breakfast than a roadside motel. The Oakdell has twenty-two semi-efficiencies; each room has fridge, microwave, private bath, cable TV, phone, and either one or two double beds. Outdoor pool and barbecue grills. Complimentary continental breakfast. Open year-round. Nightly and weekly rates. $$–$$$

Spring Hill Suites by Marriott 401 Frontage Road, off I–95 exit 82 or 83 (860–439–0151). Brand-new hotel right off the highway near New London border. Each of the eighty rooms has two queen-size or one king-size bed plus a pull-out couch, microwave, sink, refrigerator, and coffeemaker. Indoor pool and exercise room. Complimentary continental breakfast. Open year-round. $$$–$$$$

Public Boat Launches

Niantic River State Boat Launch Located approximately a quarter-mile northeast of the Route 156 bridge across the Niantic River. From the Waterford side of the bridge, take the first left-hand turn onto West Street; take another left at the stop sign and then a quick right, which will lead you down to Mago Point Park. Parking for one hundred cars is at the river's edge straight ahead. Fee in summer. Access to both the Sound and the Niantic River and Bay.

Jordan Cove at Pleasure Beach Route 213, then south on Goshen Road and straight to Dock Road. Launch is straight ahead. No fee. Very crowded on weekends. Parking for forty-five cars.

For Further Information

Waterford Parks Department (860–444–5881) or **Waterford Beach Park** (860–437–4385). Information on nonresident use of the town beach. Nonresidents can pay at the gate to enter the beach ($10 weekdays; $20 weekends), or they can buy a season pass ($60) at the Parks Department office at 1000 Hartford Road. Waterford Beach Park has a playground and picnic area, volleyball courts, rest rooms, and showers. The park is off Great Neck Road, adjacent to the O'Neill Theater.

New London

Many a New London boy turned his back on the land and took to the sea right from the wharves of this city. Like its sister city, Groton, across the Thames River, New London has a long maritime history that has influenced its development into a center of commerce and industry. No other city on the Connecticut shoreline has an economy more closely connected to the sea. A quick tour of the places where New London touches the Sound and the river reveals ferries, lobster boats, shipyards, and yacht brokers, and all of the businesses that supply and support them—sail lofts and suppliers of navigation equipment, tackle shops and boat riggers, marinas and seafood shacks. In the air are the sounds of bell buoys and foghorns, of Jet Skis and powerboats and even the Coast Guard band. In good weather and bad the Thames is crowded with boat traffic from single scull to Sunfish to submarine. There's no doubt that New London boys are still heading for the sea.

Settled in 1646 as Pequot Plantation by John Winthrop, Jr., New London had agrarian beginnings like other Connecticut shoreline settlements, but its river also formed the largest and the deepest harbor on the Connecticut coast. By 1846 it had become the second largest whaling port in the world. Long a manufacturing and shipbuilding city, its eclectic assortment of attractions frequently allude to the history and importance of the city as a center of maritime activities both industrial and recreational.

The Best of New London

United States Coast Guard Academy

On land donated to the federal government by the people of New London, the beautiful hundred-acre campus of the U.S. Coast Guard Academy overlooks the Thames River. Beginning in the 1790s as the Revenue Cutter Service in charge of enforcing customs and tariffs on maritime commerce, the Coast Guard now protects fisheries, ports, waterways, and people—responding to an average of 70,000 search and rescue calls each year. The academy is the place where cadets are educated and trained. A museum here traces the history of this branch of our armed forces, and a visitors' center features a multimedia show on

NEW LONDON WATERFRONT PARK

A beautiful, wide half-mile-long esplanade is the highlight of the new park along the Thames River in downtown New London. See historic sites, enjoy the activities of the ferry terminals, or soak up the views of the river and waterfront. A good place to enter the area is behind the railroad station near the Fishers Island Ferry, or at City Pier at the foot of State. Free live entertainment and special events are frequent on the stage at City Pier Plaza; the new Children's Discovery Pier has permanent displays about local marine wildlife; Amistad Pier offers fishing space, and the Custom House Pier hosts vessels of all sizes, including tall ships and luxury cruise liners.

cadet life. Pick up a self-guided walking tour brochure at the visitors' center if you'd like to explore the campus. Tours of the tall-ship training vessel, the barque USCG *Eagle,* are offered whenever it is in port (call 860–444–8595 to check its schedule). Dress parades and concerts by the Coast Guard Band are held on a seasonal schedule, usually on Fridays at 4:00 P.M. in the spring and fall.

15 Mohegan Avenue, off Route 31 (Public Affairs Office 860–444–8270). Campus open daily year-round 9:00 A.M. to sunset. Visitors Pavilion open May through October 10:00 A.M. to 5:00 P.M. Museum open year-round 8:00 A.M. to 4:00 P.M. on weekdays and 9:00 A.M. to 5:00 P.M. on weekends and holidays. The training vessel, when in port, is open for tours Friday through Sunday 1:00 to 5:00 P.M. Free.

Hempsted Houses

These two homes in the historic downtown area include one of the oldest documented houses in America; both are among the few New London structures to have survived the burning of the city in 1781 by British troops under the command of Benedict Arnold. Ten generations of the Hempsted family lived on this soil since the town's early history as a seaport, and the diaries of rope-maker Joshua Hempsted have contributed greatly both to the excellent interpretation of the house itself and to our knowledge of eighteenth-century colonial American life. The 1678 Joshua Hempsted House is one of the oldest frame buildings in New England. It also is the only Underground Railroad site that is open to the public in Connecticut. The 1759 Nathaniel

Hempsted House is one of the most unusual historic homes in New England—it has 2-foot-thick stone walls, a gambrel roof, and an exterior projecting beehive oven.

Hands-on activities are offered on special weekends once each month. On Labor Day weekend a special focus is put on women's work of the eighteenth century. A Hempsted Thanksgiving is celebrated on the Saturday after Thanksgiving. Costumed docents, open-hearth cooking, and food samples are part of the celebration.

11 Hempstead Street (860–443–7949 or 860–247–8996). Open mid-May to mid-October on Thursday through Sunday; tours are given from noon to 4:00 P.M. Adults $4.00, children $2.00.

Monte Cristo Cottage

An aura of sadness seems to pervade the boyhood home of Pulitzer and

NEW LONDON'S HISTORIC CENTER

These important points of interest are near or within New London's historic district.

1833 Robert Mills U.S. Custom House and Museum of American Maritime History 150 Bank Street (860-447-2501). On the banks of the Thames is the oldest customs house in the United States, now restored, with a museum on the American customs service and exhibits on maritime history and industry. Hours are limited; call for information. Free

Fort Trumbull State Park 90 Walbach Street (860-444-7160). Built on the site of Revolutionary War fortifications, this park has spectacular views of the river and sea. Guided tours, fishing pier, visitor center. Open year-round daily.

Nathan Hale Schoolhouse Foot of State Street (860-449-1110). One of the two schools in which Hale taught before losing his life in the American Revolution. Open Saturdays in summer.

Whale Oil Row Huntington Street. Restored row of 1832 Greek Revival houses owned by whaling tycoons.

Ye Townes Antientist Burial Ground Huntington Street. Oldest graveyard in New London County; interesting headstones.

CONNECTICUT COLLEGE

The picturesque campus and wonderful liberal arts tradition at **Connecticut College** (270 Mohegan Avenue; 860-447-1911) draw students from every corner of the nation. Visitors are also drawn to the 750-acre **Connecticut College Arboretum** (enter on Williams Street; 860-439-5020) of native trees and shrubs arranged in naturalized plantings with ponds, benches, and walkways throughout the property. Admission is free from dawn to dusk daily throughout the year, and free tours are given on Saturdays and Sundays at 2:00 P.M. from April through October. The galleries of the college's **Cummings Art Center** (860-439-2740) offer student and faculty exhibitions, plus a performing arts series featuring international artists in music, dance, and theater from September through May. The beautiful **Harkness Chapel** (860-439-2450) offers religious services as well as such musical events as the June concerts of the **Connecticut Early Music Society Festival** (860-444-2419). Also on campus is the **Connecticut Storytelling Center** (860-439-2764), which invites the public to its Connecticut Storytelling Festival held annually in late April.

Nobel Prize–winning playwright Eugene O'Neill. It's not that the house is not impeccably kept or that summer sunshine doesn't stream through the bare or lightly dressed windows of this modest 1840s cottage. Decay and neglect are nowhere apparent, in fact, and yet the house has a disconcerting effect of ghostliness. Perhaps the visitor is simply struck by the astonishing re-creation of the room and views that O'Neill described so minutely in his stage settings for *Long Day's Journey into Night*; perhaps the tales of the family's life told in a video presentation and on the tours add to some sense of pain or longing that seems to have plagued the home's former occupants. In any case, the cottage is fascinating, and its beautiful views of the harbor account for O'Neill's love for the sea and its sailing ships. Look for O'Neill's statue, sweetly portraying his boyhood, on a rock overlooking the harbor near Union Station and the ferry terminals, just off New London's old Main Street, now renamed Eugene O'Neill Drive.

325 Pequot Avenue (860-443-0051). Open Memorial Day to Labor Day, from Tuesday through Saturday 10:00 A.M. to 5:00 P.M. and Sunday 1:00 to 5:00 P.M. Adults $5.00; children under 12 admitted free.

Shaw-Perkins Mansion

Built for wealthy Captain Nathaniel Shaw in 1756 and used as a naval war office during the American Revolution, this house is owned and operated by the friendly and helpful New London Historical Society. Eighteenth-century furniture and artifacts, gardens, and portrait collection are what you will see on a self-guided tour. Guided tours focus on early New London history and the West Indies trade. Stories of the Shaws and their roles in the shipping trade and the Revolution are tailored to visitors of all ages.

11 Blinman Street (860–443–1209). Blinman Street is a small, one-way street separated from Bank Street by a grassy strip; look for the firehouse, then the gorgeous Georgian mansion. Open year-round, Wednesday through Friday from 1:00 to 4:00 P.M. and Saturday from 10:00 A.M. to 4:00 P.M. Closed on major holidays. Adults $5.00, seniors $4.00, students $3.00, children ages 6 to 12 $1.00; under 6 free.

Lyman Allyn Art Museum
Children's Art Park

The Lyman Allyn owns one of Connecticut's little-known but exceptional small art collections. Located in a pristine setting near Connecticut College and the U.S. Coast Guard Academy, this beautiful neoclassical museum contains 30,000 pieces of fine and decorative arts from America, Europe, Asia, and the South Pacific. From an Egyptian falcon mummy to Old Master drawings to contemporary American works, the museum presents a good overview of world art history, but the American collection is especially fine. The entire first floor is given over to the American works. Silver, glass, porcelain, furniture, and paintings are arranged in a chronological development to show the progression of the American style from the late 1600s onward through American Impressionism.

Outside on the museum's front lawn is the **Children's Art Park**, a sculpture garden designed to demonstrate the evolution of art. Children are welcome to climb on, play in, and ponder each object in the park. Back inside, a wonderful museum shop with gifts of great appeal to children and young artists is also here.

Admission is free every Sunday afternoon, and the first Sunday of each month features special activities, from live music performances to storytellings, poetry readings, or gallery tours. Art classes and other special events are offered from time to time throughout the year.

625 Williams Street (860–443–2545). Open year-round Tuesday through Saturday 10:00 A.M. to 5:00 P.M. and Sunday 1:00 to 5:00 P.M.; closed on major holidays. Adults $4.00, seniors and students $3.00, children 6 and under free. The admission fee allows entrance to the Deshon Allyn House as well. See next entry.

Lyman Allyn Dolls and Toys

One of Connecticut's newest museums houses one of the state's most endearing collections. An extension of the Lyman Allyn Art Museum, it is housed in the 1827 Deshon Allyn mansion on the same grounds as the larger art museum. This building invites children of all ages to enjoy an elaborate display of dolls and toys from yesteryear to the present.

The museum's notable collection includes nineteenth- and twentieth-century dolls, dollhouses, and toys. Freshly refurbished, the collection is inventively exhibited in settings that evoke the eras of the dolls and toys themselves. Hundreds of dolls, puppets, wind-up cars, tin boats, model trains, toy construction and emergency vehicles—even puzzles and cast-iron banks are a part of the fun here.

Visitors will find some irresistible interactive exhibits designed to appeal to the child's imagination and creativity. Doll-size farmhouses and farm equipment, along with livestock and miniature inhabitants, displays of tin boats and other maritime toys, road and highway vehicles, and fire, rescue, and other emergency vehicles are among the toys here. Doll lovers may wish to simply soak up the sights within the *Hall of Dolls,* home to more than a hundred antique poppets and dozens of more modern ones.

Sure to charm both young explorers and adult collectors, the Dolls and Toys Museum is a pleasing link to all the joys of childhood. Combined with visits to either or both the Lyman Allyn Art Museum and the Children's Art Park, this museum guarantees an enchanting outing.

Deshon Allyn House, 625 Williams Street (860–443–2545). Admission to the Lyman Allyn sites is $4.00 for adults; $3.00 for students; children under 6 free. That fee will admit visitors into both of the Lyman Allyn buildings.

Science Center of Eastern Connecticut

Emphasizing the life sciences and nature, this museum gives children a chance to see, touch, and feel the principles of science demonstrated in accessible and interactive exhibits, laboratories, and discovery stations. The invitation to learn is irresistible in Science Explorer's Hall, where there are more than one hundred stations related to discoveries about light, sound, microbiology, electricity, optics, animals, tools, and simple machines. A shop area includes an opportunity for children to build a wooden boat or a birdhouse; in another area, children learn about chromatography by experimenting with water and filter paper. An observation beehive and a marine touch tank are among the animal exhibits. Other special features are a science theater offering daily programs, a photographic darkroom, a greenhouse, and access to the trails in the Connecticut College Arboretum, where the science center is located. A picnic on the lovely property, which includes trees and shrubs native to eastern North America, is a nice way to end a visit here.

33 Gallows Lane (860–442–0391; Web site: www.scec.conncoll.edu). Open year-round Tuesday through Saturday 10:00 A.M. to 6:00 P.M. and Sunday 1:00 to 5:00 P.M.; closed on major holidays. Adults $6.00, children under 12 $4.00.

Garde Arts Center

If you have never been to a real movie palace, the kind with gilded architecture and acoustics to spare, plush seats, and a giant movie screen revealed at the opening of sweeping velvet curtains, go to the 1926 Garde Theater, downtown in the historic district. A $19 million restoration/expansion has transformed this already grand lady into a state-of-the-art performing arts center on par with others in New Haven, Boston, and New York. The stunning results of the first phase are already in place in the form of a new grand entrance and circular marquee that usher audiences into three floors of Moroccan-style lobbies.

In addition to its noteworthy new and classic film series, the 1,500-seat theater presents nationally and internationally known live performance arts throughout the year. Subscriptions as well as single tickets are available to a Broadway series, a Family Theatre series, plus country music, dance, and comedy series and single-night special events. The Garde is also the home of the Eastern Connecticut Symphony Orchestra. Call for details of its four-concert classical and pops series.

325 State Street (calendar of events and other information 860–444–6766; box office 860–444–7373 or 888–ONGARDE). Web site: www.gardearts.org.

Ocean Beach Park

For the kind of seaside fun wherein everybody gets wet, come to a place that offers not one but *three* ways to get soaked. Right on the Sound, Ocean Beach Park is both old-fashioned public beach resort and new-fangled party/conference facility. A half-mile-long, very clean white sand beach is the focal point of the park. Owned by the City of New London, Ocean Beach Park also has Connecticut's only wide wooden boardwalk down the length of the beach. It leads past food concessions, a pinball and electronic game arcade, a kiddie playground, volleyball nets, and an eighteen-hole miniature golf course ($4.00 per round).

The park and the beach are open year-round, and off-season access is offered at no charge. The pool, water slide, and other entertainments are seasonal only, and they generally open on the Saturday before Memorial Day and close after Labor Day. A full staff of lifeguards and a first-aid station help make this a popular destination for families. Entertainment on the boardwalk on Friday, Saturday, and Sunday is provided for all park visitors. An immaculate Olympic-size swimming pool and a beautiful bathhouse with changing rooms, lockers, and showers are available for individual fees, currently $4.00 per person; plus a refundable key deposit of $3.00.

Once home to carnival-style kiddie rides, the park now has one remaining amusement-park-style water slide. A triple-run, three-speed tower of serpentine slides, this is a humdinger of a ride and, with the exception of the beach itself, the most popular attraction here. A height requirement of 46 inches helps to keep the ride safe for all visitors. The three flumes begin about 50 feet up at the top of a challenging set of stairs, so depending on your speed and stamina, you'll get ten to fifteen runs down the flume of your choice in a half-hour time slot. Each person pays $7.00 for a half-hour, $11.00 for an hour, or $17.00 for unlimited rides throughout a whole day.

While you are here, check out the new handicapped-accessible observation deck and nature walk at Alewife Cove. It's a coastal paradise for birds and bird lovers, which also offers truly beautiful views of the marine and estuarine habitat.

1225 Ocean Avenue (860–447–3031 or 800–510–SAND). Access to beach and park at no charge year-round, dawn to dusk. Entertainments and concessions open Memorial Day weekend through Labor Day weekend, 9:00 A.M. (8:00 A.M. on weekends) to 11:00 P.M. Admission collected through a parking fee of $8.00 per car on weekdays and $12.00 on weekends; parking on holidays is $20.00.

Boat Excursions and Charters

The following boats offer fishing charters for up to six passengers. Full- and half-day trips can be arranged by most captains. Inshore as well as deep-sea trips are offered, usually from April or May through October.

All trips are planned by reservation only. *A'Vanga:* Captain Byron Smith, Jr., (860–848–0170), Burr's Yacht Haven. **Fish:** Captain Peter Fisher (860–739–3611), Thamesport Landing. *Lady Margaret:* Captain Claude Adams (860–739–3687), Thamesport Landing. *West Wind III:* Captain Cecil Brooks (860–526–9453), Captain Scott Lobster Dock. *White Lightning:* Captain Ted Harris (860–739–6906), Burr's Yacht Haven.

Seapony Express Sightseeing Cruises Captain Claus Wolter (860–444–0585; Web site: www.seapony.com). From Crocker's Boatyard on Howard Street, this 36-foot, Coast-Guard approved Down East lobster boat has a wide-open cockpit and a forward cabin with large windows for great visibility. Charter the vessel for customized New London harbor cruises that explore the mouth of the Thames River and offer sights of submarines, lighthouses, and other New London maritime points of interest. Holds up to twenty passengers; rates are typically $10.00 per person per hour depending on the size of your group. Arrange a trip to fit your schedule or come for one of the regular trips on Saturdays at 11:00 A.M. and 2:00 P.M. Longer cruises to Fishers Island, Sag Harbor, and the Hamptons can also be arranged.

New London Ledge Lighthouse Cruises (800–364–8472). From Avery Point Campus in Groton, take Project Oceanology's Enviro-Lab for a two-hour cruise of the Thames River and New London harbor and a walking tour of the partly restored 1909 lighthouse. Reservations required. Adults $13.00, children under 12 $9.00; children under 6 cannot take this cruise.

Block Island Ferry (860–442–7891). Leaves from 2 Ferry Street (across from Union Station) once daily from the second Saturday in June to the second Sunday in September for round trips to Old Harbor, Block Island. The huge three-deck *Anna C* leaves New London at 9:00 A.M., and arrives at Old Harbor at 11:00 A.M. (On Fridays only, a second trip departs New London at 7:15 P.M. and arrives in Old Harbor at 9:15 P.M., with no return trip the same evening.) Cars need reservations, passengers and bicycles do not. The fare is $13.50 one way for adults, $17.50 for round-trip return on the same day; children under 12 pay $9.00 one way, $11.00 for round-trip return on same day. Bicycles are $3.50 extra each way.

Fishers Island Ferry (recorded information 860–443–6851; reservations 860–442–0165. Four or more round-trips daily year-round, except Christmas Day, with as many as a dozen crossings on Fridays. No reservations necessary. One-way fare: adults $7.00, children under 12 $4.50, bicycles $20.00 plus per-person fare; car and driver $23.00.

Cross Sound Ferry Services (860-443-5281). At 2 Ferry Street (across from Union Station). Year-round high-speed vehicle and passenger-only service to and from Orient Point, Long Island. Vehicle ferries take one and a half hours one way; passenger-only high-speed ferries (April through December) take forty-five minutes. Call for vehicle reservations and ferry schedule, plus information on attractions in Orient Point and the North Fork, Long Island's picturesque farming and wine-making district. Visitors to Connecticut from Long Island will find easy connections to casinos, local attractions, and taxis.

Viking Fleet (631-668-5700). Web site: www.vikingfleet.com. This ferry and sightseeing service from New London to Montauk, Long Island, is Montauk-based, offering late May through early September passenger-only service from New London to Montauk once each Friday and Sunday evening. The adult one-way fare is $20.00; children 5 to 12 pay $10.00; bicycles are $7.00 extra each way. No reservations are necessary; payment is in cash on the boat. The ferry departs New London from the Montauk Ferry Dock near the New York City Ferry Terminal off Crystal Avenue. The Viking Fleet also offers passenger and vehicle service from Montauk to Martha's Vineyard and Block Island, plus special excursions such as casino cruises, whale-watching trips, fall foliage cruises, wine-tasting cruises to Long Island's North Shore, and a great variety of sportfishing trips.

Places to Eat in New London

Lighthouse Inn's Mansion Restaurant 6 Guthrie Place, off Lower Boulevard (860-443-8411). In a beautifully restored 1902 mansion offering lodgings to travelers for more than seventy years, this award-winning shoreline restaurant is perhaps New London's finest dining experience. Dinner is classically American with a focus on seafood but with fair attention paid to treats like roasted duck and tenderloin of beef. Don't pass up the tantalizing desserts. In a chandeliered dining room, the well-trained staff graciously serves breakfast daily from 7:00 A.M., lunch Friday and Saturday from 11:45 A.M. to 2:30 P.M., dinner daily from 5:00 P.M., and an outstanding all-you-can-eat buffet Sunday brunch ($19.95; $14.95 children 3 to 12) year-round. On Wednesdays, you might try the Pasta Bar ($10.95 adults, $6.95 children 3 to 12), where a variety of pasta is served with a variety of sauces and toppings to your order. $$$

Timothy's 181 Bank Street (860-437-0526). Everyone's raving about this downtown establishment serving continental cuisine in the form of grilled poultry and seafood, tasty signature crab bisque, good pastas, great salads, and appetizer portions for small appetites. Lunch Tuesday through Friday; dinner Tuesday through Saturday. $$

Bangkok City 123 Captain's Walk (State Street) (860-442-6970). If you like Thai cuisine, come to this casual downtown eatery offering authentic scorchers as well as milder delicacies for tender Western palates. Delicious. Open daily for lunch from 11:30 A.M. to 3:30 P.M. and for dinner from 4:30 P.M. $-$$

Fred's Shanty Pequot Avenue, overlooking Thamesport Marina (860-447-1301). The quintessential seafood shack, immortalized in Mark Shasha's children's picture book *Night of the Moonjellies*. Read the book and go have a great time getting into the act. Boats, gulls, "long dogs," fries, great seafood, burgers, outdoor-only seating. Open mid-March through mid-October, daily from 10:00 A.M. to 9:30 P.M. $

Captain Scott's Lobster Dock Restaurant 80 Hamilton Street at T.A. Fisheries (860-439-1741). Excellent fish and chips, fresh lobster just moments from the boat, clams, chowder. A New London casual classic, with picnic tables in the open air on Shaw's Cove. Open daily from April to October, 11:00 A.M. to 9:00 P.M. $-$$

Zavala 2 State Street (860-437-1891). Authentic Mexican cuisine near Waterfront Park from owner Martin Zavala, including excellent chile rellenos and superior seafood. A not-to-be-missed newcomer downtown. Open for lunch on weekdays and dinner daily, except closed on Tuesday. $$-$$$

Places to Stay in New London

Lighthouse Inn 6 Guthrie Place, off Lower Boulevard off Pequot Avenue (888-443-8411). In business as an inn for seventy-five years, this grandly restored 1902 mansion overlooking Long Island Sound near the mouth of the Thames River offers ocean swimming at its private beach and casually elegant dining at the well-respected Mansion Restaurant, open to the public for breakfast and dinner daily and lunch Fridays and Saturdays. Mahogany staircases lead to fifty luxuriously decorated and spacious rooms. Continental breakfast. $$$$

Queen Anne Inn 265 Williams Street (860–447–2600 or 800–347–8818). This elegant Victorian inn right in the center of the city has ten antiques-filled rooms with eight private baths, plus a tower suite. A third-floor bath with a Jacuzzi may be used by all guests. Many of the air-conditioned rooms have fireplaces and romantic touches like tall, four-poster canopied beds and lovely nautical artwork on the walls. Full gourmet breakfast and afternoon tea. Open year-round. $$$$

Holiday Inn Frontage Road (860–442–0631 or 800–HOLIDAY). One-hundred thirty-six units including twenty-four efficiencies and deluxe rooms with extras like coffeemakers, hair dryers, and whirlpool tubs. Outdoor pool, exercise room. Restaurant serves breakfast and lunch; sports bar lounge serves lunch. Shuttles to casino. $$$ –$$$$

Radisson Hotel New London–Mystic 35 Governor Winthrop Boulevard (860–443–7000). One-hundred twenty newly renovated deluxe rooms, including three suites with living areas, microwaves, fridges, and wet bars. Indoor pool and Jacuzzi. Restaurant, lounge. Complimentary transportation to Amtrak, ferries, casinos. $$$

Public Boat Launch

Thames River Access From I-95 exit 84, follow signs to Crystal Avenue and State Pier. Launch is directly under I-95 on the west side of the river. Parking for fifty cars; seasonal fee on weekends and holidays.

For Further Information

Trolley House Information Station in the public parking lot at the corner of Eugene O'Neill Drive and Golden Street (860–444–7264). Open 10:00 A.M. to 4:00 P.M. daily from June 15 to September 15 and on Friday through Sunday from May 1 through June 14 and September 16 through October 31. Maps, brochures, directions, information on lodging, attractions, restaurants. The station can also lend visitors an audiocassette and booklet for a self-guided driving tour of New London historic sites; ask for the Thames River Valley Heritage Tour prepared by the New London Historical Society.

Southeastern Connecticut Chamber of Commerce 1 Whale Oil Row, New London 06320 (860–443–8332).

Groton

With a good imagination, you can see that Groton must once have been a thoroughly beautiful place, with its wooded uplands sweeping down from the northern hills to the raggedy-edged quasi-peninsula formed by the Thames River to the west, Long Island Sound to the south, and the smaller Mystic River to the east. Raggedy because of its many coves and smaller estuaries near the Sound, the Groton area was a favored summer encampment of the Pequots, a savvy group who enjoyed the bounty of the sea as much for its savory nutritive value as for its economic value: Control of the shellfish beds and the shells used as trading wampum was among the many reasons that the Pequots were the most powerful tribe of the Algonkian people.

Unfortunately for nearly all concerned, the fierce Pequots had already made more than a few enemies by the time Dutchman Adriaen Block came on the scene in 1614. When the Dutch began trading with the Pequots for furs, some nasty confrontations between the Pequots, the other tribes, and the Europeans ensued. Far from benign, the Pequots took on the Dutch and English settlers and the natives alike, and the English took it upon themselves to rid the land of the warrior tribe that threatened their peace, safety, and prosperity. Soon the salty

NATIONAL SUBMARINE MEMORIAL

In honor of the 3,600 American seamen who lost their lives in U.S. submarines in World War II, a memorial monument has been placed near the banks of the Thames River in Groton, the last place where many of the men touched dry land. A moving reminder of their sacrifice, the polished black granite wall of honor includes fifty-two plaques, one for each lost sub, each one engraved with the names of its lost men. The V-shaped monument stands next to the conning tower of the USS *Flasher*, a World War II sub that had the most successful patrols of all subs employed during the war. Close to the Thames Street docks and marinas, the monument is at the corner of Bridge and Thames Streets and is accessible at no charge year-round.

AVERY POINT AND GROTON LONG POINT

Among the shore areas offering beautiful views of the Sound are Avery Point on the western side of the city and Groton Long Point toward the east. **Avery Point** is the place where the University of Connecticut has its marine science institute and where the *Enviro-Lab* boats depart for exploration of the Sound. The campus is largely open to the public. A gazebo and picnic tables overlook the water, and visitors are welcome to use the public areas for picnicking, biking, in-line skating, and walking. To find the campus, take Benham Road south 1.5 miles to the campus entrance off Shennecossett Road.

Groton Long Point, accessible from Groton Long Point Road (Route 215), is one of Connecticut's prettiest shore points. Largely residential, the area can be toured by car, but strictly limited parking makes the area much more easily accessible to walkers and bikers. Shore Avenue, South Shore Avenue, East and West Shore Avenues, and Sound Breeze Avenues are the main thoroughfares in this pristine enclave of sun-washed cottages. **East Beach, Main Beach**, and **South Beach** are open to all visitors, but cars must have stickers indicating their membership in the Groton Long Point Association. Day-trippers will have to walk in or bicycle in after leaving their cars elsewhere. Some people park at the **Esker Point Beach** just before Groton Long Point. From late May to September, you can stop for a casual meal at the **Point Spa Luncheonette** (860-572-1567) at the Casino, a 1920s gambling house that now houses the Groton Long Point post office, police station, and community activity rooms. You might find a place or two to park out front if you're here just for a quick bite. If you feel the need to linger, call Jennifer at the **Shore Inn** (860-536-1180), a B&B right on the water at 54 East Shore Avenue.

tides of the Sound were flooded with the bloodshed of hundreds, as the Pequot fort on the Mystic River was attacked at dawn in the spring of 1637 by an army under the command of Captain John Mason of the Connecticut Colony. The massacre of nearly the entire tribe of more than 600 Pequot men, women, and children cleared the way for the English development of the peninsula.

In 1646 John Winthrop of the Massachusetts Colony established a settlement on the western bank of the Thames and named it, astonishingly, Pequot Plantation. Groton developed simultaneously on the eastern bank. Soon the pretty vistas down the Thames River were forever changed as wharves, warehouses, and mills sprang up on both banks. Groton piers rang with the sounds of wooden boat building, and Groton seamen sailed to all corners of the globe in search of whale oil and seal furs.

In 1868, 112 acres at the eastern edge of the Thames became a federal navy yard, and in World War I it was officially commissioned as a submarine base. For much of the last century, Groton, often called the Submarine Capital of the World, has been most famed as the home of the Electric Boat Division of General Dynamics, the leading designer and manufacturer of nuclear submarines.

Less well known is Groton's marine science institute on the University of Connecticut's campus at Avery Point and its huge complex of Pfizer pharmaceutical corporation facilities. Groton also is the site of two state-owned land and wildlife conservation areas—a tribute to the efforts of Groton citizens and the state of Connecticut to preserve and protect the open space that reminds visitors of Groton's beauty as a coastal town.

The Best of Groton

USS Nautilus *Memorial and Submarine Force Museum*

A visit to Groton has to include a visit to the USS *Nautilus,* the world's first nuclear submarine and now a National Historic Landmark. The USS *Nautilus* Memorial near the submarine base on Route 12 includes tours of the *Nautilus* and an award-winning museum that explores the history and technology of submarines.

Excellently presented in a state-of-the-art facility, the museum exhibits celebrate the achievements of the human mind in devising this technology. Visitors can stand in the re-created sub attack center and hear the sounds of battle. They can operate any of three working periscopes. They can watch films of submarine history, and they can explore four mini-subs outside and a variety of models inside. Many other outstanding exhibits explain the important uses of the submarine both in defense and underwater exploration.

THAMES RIVER FIREWORKS AND SAILFEST

If you can get to Groton and New London on the second weekend in July, your visit will coincide with the annual Sailfest, a three-day celebration of life on the water. Sailing regattas, musical entertainment, boat shows, craft shows, a flea market, children's activities, a parade through historic New London, and much more are on the schedule that touches both cities on the Thames. Most activities center on New London's Bank and State Streets from noon on Friday, all day on Saturday, and from noon to 6:00 P.M. on Sunday.

The crowning event has to be the enormously popular and absolutely fantastic simulcast Grucci Brothers Fireworks Show. Sponsored by the Mashantucket Pequot Tribal Nation, the fireworks are launched from three barges in the middle of the Thames River. The second largest display in the United States (Macy's New York still beats 'em), this is a must-see show, but you have to like crowds. Groton's Fort Griswold State Park is the best viewing site; get there by 7:00 P.M. for the very best spots. Call for exact dates and further information (860–444–1879); if that number has changed, try the Southeastern Connecticut Chamber of Commerce (860–443–8332) or the Southeastern Connecticut Tourism District (800–863–6569).

Aboard the *Nautilus*, visitors explore the sonar and torpedo rooms and the navigation and control room, as well as the crew's living quarters, the galley, the captain's quarters, and much more. The impact of the huge size of the ship is somewhat lost due to the way it is moored to give visitors access, but once inside visitors will easily imagine life and work aboard this amazing vessel that explored beneath Arctic ice and the 20,000 leagues of the deep ocean.

Adjacent to the U.S. Naval Submarine Base on Crystal Lake Road off Route 12 (800–343–0079 or 860–449–3174). Open from May 15 to October 31, Wednesday through Monday 9:00 A.M. to 5:00 P.M. and Tuesday 1:00 to 5:00 P.M., and from November 1 to May 14, Wednesday through Monday 9:00 A.M. to 4:00 P.M. Closed the first full week of May and the last full week of October, plus Thanksgiving, Christmas, and New Year's Day. Handicapped access to the submarine is limited. Gift shop. Submarine Force research library open by appointment (860–694–3558). Free.

Fort Griswold Battlefield State Park and the Ebenezer Avery House

Revolutionary War buffs might want to visit this site of the 1781 massacre of American defenders under the command of William Ledyard by British troops under the command of Benedict Arnold. Originally, the square fort with 12-foot-high stone walls was surrounded by ditches on the high banks of the Thames River. When the British finally broke through the fortifications after several bloody assaults, Ledyard surrendered his sword to a Tory officer, who abruptly ran him through. The Patriot militiamen, who had also thrown down their arms, attacked the enemy with sheath knives and fists, but the British slaughtered dozens of them in a swift counterattack.

Today the site includes ramparts, battlements, and buildings dating from the Revolution as well as a 134-foot granite monument to the defenders. Climb the 166 stairs to the top of the obelisk for beautiful views of the river, the cities, and the countryside. When you descend, visit the museum that tells the full story of the battle. Other exhibits tell the history of early Groton and other areas of southeastern Connecticut. You may guide yourselves or ask to be accompanied by an interpretive guide (well worth it). Ask for the dates of the Revolutionary War reenactment in early September.

Also on the park grounds is the 1750 **Ebenezer Avery House**, which, in its original site on Thames Street, had been a repository for some of the wounded Patriots. The house was moved to the park in 1971. Its kitchen and weaving room are furnished as they might have been in the eighteenth century. Tours are also offered there.

Monument Street and Park Avenue (860–445–1729). Battlefield and fort ruins open daily year-round 8:00 A.M. to sunset. Picnic areas and rest rooms available. The Monument House Museum (860–449–6877) and the monument are open from Memorial Day to Labor Day 10:00 A.M. to 5:00 P.M. and from the weekend after Labor Day until Columbus Day on weekends only at the same hours. The Avery House (860–446–9257) is open only on weekends from Memorial Day to Labor Day 1:00 to 5:00 P.M. Free admission to all sites.

Bluff Point Coastal Reserve

Those who prefer to explore the shore on foot may do so at this 800-acre preserve. From the parking area on Depot Road, it might take up to a half-hour to walk the 1.5-mile main trail through upland forest to the rocky bluff for which the park is named. Below this headland lies a mile-long sand spit and a tidal salt marsh overlooking Mumford Cove, the Poquonnock River, and the Sound. Make your way through the colorful beach peas and roses in summer and early fall to enjoy saltwater fishing, shellfishing, beachcombing, swimming, snorkeling, and scuba diving at the narrow tombolo beach that curves to the west. No lifeguards are stationed here, and those who venture into the water do so at their own risk.

A wonderfully wild place from which to enjoy the sea, Bluff Point offers limited facilities. Pit toilets are the only amenities, so pack in your own drinking water, first-aid supplies, and snacks or picnic if you are planning on making the full hike out to the beach. No campfires or cooking fires are allowed in any part of the park.

You can horseback ride, hike, and mountain bike on side trails throughout the park, but no maps of the area are provided for visitors. Signage is fairly clear, but be sure you pack in water if you're trekking off the main trail. Tick repellent or proper clothing is a must for protection against deer ticks. The trails are sometimes used for cross-country skiing in the wintertime.

Folks who like life *on* the water, not in, can bring powerboats, Jet Skis, or sea kayaks and such to launch from the sand ramp near the park entrance.

Depot Road off Route 1 (go to the very end of Depot Road under the railroad overpass to reach the parking lot). Open year-round 8:00 A.M. to sunset at no charge. For information, call the rangers at Fort Griswold (860–445–1729) or the Monument House Museum (860–449–6877).

Haley Farm State Park

This 204-acre state park is on a former farm site at the north of Palmer Cove not far from Groton Long Point and the village of Noank. Signage near the park entrance and parking area explains the history of the site, and ruins of farm buildings adjacent to the parking area provide an intriguing incentive to get out of the car or off the bicycle to explore here a while. Trails lead throughout the park, and recreational use through the year includes hiking, running, and cross-country skiing. Bikers are also welcome to use the park trails, but they are urged to offer the right-of-way to joggers and walkers.

Bird-watchers and other nature lovers will appreciate the large variety of plant and animal life at this pretty, quiet place. Facilities are limited to portable toilets, so pack in whatever you might need. No cooking fires are allowed on the property.

Haley Farm Lane off Brook Street, which is off Groton Long Point Road (Route 215). For information, call the ranger at Fort Griswold (860–445–1729 or 860–449–6877). Open year-round 8:00 A.M. to sunset at no charge.

Boat Excursions and Charters

Project Oceanology. The lure of the sea may be irresistible in Groton. If so, head to the Institute of Marine Science at the Avery Point campus of the University of Connecticut, where you can board the 55-foot *Enviro-Lab* for a two-and-a-half-hour cruise called Project Oceanology. *Enviro-Lab's* instructors are marine scientists who accompany each group of about twenty-five passengers for an afternoon or morning of study. Passengers measure and record data about the geology and biology observed; learn the uses of nautical charts and navigation instruments; collect and test water, mud, and sand samples; and pull trawl nets and examine the plants and animals swept from the bottom. All the while, the crew and captain provide a wonderfully interesting narration about the islands, lighthouses, and watercraft that surround your area of exploration.

In summer, wear sunscreen or a hat and sneakers, and bring a sweatshirt or windbreaker. In winter, dress appropriately for cold weather. Project Oceanology's headquarters are in a waterfront laboratory building near its boat docks. A seawater aquarium system, classrooms, a library, several labs, and a hostel are housed there, and a cafeteria where visitors can purchase snacks and lunches is available to daytrippers. You can also picnic on the campus before or after a cruise if you bring your own makings.

Inquire also about the seal observation cruises in the wintertime. Usually offered, weather permitting, in February and March, these cruises feature the harbor seals that inhabit the Sound in cold weather. Some folks may also be interested in the walking tour of the still-operating New London Ledge lighthouse in the middle of New London Harbor; call for details on this special cruise.

104 Shennecossett Road, at foot of Benham Road, Avery Point Campus of UConn (call 800–364–8472 between 9:00 A.M. and 4:00 P.M.). Web site: www.oceanology.org. Public oceanography cruises from mid-June to Labor Day at 10:00 A.M. and 1:00 P.M. Seal watching cruises, February through April, weekends only. Adults $18, children under 12 $12. Reservations strongly recommended; Visa or MasterCard required to hold reservation.

Captain Bob's See Submarines by Boat Cruises Thames Harbour Inn and Marina, 193 Thames Street (860-434-5681). *Captain Bob II* expeditions cruise upriver and down for fairly close-up views of the submarine base and the world's first nuclear-powered submarine, the USS *Nautilus,* plus the U.S. Coast Guard Academy and its tall ship, the bargue *Eagle,* the high-speed ferries, and the Electric Boat facilities. Cruises depart hourly Tuesday through Friday 11:00 A.M. to 3:00 P.M. and Saturday and Sunday 11:00 A.M. to 6:00 P.M. Adults $9.00, seniors $8.00, children 5 to 15 $3.00, children under 5 free. Free parking at the dock. Romantic evening cruises and fishing trips also available, by charter only.

Hel-Cat II Hel-Cat Dock, 181 Thames Street (860-535-2066 or 860-445-5991). Web site: www.helcat.com. Captain Brad Glas offers fishing trips for striped bass and bluefish in summer (daily from June through October) and for cod, pollock, mackerel, blackfish, sea bass, and more in winter and spring (weekends and holidays from January through May) on a 114-foot party boat. No reservations required. Leaves Groton at 9:00 A.M., returns 3:00 P.M. Adults $30; children 12 and under half-fare. Rental tackle $5.00; bait provided; help and instruction from deck technicians. Non-fishing adults pay half-fare; nonfishing children pay $5.00. Onboard restaurant and rest rooms. Night fishing and evening charters for private parties also available.

Places to Eat in Groton

The Fisherman 937 Groton Long Point Road (860-536-1717). Very popular for its views and its classic American seafood dishes, this establishment at the entrance to Groton Long Point Road between Palmer Cove and the Sound serves fresh fruits of the sea, steaks, poultry, and pasta in the main dining room. Lighter fare, including fish platters, sandwiches, chowders, and salads, is served in the lounge. Be sure to share a piece of the house signature dessert: chocolate peanut butter pie. Outdoor seating in season. Open year-round daily for lunch and dinner from 11:30 A.M. $-$$

Octagon 625 North Road (860-326-0360). Sleek and sophisticated, this new restaurant in the Mystic Marriott Hotel specializes in top-quality steaks grilled to perfection on its 16-foot octagonal open-flame exhibition grill. A Roy Carruthers painting called *Le Sommelier* sets the tone and complements the climate-controlled wine display in the dining area. Excellent appetizers and sides match the superior touch shown in the steak and seafood dishes; chef Sean Dutson is the expert in charge of your complete satisfaction. Open daily for lunch and dinner. $$$-$$$$

Paul's Pasta Shop 223 Thames Street (860–445–5276). Specializing in freshly made-in-house pastas and pasta companions, this marvelous pasta shop with full-service restaurant offers a lunch and dinner menu of cold and hot pasta specials with seafood, meat, poultry, and vegetarian toppings, plus garlic bread, several salads, a fresh house-made soup daily, and a great selection of desserts. Wine and beer. Open daily 11:00 A.M. to 9:00 P.M. $

Places to Stay in Groton

Best Western/Olympic Inn 360 Route 12 (860–445–8000 or 800–528–1234). One hundred forty rooms, three suites); restaurant, lounge, health club, sauna. $$$$

Groton Inn and Suites 99 Gold Star Highway (Route 184) (860–445–9784 or 800–452–2191). One hundred fifteen units, with ten efficiencies and twenty-five suites; in-room refrigerators, TV; restaurant, lounge. Senior rates. $$–$$$$

Shore Inn 54 East Shore Avenue (860–536–1180). Seasonal B&B in Groton Long Point; five immaculate but casually comfortable guest rooms, each with a private bath, in a beautiful setting directly on the water. Continental breakfast with homemade treats and fresh fruits. Passes to three other beaches in walking distance; bring a fishing pole. $$$

Thames Inn and Marina 193 Thames Street (860–445–8111). Twenty-six efficiencies; overnight and seasonal boat dockage on the Thames River. Fishing. Senior rates. $$$

The Sojourner Inn 605 Gold Star Highway (Route 184) (860–445–1986 or 800–MY-SUITE). Forty-five rooms of varied sizes, all with kitchenettes, some with Jacuzzis and suitelike floor plans; pull-out couches for extra guests. Laundry room, valet dry cleaning, passes to community exercise center. Continental breakfast. Kids under 12 stay free; senior rates. $$–$$$$

Mystic Marriott Hotel and Spa 625 North Road (860–446–2600; 866–449–7390). Enormous new 285-room hotel; luxury appointments, indoor pool, Octagon restaurant, lounge, Elizabeth Arden day spa, health club, much more. $$$$

Public Boat Launches

Bluff Point State Park Route 1 to Depot Road; go to end of Depot Road under the railroad overpass. Sand ramp with direct access to Long Island Sound, just inside park entrance.

Bayberry Lane Long Island Sound access off I–95 exit 87 to Route 349 (also called Clarence Sharp Highway), which becomes Shennecossett Road. Follow this road south to a left on Bayberry Lane. Parking for sixty-five cars. Seasonal fee weekends and holidays.

Mystic River Long Island Sound and river access for cartop/carry-in boats only. I–95 to Allyn Street exit or River Road north from downtown Mystic. Parking for eight cars; no fee.

Thames River Long Island Sound and river access from Bridge Street to a right on Fairview Avenue; Ken Streeter launch is on the left under the bridge. Parking for twenty-five cars; no fee.

Noank

One of Connecticut's most picturesque shoreline enclaves, 300-year-old Noank rivals Stonington for its qualities as an authentic New England seaside village. Quiet, narrow streets, historic buildings, lobster boats, and small shops and markets create the aura of a step back in time, while the cottages, marinas, pleasure boats, and barefoot children add to the beach-town atmosphere.

On a peninsula that juts out into Fishers Island Sound at the mouth of the Mystic River, Noank was once a summer encampment area of the Pequots, who controlled the extensive shellfish beds of the nearby estuaries. Later settled by English farmers who held a lottery in 1712 to draw their plots of land, Noank soon evolved into a shipbuilding, whaling, fishing, and maritime trade center. Today its harbor and coves are dotted with marinas and lobster pots, and the faces of its sun-kissed citizens are dotted with freckles. Perfect in summer, Noank is also lovely in winter and a veritable paradise on a warm afternoon in early fall.

A VILLAGE STROLL

Noank's streets are lined with an intriguing collection of nineteenth- and early twentieth-century houses and churches. Although signs of modernization are evident on some homes, old-fashioned details are far more apparent on beautifully restored and original structures ranging from neocolonial to Greek Revival to Victorian and other styles. Stroll wherever you can throughout town. Be sure to soak up the views from **Snake Hill**, which you'll reach from Palmer Court off Pearl Street. On a clear day, the vista is breathtaking, but even on hazy days you'll see far and wide across the water to Stonington, Watch Hill, Fishers Island, and more. On a walk through the mile-wide village, stop also to admire the 1843 **Noank Baptist Church** on the hilltop of Church Street. Wander as far as you can down to Morgan Point. Parts of this pretty area are private, including the beautiful black-capped stone lighthouse at its end, but walkers can look for the COASTAL PUBLIC ACCESS sign that shows where you can go to reach West Cove.

Before you head back to the present time period, take a memento of this lovely Brigadoon with you. Browsers and serious buyers alike may want to peruse the **Pratt Wright Galleries** (48 Main Street; 860-536-9243). Fine American landscapes and seascapes are among the beautiful works for sale here. Around the corner at the **Stone Ledge Art Gallery** (59 High Street; 860-536-7222), you may find an exhibit of the works of regional artists; call ahead to be sure a show is on the walls of this gallery, open since 1939. If you are here in lobster season, stop for some fresh beasts at the picturesque and much-photographed **Ford's Lobster House** (860-536-2842) on Riverview Avenue. One of Connecticut's last wooden lobster boats brings you the Sound's finest crustaceans. You'll have to steam them yourself, but you won't forget Noank for a long time after you scrape the last morsel from each claw.

The Best of Noank

Latham-Chester Store Museum

Once a marine hardware store owned first by the Lathams and then by the Chesters, this restored structure near the foot of Main Street and close to the town landing is opened in the summertime for an annual exhibition by local artists. Oil and watercolor paintings and photographs

ON THE WATER

Recreational sailing and fishing are the primary water activities in Noank, but swimmers also can explore the quiet waters of protected Fishers Island Sound. **Esker Point Beach** (860-572-9702), near the elbow of Groton Long Point Road (Route 215) and Marsh Road, surely lies at one of the prettiest points on the Connecticut coast, with beautiful views of such islands as little Mouse Island just offshore and Fishers Island farther out in the Sound. A fine wading beach for children because of its shallow swimming area, Esker Point is actually not all that terrific for older swimmers because the water is rarely more than waist high. Still, for a day in the sun by the shore, Esker Point offers lots of sand, rest rooms, a snack concession (in season, Thursday through Sunday only), and a picnic area with hibachi-style grills so you can linger through a couple of meals to catch the sunset. Parking here costs $1.00 per vehicle. On Thursday evenings in the summertime, free concerts suitable for all ages are held at the beach at 6:30; parking for the concerts is $3.00.

Walkers may also want to check out the tiny beach at the **town dock** at the foot of Main Street. Slightly larger than a few good-sized beach blankets, it can also be a nice place to take a quick dip, or relax on benches while you soak up the view. The **Noank Play Area** in the park on Main Street and Ward Avenue has a children's playground and a picnic area perfect for taking a break from a village stroll. **Spicer Park** on Spicer Avenue (go back across the railroad bridge on Mosher Avenue to Route 215 and then a block to Spicer Avenue) overlooks pretty Beebe Cove and has grills and picnic areas open to all visitors. Beebe Cove is well known among bird-watchers, who say it is a fine spot for sighting nesting shorebirds and seabirds.

are among the works that are displayed. Call ahead to see what's on the current schedule.

108 Main Street (860–536–7026). Hours are usually limited to Wednesday, Saturday, and Sunday afternoons in the summertime (typically 1:00 to 4:00 P.M.) or at other times for special events; call ahead. Free.

Noank Historical Society

Maritime exhibits and local memorabilia are the focus at this social and marine history museum housed in the beach-stone-sheathed Grace Episcopal Church, built in 1902 to serve Noank's summer visitors. Among the many artifacts are hand-hewn tools and nautical gear. Exhibits focus on fishing methods and the Noank fishing industry, methods of building wooden boats, and the history of the Noank shipyards. Ask curator and Noank native Ken Hodgson about the adventures of Captain Dan Chester and the clipper ship *Dauntless,* the Noank single-room schoolhouse, and the Central Park obelisk that journeyed across the Atlantic in a specially outfitted Noank clipper ship.

Sylvan Street (860–536–7026) or call Ken Hodgson (860–536–3827). Open July 4 through October 12 on Wednesday, Saturday, and Sunday from 2:00 to 5:00 P.M. or by appointment. Free; donations gratefully accepted.

Boat Excursions and Charters

Coastline Yacht Club Eldridge Yard, Marsh Road (860–536–2689 or 800–749–7245). Twenty-two vessels for bareboat or skippered charters on classic motor or sailing vessels. Food and beverage services. Boat-and-breakfast accommodations available, with evening cruise, overnight lodging onboard back at the dock, and continental breakfast brought aboard in the morning.

All of the following charted fishing trips hold up to six passengers, and have captains licensed by the U.S. Coast Guard and registered by the State of Connecticut. **Trophy Hunter Sportfishing:** Captain Ron Helbig (860–536–4460), Noank Village Boatyard. Half- and full-day charters for inshore bass and bluefish or offshore tuna, shark, and marlin. See the whales while you fish. Experts and novices welcome; crew offers help, instruction. **Mataura and Mataura Lite:** Captain Tom McLaughlin (860–536–6970 or 800–605–6265), Riverview Avenue Dock. Saltwater fly-fishing for blues, bass, and bonita or deep-sea fishing for tuna and shark. Half- and full-day charters for up to six passengers. **Anna R.:** Captain Franklin Rathbun (860–536–0529), Rathbun's Dock. **First Light:** Captain Bob Romeo (860–632–8455), Noank Shipyard. **Magic:** Captain Art Goodwin (860–429–9276), Spicer's Noank Marina. **Flying Fish:** Captain Thomas Shipman (860–886–1838), Spicer's Marina.

Places to Eat in Noank

Carson's Store 43 Main Street (860–536–0059). Pull a stool across black-and-white floor tiles to the Formica counter of this market-cum-luncheonette and order freshly made-to-order American favorites like egg sandwiches and French toast or a frosty malt or milkshake. Established in 1907 to provide "Ice Cream, Coffees, Sundries, and Conversation," Carson's is also the place to buy a copy of *National Fisherman* or penny candy, post-cards, or a souvenir sweatshirt. The charm and friendly service are free to all patrons. Open year-round daily; summer hours are 6:00 A.M. to 8:00 P.M., winter 6:00 A.M. to 5:00 P.M. Free entertainment on the front porch every Friday evening at 6:00 from late June to late August. Bring a folding chair and a picnic or buy one of Carson's Friday-night dinner specials. $

Mystic River Baking Company 19 Pearl Street (860–536–0182). Once the home of the Noank post office, owner Liz Prete's bakery is open from 7:00 A.M. to 5:30 P.M. Monday through Friday and until 3:00 and 1:00 P.M. respectively on Saturday and Sunday. Come early to buy break-fast, lunch, and dinner fare to go. Great baked goods and beach and pic-nic treats. Choose breakfast and lunch sandwiches, incredible pies and scratch-made breads, soups and salads. Liz keeps tourists and villagers well-fed from March 1 through December 31. $

Abbott's Lobster in the Rough 117 Pearl Street (860–536–7719). Fifty-plus years of extraordinary seaside ambiance with views of fisher-men, bobbing sailboats, and the offshore islands. Eat out in the breeze and sun on picnic tables, under the striped tent, or inside the casual dining room. Lobsters, steamers, oysters, steamed-in-the-husk corn on the cob, seafood sandwiches, barbecued chicken, and classic strawberry shortcake. Bring your own bottle. Open May through Labor Day, noon to 9:00 P.M. daily, then weekends only (including Fridays) through Columbus Day from noon to 7:00 P.M. $–$$

The Seahorse 65 Marsh Road (860–536–1670). A local favorite tucked near Spicer's Marina, this seafood restaurant doesn't have the same views as Abbott's, but it doesn't have the crowds either. It serves fresh catch of the day from scallops to lobster, plus lots of other shore dinner choices. Sandwiches, salads, chowder, and meat dishes. Open for lunch and dinner daily from 11:00 A.M. to 10:00 P.M. $$

Costello's Clam Company Pearl Street (860–572–2779). Right on the dock at the Noank Shipyard, this casual, all-outside-seating establishment operated by Abbott's is the place to come for mostly fried seafood, a twin lobster special (two one-pounders for $13.99), steamed shrimp and clams, chicken sandwiches, raw bar, chowder, and other such shoreline fare for lunch and dinner daily from noon to 9:00 P.M., from late May through Labor Day. $–$$

Universal Food Store 17 Pearl Street (860-536-3767). In business the better part of a century, this is a great, old-fashioned place to stop for fresh produce, salads, grinders, calzones, strombolis, deli meats, beverages, fresh pizza, and lasagna. Open year-round on Friday and Saturday from 8:00 A.M. to 8:00 P.M. and until 7:00 P.M. the rest of the week. $

Public Boat Launch

Mystic River Access to river and Fishers Island Sound. From I-95 exit 89, go south on Allyn Street, then take the first left on Sandy Hollow Road. At the end, take a left on High Street and take the next right on Bindloss Road. At its end, take a left on River Road. Launch is on the west bank of the Mystic River, just north of I-95. Cartop/carry-in boats only. Parking for eight cars. No fee.

For Further Information

Town Parks and Recreation Department (860-441-6777).

Mystic

Rich in history that harks back to the earliest days of the Connecticut Colony, Mystic is a community that has witnessed the first of the painful compromises between settler and native, the glory days of whaling and shipbuilding, the rise of industrialization and the decline of agriculture. Throughout nearly three centuries, Mystic has remained a vital community that comprises diverse citizens engaged in the simple craft of building an American tradition.

For many years in this century, Mystic has been a tourist destination, most notably because of Mystic Seaport, arguably the nation's most outstanding maritime history museum. Now home to other notable attractions, Mystic is a destination for more tourists than ever before in its existence. Even its wonderful downtown, until somewhat recently unknown to out-of-towners, is now a thriving center enjoyed by tourists as well as townies.

The Best of Mystic

Mystic Seaport, The Museum of America and the Sea

The first stop in Mystic for most visitors, the seaport's seventeen acres of historic buildings and re-creations represent a nineteenth-century New England whaling and shipbuilding village. An incredible array of educational and entertainment activities are offered here throughout the year. From rope-making to printing to oystering, from sailor to chandler to merchant, the arts, crafts, and occupations of an early American seaport are celebrated.

Among the major exhibits are the *Charles W. Morgan*, the last surviving wooden American whaling ship; the 1882 training vessel *Joseph Conrad*; and the *L. A. Dutton*, a 1921 fishing schooner. In the winter months (generally November through April), visitors may also see and board the *Amistad*. A permanent exhibit on the re-creation of this vessel is displayed at the Shipyard Gallery; an exhibit on the *Amistad* incident is in the gallery of the P.R. Mallory Building. (See the New Haven chapter for the story of this vessel or visit the Web site www.amistadamerica.org. During the summer months, the *Amistad*'s home port is New Haven.)

Horse and buggy rides, planetarium shows, sea chantey sing-alongs, chowder festivals, lantern-light holiday dramas, tall ship tours, hands-on activities of all sorts, and an outstanding calendar of special events are parts of the key to the Seaport's success. Summer camps, living history workshops, lectures for children and adults, boat excursions, concerts, and much more are among the opportunities for families and individuals. After your adventures, shop in the Seaport's excellent five-part museum shop for a memento of your trip. The Galley restaurant provides very casual fare for on-site dining.

75 Greenmanville Avenue (Route 27) off I–95 exit 90 (860–572–5315). The Seaport is open year-round, daily except for Christmas Day. From April through

BELUGA ENCOUNTER

The Mystic Aquarium now offers a program that allows the public to swim with its whales. Adventurers 5 feet tall and over can make arrangements to spend time in the pool with the aquarium's beluga whales. An expensive adventure for most families, it may still be a once-in-a-lifetime experience worth the splurge to animal lovers. Call the aquarium for more details on this exciting program.

October, the schedule is 9:00 A.M. to 5:00 P.M.; from November through March, 10:00 A.M. to 4:00 P.M. Adults $17.00; children 6 through 12 $9.00; 5 and under free. Second consecutive day is free.

Mystic Aquarium and Institute for Exploration

The redesigned and expanded Mystic Aquarium is busy establishing itself as the premier aquarium of the Northeast. Twenty-four new or newly renovated exhibits represent the trio of "islands" of marine life found across the globe: the estuaries, the coral reefs, and the upwelling zones. From a New England tidal marsh to a brand-new 30,000-gallon coral reef re-creation to the Roger Tory Peterson penguin paradise, indoor and outdoor exhibits focus on 6,000 fascinating mammals, fish, and invertebrates of the sunlit seas, with a focus on the vital importance of all the essential elements of a healthy ocean ecosystem. The outdoor seal and penguin exhibits are exceptional representations of the animals' natural habitats. The first has been designed to reflect the habitats of northern fur seals and Steller's sea lions of the North Pacific Pribilof Islands. The latter allows visitors to see both above and below water in the African black-footed penguin rookery. The newly renovated skylit marine theater, World of the Dolphin, allows staff marine biologists to demonstrate the dramatic talents and capabilities of Atlantic bottlenose dolphins.

From the deep, dark ocean to the sunny California coast, visitors now make an entertaining and educational journey across the planet, gaining throughout an understanding of the interrelatedness of all life. Conserving Our Oceans exhibits highlight those species facing particular pollution and habitat destruction issues. A viewing window into the veterinary care lab gives visitors a close-up look at the work of aquarium scientists. The aquarium has an exciting relationship with underwater

explorer Robert Ballard in the Institute for Exploration, which intro-
duces visitors to undersea technology, oceanographic exploration, and
marine archaeology.

The aquarium has a new cafe and an excellent gift shop/bookstore,
which shoppers may browse without an admission ticket. Workshops,
classes, and special events are held throughout the year.

*55 Coogan Boulevard, off I–95 exit 90 (860-572-5955). Open daily (except
New Year's Day, Thanksgiving, and Christmas). Admissions from 9:00 A.M. to 5:00
P.M., visitors may remain until 6:00 P.M. (Visitors may remain until 7:00 P.M. in
summer.) Adults $16.00, seniors $12.00, children 3 to 12 $11.00, 2 and under free.*

Downtown Mystic

A few years back only the locals knew the secrets of the "real" historic center of Mystic. Now the whole downtown area rocks and rolls with the
tourist crowd that has discovered the inner core of the village. If your
appetite for the sea has simply been whetted by the sights upriver, head
downtown to Route 1 via Route 27 and the famed counterweighted bas-
cule drawbridge that leads you to picturesque Mystic center. Linger awhile
on the bridge itself (park the car somewhere else first) and watch the jelly-
fish and other flotsam on their way to beautiful Fishers Island Sound. Stay
to see the hourly raising of the bridge and the passage of the yachts and
sailboats as they cruise up or down the river. Then stroll the boutiques,
the art galleries, the bookstores, the candy shops, the restaurants.

This wonderful village encapsulates a unique blend of old and new.
Discover your own favorite places, but be sure to linger a while at the
Mystic River Park, the incredible Mystic Army Navy Store, the excellent
Mystic Art Association Museum and Gallery (9 Water Street;
860-536-7601), the fanciful as well as practical Emporium, the Mystic
Drawbridge Ice Cream Company, and the incomparable Sea Swirl
seafood shack. You'll find them all easily in the 1-mile historic district.
If you can, come in mid-August for the famed **Outdoor Art Festival**
(860-572-5098), a two-day juried show of 300-plus artists who bring
their wares from all parts of the nation to the sidewalks, parks, and
riverbanks of downtown Mystic. The most beautiful of all annual
events that can be enjoyed south of the Seaport and downtown is the
Antique and Classic Boats Rendezvous (860-572-5315) in late July.
Sponsored by the Seaport, this colorful reunion of restored wooden
power and sailboats built before the 1950s features a Sunday parade
downriver of all the boats and their authentically costumed crews.

West and East Main Street (Route 1), Water Street, Bank Street, Pearl Street, and other nearby streets.

Olde Mistick Village

A mere shopping center built as a re-creation of a circa-1720 New England village, this complex contains pretty paths, reproduction free-standing shops, and ponds, fences, stone walls, and waterwheels that all make for a very pleasant shopping experience. Franklin's General Store and Elizabeth and Harriet's Fine Handcrafts are personal favorites among the sixty-plus restaurants, tea shops, jewelry, clothing, and toy shops, and gourmet coffee and chocolate shops here.

Olde Mistick Village is especially pretty in summer when its ponds are busy with waterfowl, its gazebo is the site of free concerts, and its flowers and trees are in bloom. During December the village and its New England church replica are aglow with holiday light displays, and complimentary festivities and promotions in individual shops lure cheerful holiday shoppers along the luminaria-lined pathways.

At the junction of Route 27 and Coogan Boulevard (860–536–4941), immediately adjacent to the Mystic Aquarium. Open year-round Monday through Saturday from 10:00 A.M. to 6:00 P.M. and Sunday from noon to 5:00 P.M. Summer and holidays hours are often extended.

Denison Pequotsepos Nature Center

If you need a break from marine and historical themes, visit this 125-acre preserve with 7 miles of trails through woods and meadows and past ponds. Wildflower and fern gardens are among the areas created to encourage home owners to create their own similar backyard habitats. Here you may see otter, mink, and other mammals native to southeastern Connecticut, plus 150 species of birds, including bluebirds and scarlet tanagers.

A trailside natural history museum includes indoor native wildlife exhibits and outdoor flight enclosures for non-releasable raptors. You'll have a look at a great horned owl and other live birds of prey. The Trading Post gift shop sells field guides, children's books, birding supplies, great natural science materials for children, and locally made items like painted walking sticks and hinged birdhouses with peek-in windows. A full schedule of guided walks, summer camps for children ages 3 to 16, birding activities, and field trips can be obtained at the natural history museum.

The nature center also owns the Peace Sanctuary on River Road on the western bank of the Mystic. Atop rocky ledges, this wooded, thirty-acre preserve offers trails overlooking the river. Ask for directions when you visit the main center. Open at no charge from dawn to dusk, it is well named and especially lovely to explore during the early morning and close to dusk, when the birds are most active and visible.

109 Pequotsepos Road (follow Coogan Boulevard to its eastern end, turn right on Jerry Browne Road, then right on Pequotsepos) (860-536–1216). Open year-round Monday through Saturday from 9:00 A.M. to 5:00 P.M. and Sunday from 1:00 to 5:00 P.M. Adults $6.00, children 6 to 12 $4.00, 5 and under free. Trails open dawn to dusk; leave a donation in the box. Cross-country skiers welcome, weather permitting. Pets, leashed, are welcome; picnicking is allowed.

Boat Excursions and Charters

Mystic Whaler Cruises If you have the time and the money, these just may be the cream of the crop in terms of boat excursions along the entire Connecticut coastline. The cruise options are varied to suit nearly any desire, the schooner is an awe-inspiring 110-foot beauty carrying 3,000 square feet of sail, and the crew cheerfully invites both landlubbers and skilled show-offs to hoist the sails, plot the course, or take a turn at the wheel. If you can spring for an overnight sea trek, you

LAMPLIGHT TOURS AT THE SEAPORT

During the month of December (call 860-572-5315 for the exact schedule) Mystic seaport offers lantern-light tours that reenact the scenarios that may have enlivened a similar town of the nineteenth century at holiday time long ago. Costumed reenactors set the scenes in a dozen or so sites throughout the village. You and your family eavesdrop on the goings-on as your host or hostess leads you by lamplight through the darkened streets. You'll enter parlors and taverns and shops, and even go down to the crew's quarters on the whaler *Charles W. Morgan*. The wind may wail, rain may lash at your cheeks, or perhaps snow will fall lightly on your path, but it all merely enhances the special effect of these marvelous portrayals. Reservations are a must.

OTHER MYSTICAL ATTRACTIONS

Mystic County Fair Carousel and Fun Center 193 Greenmanville Avenue (Route 27) (860-572-9949). Need to satisfy the urge to ride a carousel? This family entertainment center (read noisy, busy pay-as-you-play amusement arcade) has a full-size operational carousel and antique band organ. Take a whirl! Open daily year-round.

Denison Homestead Museum Pequotsepos Road (860-536-9248). If the Seaport fails to satisfy a history craving, this unusual 1717 house might do the trick. Still owned by descendants of the Denison family and furnished with original Denison belongings, its rooms represent periods from the 1720s to the 1940s. Across the street from the Denison Pequot-sepos Nature Center, it is open from May through October; call for the current hours. Adults $4.00, seniors and students $3.00, children $1.00.

Portersville Academy 74 High Street (860-536-4779). This Greek Revival two-story schoolhouse with belfry, separate entrances for boys and girls, and a one-room school on the second floor is furnished as it was in 1840. The first floor, which resembles a courtroom, served as a district voting hall and now is used for changing exhibitions on topics of local historical interest. Open mid-May through mid-October on Tuesday 10:00 A.M. to noon, on Thursday noon to 3:00 P.M., and on the first and third Saturdays of the month from 11:00 A.M. to 3:00 P.M.; call for off-season hours.

Williams Beach Park at Mystic Community Center off Mason's Island Road (860-536-3575). Saltwater beach with playground, picnic and snack bar pavilions, grills, sports fields, and more. Open at no charge to visitors. Fitness center with Nautilus equipment and more (day-use passes $12.00 per person over the age of 14). Indoor pool (day-use passes $12.00 adult, $3.00 children). Beach open June to Labor Day; no lifeguards.

can choose from five accommodations options, including the tiny Sloop, the Great Room that gives a taste of life below decks for the common sailor, and the Clipper cabins that provide luxuries like sky-lights, private showers, and double beds.

Three-hour lobster dinner cruises include steamed lobster and fresh clam chowder served on deck under sail. Six-hour day sails include a hearty barbecue lunch, fresh off the onboard grill, served while cruising

Fishers Island Sound; if the wind is right, the trip includes a swim in a sheltered cove before returning to Mystic. Musicians are on board for nearly all cruises. Overnight sails of one, two, three, and five days include such ports of call as Mystic itself, Block Island, Shelter Island, Sag Harbor, Newport, Cuttyhunk, and Martha's Vineyard. Among the three-day specialty cruises are lighthouse cruises and whale-tale cruises. These maritime mini-vacations that Captain John Eginton plans to tempt you aboard include entertainment such as music and story-telling, lively narratives regarding regional lore and natural history, and all meals. You may have the adventure of a lifetime.

P.O. Box 189, Mystic 06355 (860–536–4218 or 800–697–8420) Web site: www.mysticwhaler.com. Sails May 1 to November 1; cruises range from $75 (for lobster-dinner cruises) to $1,095 (for overnight cruises) per person. Children 10 and older welcome on overnight voyages at full fare; children 5 to 10 welcome on day sails and evening cruises at half-fare. Reservations required. Cruises depart from 15 Holmes Street in Mystic.

Voyager Cruises The *Argia,* a replica nineteenth-century gaff-rigged schooner, takes passengers on two- or three-hour morning, afternoon, or evening sails in scenic Fishers Island Sound. Skippered by Captain Jodie Ferraro, this beautiful 81-foot white bird glides gracefully across the Sound's sheltered waters, providing a gentle ride that cannot fail to relax and refresh weary day-trippers.

Sunset cruises offered at twilight (6:00 to 8:10 P.M.) daily are the most romantic of the *Argia* options. The other daily public sails leave at 10:00 A.M. and 2:00 P.M. and last three hours and ten minutes each.

73 Steamboat Wharf (860–536–0416). Daily (weather permitting) from mid-April to mid-October at 10:00 A.M., 2:00 P.M., and 6:00 P.M. Adults $34 Monday through Friday afternoon, $36 Friday evening through Sunday; children under 18 pay $24 for weekdays, $26 on weekends; children under 2 sail for free. Seniors get a $3.00 discount off the adult fare. Reservations recommended.

Sail the Sounds (860–536–5486). Located at Mystic Shipyard, this American Sailing Association Training Center and Yacht Charter company offers bareboat or captained day rentals or extended cruises on a variety of U. S. Coast Guard–approved vessels. Fully equipped for family vacations, romantic getaways, or weekend outings. Fully licensed captains. See the Web site (www.sailthesounds.com) for descriptions of equipment, inventories, fares, and special events.

Sabino *Mystic River Cruises* The *Sabino* is the last coal-fired passenger steamboat in operation. Built in 1908 in East Boothbay, Maine, for passenger service on the Damariscotta River, it is now a working exhibit of the Seaport Museum. Board as the steam whistle calls passengers to the double decks for a cruise downriver. Watch the crew shovel anthracite coal into the glowing maw of the steam plant, then shift your gaze to the beautiful historic homes that grace the banks of the peaceful Mystic River. For the evening cruise, bring a picnic dinner aboard or ask about the boxed dinner and beverage service. Bring a sweatshirt or jacket and settle in for the hour-and-a-half journey down the river and into Fishers Island Sound.

Sabino Dock at Mystic Seaport; use the south parking lot across from the main Seaport entrance (860–572–5315). Call for rates and reservations after 10:00 A.M. Daily half-hour cruises leaving on the hour, from 11:00 A.M. to 4:00 P.M., from the third week in May to Columbus Day; extra cruises in midsummer. Adults $3.50, plus Seaport admission; children 6 to 12 $2.00, plus admission; children under 6 free. Evening cruises at 5:00 P.M. in early and late parts of the season; 7:00 P.M. in midsummer. Adults $8.50, children $7.00, no Seaport admission necessary for evening cruises.

Brilliant Mystic Seaport, 75 Greenmanville Road (860–572–5315). No experience is necessary to join the crew of this 61-foot schooner and try your hand at navigation, sail handling, and even onboard cooking (no easy feat!). Weekend programs are offered in spring and fall for adults; multi-day summer programs are open to youth.

Shaffer's Boat Livery 106 Mason's Island Road (860–536–8713). Rentals of 16-foot fiberglass skiffs with six-horsepower engines for exploring and fishing in Mystic River, Fishers Island Sound, Noank, and Stonington. Full selection of bait and tackle available. Ramp.

Sterling Yacht Charters 44 Water Street (860–572–1111). Traditional or contemporary yachts of nearly any size for private or corporate parties or cruises.

Places to Eat in Mystic

The Mooring 20 Coogan Boulevard in the Mystic Hilton (860–572–0731). One of the finest restaurants in Mystic is this nautically dressed establishment with a sophisticated ambiance and a sure-handed focus on seafood and steak. Among the continental and American dinners are its famed seafood pie, poultry and pasta specials, traditional veal and beef dishes, and inventive choices like duck strudel. Soundings Lounge. Breakfast and lunch also available. Open year-round daily for breakfast from 6:30 A.M., lunch from 11:30 A.M., and dinner from 5:30 P.M. $$$

The Flood Tide Junction of Route 1 and Route 27 (860–536–8140). For an exceptionally gracious dining experience on the picturesque grounds of the Inn at Mystic overlooking the harbor and the town, come to the Flood Tide for American cuisine with continental over-tones. Roast duckling, chateaubriand, rack of lamb Dijonaise, excellent pastas, and fresh seafood. Piano player at dinner nightly and on Sunday afternoons. Impressive and reasonably priced buffet breakfasts and luncheons and beautiful Sunday brunches. Patio seating in summer. Open daily year-round for breakfast from 7:00 A.M., lunch from 11:30 A.M., dinner from 5:30 P.M., and Sunday brunch 11:00 A.M. to 2:30 P.M. $$$$

Captain Daniel Packer Inne 32 Water Street (860–536–3555). In the eighteenth-century National Historic Register home of a Mystic whaling captain is this charming bi-level restaurant overlooking the Mystic River. The first-story pub is a cozy affair with a large fireplace that makes for a delightful winter afternoon here. Upstairs are two dining rooms and five more fireplaces. The fare is basically American with a few Asian touches. The house signature dish is its Steak Black Jack, a beautifully seared sirloin splashed with Jack Daniels. Duck, veal, and poultry share the spotlight. The pub menu features full dinners and lighter fare for lunch. Live jazz, blues, and pop in the pub on weeknights. Open year-round Monday through Sunday for lunch 11:00 A.M. to 4:00 P.M. and dinner 5:00 to 10:00 P.M. $$$–$$$$

Seamen's Inne Greenmanville Avenue, just outside the north entrance to the Seaport (860–536–9649). With a special Connecticut Yankee ambiance, this tavernlike restaurant is a great place for regional American seafood cuisine like shrimp Creole, Maryland crab cakes, and New England seafood potpie in a pastry-sealed crock. At dinnertime, lobster and prime rib probably outsell all of these, however. At lunch, soups, salads, stews, sandwiches, and seafood rolls are de rigueur. The Samuel Adams Pub offers beer and ale on tap and entertainment nightly. Come back for the popular Dixieland Sunday brunch, which offers southern-style fare. Open daily for lunch and dinner; Sunday brunch. Lunch $; dinner $$–$$$

Go Fish Corner of Coogan Boulevard and Route 27 in Olde Mistick Village shopping center (860-536-2662). Touted as the best new restaurant in New London County and one of the best seafood establishments in the state, Go Fish is a wonderfully imaginative, contemporary place. It offers an enormous sushi bar, a wine bar, and a coffee bar—as if the perfectly prepared seafood were not enough. Must-tries are the excellent seafood bisque and the superb bouillabaisse. Open for lunch Monday through Saturday 11:30 A.M. to 2:30 P.M., dinner Thursday through Saturday from 4:30 to 10:30 P.M., and Sunday through Wednesday from 4:30 to 9:30 P.M. $$-$$$:

Places to Stay in Mystic

The Inn at Mystic Junction of Routes 1 and 27 (860-536-9604 or 800-237-2415). Web site: www.innatmystic.com. Beautiful resort complex overlooking the town and the sea. Five suites in the inn, which is on the National Register of Historic Places; forty-seven rooms, suites, and efficiencies in the cream-of-the-crop motor inn; five fireplace rooms with a whirlpool in the gatehouse; and ultra-luxe rooms with balconies overlooking the harbor in the East Wing. Indoor and outdoor pools, Flood Tide restaurant, tennis, boating, exercise room, gardens. $$$$

Harbour Inne and Cottage 15 Edgemont Street (860-572-9253). At the edge of the Mystic River, this inn has four charming, air-conditioned guest rooms, each with a private bath and kitchen privileges. Common room with piano and fireplace; waterfront gazebo and picnic tables. Private three-room cottage with bedroom with two double beds and fireplace, fully equipped kitchen, living room with pullout couch, and furnished deck with hot tub. Pets are welcome. $$$-$$$$

Steamboat Inn 73 Steamboat Wharf (860-536-8300). This intimate establishment is right at the docks on the Mystic River and offers luxurious privacy just steps from all the activity at the heart of downtown. Each of the ten elegant rooms has a private bath and whirlpool; second-level rooms have fireplaces, dock-level rooms have small kitchens with refrigerators and coffeemakers. Fully air-conditioned. Continental-plus breakfast and afternoon sherry or tea in the Common Room. $$$-$$$$

Whaler's Inn 20 East Main Street (860-536-1506 or 800-243-2588). Beautiful white clapboard historic inn with forty-five comfortable and recently redecorated rooms right down by the bascule bridge. Homey ambiance; children stay free. Great restaurant called **Bravo Bravo** (860–536-3228) with an indoor dining room and outside terrace. Also the home of the C.C. Bagel Company. $$$–$$$$

Red Brook Inn 2750 Gold Star Highway, Old Mystic (860–572-0349). Web site: www.redbrookinn.com. This seven-acre country setting features the 1740s Haley Tavern and the 1770s Crary Homestead. Among the luxuries of nearly a dozen antiques-filled rooms are queen-size beds, whirlpool baths, and fireplaces. Large common areas, from cozy parlors to a game room and terrace. Full country-style breakfast and afternoon refreshments. $$$$

House of 1833 72 North Stonington Road (860–536-6325 or 800–367-1833). If you crave something close to splendor, come to this Greek Revival mansion. From the base of its tall columns to the top of its unusual cupola, the house has been impeccably restored and gorgeously decorated. It offers guest rooms with working fireplaces, luxe private baths, and some private porches. Tennis court, swimming pool, and bicycles. Gourmet breakfasts. $$$$

Pequot Hotel B&B 711 Cow Hill Road (860–572-0390). This inn was once an 1840s stagecoach stop; today it offers twenty-three wooded acres of solitude with three meticulously kept country-style guest rooms and suites. Among the varied luxuries are queen-size beds, fireplaces, and whirlpool baths. The two-bedroom suite with connecting bath works great for families. Your hostess provides a full country breakfast each morning. Nonsmoking. $$$$

Mystic Hilton 20 Coogan Boulevard (800–HILTONS). This imposing brick hotel perched on a hill near the aquarium and outlets has 184 rooms, some suites, an indoor pool, a fitness room, and an outstanding restaurant, The Mooring. Lots of special treatment for children. $$$$

Seaport Motor Inn Route 27 (860–536-2621). Practically a hotel, with 118 rooms on two levels, outdoor pool, nice grounds, lounge, and restaurant; reasonable rates considering the competition. $$–$$$

Best Western/Sovereign Hotel 9 Whitehall Avenue (800–363-1622). One hundred fifty units, restaurant, lounge, sauna, indoor pool. $$$

Comfort Inn Mystic 48 Whitehall Avenue (860–572-8531 or 800–572-3993). One hundred twenty units, health club, continental breakfast. Special packages available; complimentary shuttles. $$$

Days Inn Mystic 55 Whitehall Avenue (860-572-0574 or 800-572-3993). One hundred twenty-two units, restaurant, playground, outdoor pool. Inquire about packages and shuttles. $$$.

Residence Inn by Marriott 41 Whitehall Avenue (860-536-5150). Eighty suites with fully equipped kitchens, indoor pool, sport court, continental breakfast. $$$$.

Whitehall Mansion 42 Whitehall Avenue (860-572-7280). A recently restored historic home that has been made into an inn with five guest rooms with period furnishings, fireplaces, and modern baths with Jacuzzi tubs; complimentary wine, continental breakfast.

Old Mystic Inn 52 Main Street, Old Mystic (860-572-9422). Web site: www.oldmysticinn.com. Innkeeper Michael Cardillo knows what he's doing, and he's doing it all right. His inn's eight immaculate rooms are named for New England authors; all have queen-size beds and private baths; some have working fireplaces and whirlpool tubs. A lovely dining room is the site of delicious lamp-lit country breakfasts; the keeping room is a cozy place to read, play backgammon, and enjoy a fire. The grounds are restful and impeccable; stroll the gardens or sway in the hammock. Open year-round. Smoke-free. $$$$

Seaport Campgrounds Route 184, Old Mystic (860-536-4044). Out in the country away from the crowds is this family campground for tenters and RVs. Hookups for motorized campers; separate open and wooded sites for tents. Swimming pool, fishing pond, rec center, laundry, rest rooms and showers, playground, miniature golf, grocery store, wood, ice, dumping station. Open mid-March through late November. $

Public Boat Launch

Mystic River Access to river and Fishers Island Sound for carry-in/car-top boats only. Take River Road on the west bank of Mystic River to the parking area just north of the I-95 overpass. No fee.

For Further Information

Mystic River Historical Society 74 High Street, West Mystic (860-536-4779). The historical society has put together a wonderful small book of walking tours of historic sites. *Curbstones, Clapboards, and Cupolas* is available for $3.00 at the society's building on High Street, open Tuesday 9:00 A.M. to noon and on Wednesday and Thursday from noon to 3:00 P.M.; book also sold at the Mystic Public Library (860–536–7721) and Bank Square Bookstore (860–536–3795).

Mystic Chamber of Commerce 16 Cottrell Street (860–572–9578). Maps, brochures, and other helpful information. Boaters as well as shore explorers may want to ask for a copy of the *Mystic Waterfront Directory,* which provides a complete list of marinas, charter boats, liveries, and cruise operators in the Mystic area. Open year-round Monday through Friday 9:00 A.M. to 5:00 P.M., plus outdoor computerized visitor information center available 24 hours daily.

Mystic and Shoreline Information Center Building 1D, Old Mistick Village, Coogan Boulevard off Route 27, Mystic (860–536–1641). Open in summer season Monday through Saturday 9:00 A.M. to 6:00 P.M. and Sunday 10:00 A.M. to 6:00 P.M.; in the off-season, from September through April, the center closes one hour earlier.

Tourist Information Depot of Mystic Route 27, opposite the I–95 exit 90 southbound off-ramp (860–536–3505). Open 7:00 A.M. to 9:00 P.M. daily year-round. Stop here for discount coupons for area lodging and dining and discounted admissions to some local attractions.

SNET Visitor Information Center off exit 92 southbound on I-95 (860–599–2056). Open daily from Memorial Day to Columbus Day, 8:00 A.M. to 6:00 P.M.; 8:30 A.M to 4:30 P.M. the rest of the year.

Bed and Breakfasts of the Mystic Coast (860–892–5006). Reservations service for nearly thirty B&Bs in New London County and Westerly, Rhode Island.

Visit Mystic Web site www.visitmystic.com.

Stonington Borough, Stonington, and Pawcatuck

Bounded by the Mystic River on the west and the Pawcatuck River on the east is Connecticut's easternmost coastal town of Stonington. It includes a large part of what most folks think is the separate town of Mystic (but is not), a self-governing village called Stonington Borough, an area simply called Stonington, *and* the village of Pawcatuck. This guidebook deals with Mystic in another chapter. The collected parts of Stonington plus some lodgings in the town of North Stonington are the focus of this chapter's exploration of the eastern corner of the Connecticut shore.

Stonington Borough is the most beautiful and evocative of all Connecticut shore towns. Very quaint and very New England, it exists as if in a time warp. In Stonington Borough, it's easy to imagine the days of sea captains and West Indies trading ships.

Originally a farming community settled in 1649 by families from Plymouth Colony, Stonington was both a major whaling and sealing port and a shipbuilding town throughout the first three-quarters of the nineteenth century. In the last quarter of the century, its graceful wooden clipper ships were replaced by steamships, and the look of Stonington Harbor changed as the maritime industry decreased and the tourist industry grew. When the railroad built bridges over the rivers and began interstate rail lines linking the cities, bustling Stonington changed again. For a while, the local fishing fleet had the whole port to itself, but soon pleasure boaters began to share this pretty harbor.

Today, Connecticut's only remaining commercial fleet docks in Stonington along with the recreational boaters, and Stonington can still appear stuck in time if you overlook the expensive yachts with high-tech equipment. In the cozy village laid out neatly in 1752, the eighteenth- and nineteenth-century houses cuddled nearly gable to gable offer a glimpse backward to a time when every citizen was well-acquainted with his or her neighbors, and merchants catered to a clientele whose needs and preferences were well known and discreetly met.

Outside of Stonington Borough is the remaining town of Stonington, a little less evocative but nonetheless picturesque. East of the main town is the village of Pawcatuck, nearly in Rhode Island. Inland is the separate town of North Stonington, off the shore path but linked in spirit to the quiet way of life that city visitors may yearn for nostalgically. Come in all seasons to savor the peaceful pleasures of coastal country life.

The Best of Stonington Borough

Once you have crossed the Route 1A bridge to the borough, park anywhere and just stroll. The whole of Stonington is not that small, actually, but its borough is a great place for walking. Weave your way down narrow Water Street, stopping at the shops and galleries as you wander. Stop at **Cannon Square** to see the marker that commemorates the success of the Stonington militia in repelling the British attack on Connecticut during the War of 1812, then rest a while at a cafe or coffeehouse. Enjoy the model railroad that re-creates the setting of the Stonington Line Railroad and the town dock as they appeared in the mid-1800s; the display is in the **Anguilla Gallery** (72 Water Street) and is open to the public from 10:00 A.M to 5:00 P.M. daily year-round.

Shoppers may want to peruse hand-painted French pottery at **Quimper Faience** (141 Water Street; 860-535-1712; open Monday through Saturday 9:00 A.M. to 5:00 P.M.) or the used collection of volumes at **Battersea Books** (106 Water Street; 860-535-1622; open Wednesday through Sunday 11:00 A.M. to 5:00 P.M. or by appointment). Antiques collectors may want to search shops like Ronald Noe's **Grand and Water Antiques** (860-535-2624); **Neil Bruce Eustace Antiques** (Water Street; 860-535-2249); or, a bit farther afield, the **Stonington Antique Center** (71 Cutler Street; 860-535-8373). If you are here in summer, stop to smell the roses—literally. The borough overflows with flower beds and window boxes.

Old Lighthouse Museum

Inside the stone lighthouse at the foot of the village are six rooms displaying whaling and fishing equipment, swords and cannonballs and other instruments of defense, nineteenth-century portraits, and much more. One exhibit focuses on the wonderful treasures brought back to Stonington by the captains of the China trade route. Another shows a

THE BATTLE OF STONINGTON

In 1814 the residents of Stonington were heavily invested in their bustling village. As Patriots, they had successfully thwarted the attack of the British on their harbor during the Revolution, and they had settled down right tidily to their lives as *American* shipbuilders, sailors, farmers, merchants, and tradesmen. When the Brits showed up again in August of 1814 and blockaded Long Island Sound, the Stonington townsfolk were not about to take any guff. With five ships in the harbor carrying a total of 160 guns, British captain Thomas Hardy sent a note ashore to the Americans, warning them that they had one hour to leave town before the village would be bombarded. The feisty Stonington folk stayed exactly where they were and planned to defend their beloved homes with the town's three cannons. A three-day volley between ship and shore began, and in the end, with their own paltry supply of munitions boosted by backup shipments of cannonballs from New London, the Stonington defenders drove out the British and returned to their farming, shipbuilding, and whaling. At Cannon Square, a granite monument topped with British cannonballs commemorates the victory, and one of the cannons used in the Battle of Stonington still faces the sea—just in case.

collection of antique shoes found in the walls of old houses to protect them from evil spirits. The antique dollhouse, decoys, toys, and model ships are often especially interesting to children.

You can learn about the history of Stonington and its role in the War of 1812. You can discover the history of the lighthouse itself—the first one in Connecticut, commissioned in 1823 by the U.S. government and rebuilt in 1840. Learn the details of the railroad that once transferred passengers from luxury liners to river steamboats, and climb the stone staircase of the lighthouse tower for a view of the harbor.

7 Water Street (860–535–1440). Web site: www.stoningtonhistory.com. Open daily in July and August from 11:00 A.M. to 5:00 P.M.; open in May, June, September, and October from Tuesday through Sunday at the same hours. Adults $4.00, children 6 to 12 $2.00. Combination tickets to this and the Palmer House are $6.00 and $3.00, respectively.

Captain Nathaniel B. Palmer House

Home of the discoverer of Antarctica and his equally adventurous brother, this mid-nineteenth-century mansion at the far north end of the village has sixteen rooms filled with the clever architectural design work of the crafty captain himself. Better known for their success in the China trade and Nat's discovery of the southernmost continent in 1820 in the sloop *Hero* while on a sealing expedition, Nathaniel Palmer and his brother Alexander filled their elegant home with a variety of innovations and contraptions that intrigue young and old visitors. Lively stories told by the docents tell of the many adventures of clipper ship designer Nat and daring Alexander; the tours take one hour. Be sure to climb to the top of the home's octagonal cupola to have a look at the glorious view of Stonington Harbor that allowed the residents to identify the sailing ships that approached the harbor after long sea journeys.

40 Palmer Street at North Water Street (860–535–8445). Open May through October, Wednesday through Monday 10:00 A.M. to 4:00 P.M. (last tour at 3:00) and by appointment. Adults $4.00, children 6 to 12 $2.00. Combo tickets ($6.00 and $3.00) available for this and the Lighthouse Museum.

The Best of Stonington

Once controlled by the Pequots, who were decimated in a horrific scene in 1637, the area now called Stonington was once a part of the Massachusetts Colony and was called Southerton. When it came under the control of the Connecticut Colony in 1662, it was renamed Mystic, an Anglicization of a native word meaning "large tidal river." After a year of trying to farm the New England soil, however, the townsfolk rechristened their settlement Stonington. Today a few of the town's attractions disprove the assumption that the Stonington farmland might be a cursed plot of countryside.

Stonington Vineyards

The climate of coastal Connecticut has proven to produce some wonderful wines. Vineyards benefit from the shoreline's mild but crisp winters and sunny summers. Stonington Vineyards is among the state's most successful growers, and the fifty-eight–acre setting is the perfect destination for a summer or fall day. Though the twenty-minute guided winery tours are scheduled at 2:00 P.M. only, visitors who arrive early in

DUBOIS BEACH

Even gross hyperbole inadequately describes the beauty of tiny DuBois Beach at Stonington Point. The amenities are few, the sand is pebbly, the space is limited, the privacy is practically nil, and yet it remains the most exquisite spot on the Connecticut shore.

At the foot of Water Street, the beach parking area is open year-round, and day-trippers in cars can have a tool around and perhaps a brief walk at no charge. To park and stay at the beach, a fee of $2.00 on weekdays and $3.00 on weekends is charged per person; families pay $5.00 or $6.00, respectively. The beach is lifeguarded daily in July and August and on weekends at other times in the swimming season. For more information, call the Stonington Community Center (860–535–2476).

the day are welcome to enjoy a stroll through the vineyards themselves and may even spread a picnic blanket.

Visitors who take the guided tour will see the wine-making cellars and learn how the vintner makes 15,000 gallons of wine annually. A tasting room ensures that all guests may sample the six premium wines that have been aged to a balanced finish in French oak barrels. Both chardonnay and pinot noir grapes are used to create both crisply dry and subtly sweet fruity wines perfect for all cuisines. If you are so inclined, browse the gift shop and buy a bottle or two.

523 Taugwonk Road (860–535–1222). Open daily year-round 11:00 A.M. to 5:00 P.M., except on major holidays. Guided winery tours at 2:00 P.M. or by appointment for groups of ten or more. Free.

Adam's Garden of Eden

More than five acres of themed gardens are the focus of this nursery and garden shop. Herbs are the specialty here, but all kinds of annuals, perennials, everlastings, dig-your-own mums, pumpkins, Christmas trees, and water plants are among the traditional plants and unique horticultural treasures gardeners may find. Famed for the flower arrangements and topiaries it ships to special events from New York to Boston, Adam's began as a small dig-your-own-mum farm. Now it is an island of color and fragrance in the Stonington countryside.

THE BLESSING OF THE FLEET

Perhaps the quaintest and most touching annual event in Connecticut is the blessing ceremony that offers spiritual protection to the fishermen who ply these waters for the seaborne bounty that provides to them a living and to us a feast. Held usually on the last weekend in July, the two-day event begins with a traditional lobster/clambake under a tent at the town dock at the end of Pearl and Front Streets. Portuguese sweetbreads and sausages, chowders, corn on the cob, and all kinds of fish build everyone's stamina for an evening of dancing on the dock until midnight. The next morning the Fisherman's Mass is offered at 10:00 A.M. at St. Mary's Roman Catholic Church on Broad Street in the village, and then the street parade gets underway by 1:00 P.M., encircling the town before returning to the dock. A dockside ceremony at about 3:00 P.M. precedes the bishop's boarding of the decorated fleet's lead vessel, which moves into the harbor to bless each of the remaining boats as they pass in their own parade. Following the blessing, the vessels pass the breakwater and go out on the Sound, where the families of deceased fishermen toss into the sea floral tributes formed like broken anchors. Call for further information (860–535–3150).

A pond with a waterfall and a Victorian-style gazebo are among the features that punctuate the gardens and pathways. While it remains true that Adam's is a retail operation with a shop overflowing with floral and gardening merchandise, it is also true that the setting draws thousands of visitors who come just to share the beauty. Weddings and receptions are not uncommon here, and free annual events such as the Garlic Fest in midsummer bring crowds of happy revelers. A fall festival celebrating pumpkin season means free hayrides to the pick-your-own pumpkin fields and freshly pressed cider for all visitors. In December, return to cut your own Christmas tree or buy a decorated wreath or Christmas topiary.

360 North Anguilla Road (860–599–4241). To find the gardens, take Route 2 west to the rotary at Route 184; travel west on Route 184 to the first left; the gardens are on the left, three-quarters of a mile from that turn. Open daily except Thanksgiving and Christmas.

The Best of Pawcatuck

The easternmost village in the lower part of the county just before you cross the Rhode Island border on I-95, Pawcatuck is another speck of a place with some fun attractions. The town is 2 miles wide and about 4 miles from north to south. Its location on the Pawcatuck River and its access to shipping created a small center of manufacturing and a good-sized downtown near the junction of Route 1 and Route 2. Choose from the simple pleasures of Pawcatuck's recreational attractions, then stop downtown for a bite to eat or a stroll through the shops. Just a blink away is Rhode Island, the beautiful area of Watch Hill and Napatree Beach, and Atlantic playgrounds like Misquamicut.

CLYDE'S CIDER MILL

To visit Clyde's on a crisp day in early fall when the apples are at their peak and the cider is at its sweetest, swing north out of Stonington Borough on Flanders Road and take a left on the Pequot Trail (Route 234) and head toward the village called Old Mystic. Take a right on North Stonington Road (Route 201) and find Clyde's Cider Mill (860-536-3354) at number 129, not far up the road. A National Historic Landmark, this huge 1881 mill presses the amber juices from the apples that fill barrel after barrel to the brim.

The largest and oldest operating steam-powered cider press in New England, the mill produces both sweet cider and hard cider from September through Thanksgiving. Although pressings are usually done on a regular but unscheduled basis throughout the week, a crowd typically gathers on Saturday and Sunday afternoons when pressings are scheduled for 1:00 and 3:00 P.M. The mill store is open daily from early July until late December from 9:00 A.M to 6:00 P.M. until Halloween and until 5:00 P.M. the remainder of the season. Even before apple pressing season, Clyde's always has an aura of festivity as spectators also shop for fresh local produce, fudge, pies, breads, jams, honey, maple syrup, pumpkins, gourds, freshly ground cornmeal, and more.

Maple Breeze Action Park

For the pure fun of it, you must come to Maple Breeze Park. Just bring a bathing suit and prepare to get wet. Two 350-foot water slides are tons of fun for anyone taller than 40 inches. All riders must ride separately. You can also ride motorized bumper boats (you have to be at least 48 inches tall to ride alone, but smaller children can ride along with taller siblings or parents) or play eighteen holes of very classic miniature golf. Next to the mini-golf course are motorized kiddie karts for little tykes.

Admission to the park is free, and use of the rides and games is administered through the purchase of tokens. Bumper boats cost $3.00 per person for a four-minute ride; mini-golf is $4.50 per person; the water slide is $6.50 for a forty-minute turn. A snack bar and an ice cream stand with twenty-four flavors are also on the premises.

Off I–95 exit 92 at 350 Liberty Street (Route 2) (860–599–1232). Open in May and June on weekends only from 10:00 A.M. to 10:00 P.M. and daily from approximately July 1 through Labor Day at the same hours, weather permitting. Call to confirm hours early in the season or in questionable weather.

Davis Farm Horse-Drawn Hayrides

Davis Farm is one of southeastern Connecticut's famed farms held by the same family for more than three hundred years. The farm produces and sells its own sweet corn, sweet cider, pumpkins, and other organically grown vegetables. Once the pumpkins are ready for picking in late September, six magnificent pedigreed Belgian horses pull visitors along more than 2 miles of trails through the farm's fields and woods. These rides are free; call for hours.

Some years, an enchanted Christmas hayride treks past 150 lighted and decorated Christmas trees and other seasonal scenes on the way to Santa's cabin in the woods. Call to inquire if this seasonal event is on for this year. Private carriage rides can also be arranged.

576 Greenhaven Road (860–599–5859). $100 for private rides for groups of approximately twenty passengers. Reservations required for all rides.

Barn Island State Wildlife Management Area

Take Greenhaven Road south from the traffic light on Route 1 where a sign says BARN ISLAND STATE-OWNED BOAT LAUNCHING AREA. A nearly immediate left on Palmer Neck Road takes you past Wequetecock Cove and down to the shore, where the state manages an undeveloped wildlife area. Situated on Little Narragansett Bay between the cove and the Pawcatuck River, this pretty refuge has trails and unpaved roads across the tidal marshes and uplands of oak forest. A parking lot off Palmer Neck Road provides space for the vehicles of all visitors.

If you have a boat, launch it at the state boat ramp here and cruise the quiet inlets. Saltwater canoeing and sea kayaking are especially pleasant in this peaceful place. You can also fish here, usually without too many boaters to disturb your serenity. A great variety of waterfowl winter in the bay, and hunting is also allowed in season with permits. Those who prefer live birds will appreciate the many songbirds and shorebirds that inhabit this spot.

Palmer Neck Road (off Greenhaven Road off Route 1). For information call area supervisor John Lincoln (860–445–1729).

Cottrell Brewing Company

Old Yankee Ale is the specialty of this microbrewery, one of several Connecticut coastal enterprises aiming to brew distinctive beers with a regional flair. Discover the secrets of the process on a brewery tour, then sample some of the wares.

100 Mechanic Street (860–599–8213). Tours on Saturday at 3:00 P.M or by appointment. Take Route 1 east toward Rhode Island. Take the last right in Connecticut onto Mechanic Street; the brewery is slightly less than a half-mile down on the left; follow signs to the back of the building.

Places to Eat in Stonington Borough, Stonington, and Pawcatuck

The Yellow House Coffee and Tea Room 149 Water Street, Stonington Borough (860–535–4986). Wonderful coffees and biscotti in a sunny space splashed with cheerful colors. Tasty sandwiches, excellent soups, and other casual fare perfect for shoppers, day-trippers, and children. Open daily from 6:30 A.M. (to 6:00 P.M. on weekdays; to 10:00 P.M. on weekends) for breakfast and lunch served all day long, plus afternoon tea from 3:00 to 5:00 P.M. $

Noah's 113 Water Street, Stonington Borough (860–535–3925). Three solid meals a day are served at this warm and casual place with a down-home flair. Twirling ceiling fans and a tin ceiling add to the old-fashioned, casual ambiance. Good cookin', served with a smile, keeps

THE PEQUOT TRAIL AND MORE

From Route 1 in Pawcatuck drive west (the sign may say north) on the Pequot Trail (Route 234), the designated scenic highway that was once the supposed warpath of the Pequots. The road meets Route 184 at the village of Old Mystic near the banks of the Mystic River, and it is especially lovely to drive this way as the sun begins to set as you travel west. For a truly Sunday-drive sort of trek, take Route 184 eastward about 6 or 7 miles (again, the signs might say north) to Route 49 in North Stonington. Take a left to head north on Route 49 for a scenic ride past forests and farms along another designated highway that actually extends 19.5 miles to Sterling in Windham County. The farms and fields along these roads are spectacular in all seasons.

the place busy all day. House-made pasta, excellent soups, and great seafood. The scrod melts in your mouth. Open Tuesday through Sunday for breakfast and lunch from 7:00 A.M. until 2:30 P.M. and for dinner from 6:00 to 9:00 P.M. $-$$

Water Street Cafe 142 Water Street, Stonington (860-525-2122). This sweet survivor of a disastrous fire simply took up digs elsewhere and went on. The cafe serves a more relaxed menu than the fine dining it had offered earlier but is just as fresh and inventive as before, with some French and Asian influences as well as regional American overtones. Open for dinner daily and for lunch also, except for Tuesday and Wednesday. $$

One South, a Cafe 201 North Main Street, Stonington Borough (860-535-0418). In one of the village's charming old homes, this casual but sophisticated restaurant serves regional and international cuisine made from the finest seasonal ingredients available. Hearty scratch-made soups, creative appetizers, fresh salads, seafood (including the famed grilled mussels), steaks, pasta, and poultry leave just a little room for excellent house-made desserts. Open daily for lunch from 11:30 A.M. (except Sunday) and for dinner from 5:00 P.M. $$-$$$

Mystic Lobster Company 29 Old Stonington Road, Stonington (860-536-8299). Out of the village just off Route 1 between Stonington and Mystic, this rambling structure set back near the salt marsh is a celebration of all that is seafood, with a special focus on lobster. From the

250-gallon lobster rank in the lobby to the casually homey decor in its large dining room and pub-style club room, the restaurant is friendly both to the families and fine diners. Chef Kevin Tricarico prepares at least one, if not two, inventive lobster specials each weekend. If you're lucky, you may get to buy the Bourbon Street Bug, a roasted lobster with a mushroom/scallion sherry sauce! Come Sunday through Wednesday for affordable family dinners ($9.95) and Thursday for all-you-can-eat lobster, prime rib, or fish and chips dinners (prices vary). Open daily for dinner from 4:00 to 10:00 P.M.; pub menu 4:00 P.M. to midnight. Live entertainment on Thursday through Sunday evenings in the 2,500-square-foot game room. $–$$$

Festivals Family Restaurant 163 South Broad Street (Route 1), Pawcatuck (860-599-0880). Across from the high school, dine on chicken, surf and turf, veal, pastas, pizza, seafood, grinders, sandwiches, and a delicious Rainbow Salad. Open Tuesday through Sunday for lunch and dinner year-round. $–$$

Prime Time Cafe 1 West Broad Street, Pawcatuck (860-599-3840). On the bridge overlooking the Pawcatuck River in downtown Pawcatuck, this brightly painted, bistro-style restaurant serves breakfast, lunch, and dinner seven days a week year-round. Everything here is homemade, from scones to soups and sauces, and everything is cooked to order. Wine and beer list; American cuisine; regional art for sale on the walls; live entertainment on Thursday evenings. $–$$$

Randall's Ordinary Route 2, North Stonington (860-599-4540). Open-hearth cooking with a waitstaff dressed in eighteenth-century attire is the intriguing attraction at this rustically restored colonial country inn, just a third of a mile north of I-95. Open daily for a la carte breakfast and lunch and a prix fixe dinner ($30), the inn serves authentic fare at every meal. At dinner, guests receive cheese and crackers and hearth-baked breads, soup, a choice of three entrees (seafood, red meat, or poultry), and dessert and a beverage. Guests may also stay overnight. $$–$$$$

Places to Stay in Stonington Borough, Stonington, and Pawcatuck

Cove Ledge Inn and Marina on Route 1 on Pawcatuck side of Stonington (860-599-4130). Web site: www.coveledgeinn.com. Right near the hub of a marina, this sixteen-unit waterfront motel on five acres is picturesque and convenient, with fishing and boat launching easily available. Four efficiency units, two guest houses, two luxury suites in lovingly restored vintage main house, plus motel units. Outdoor pool, playground, continental breakfast. Kayak rentals. Guest boat docking. Open May through October. Special-events planning for events such as reunions and birthday parties. $$$

Sea Breeze Motel 812 Stonington Road (Route 1), Stonington (860-535-2843). On a little arm of the sea, thirty units offer the basic necessities, plus air-conditioning and TV. $$$

Stonington Motel 901 Stonington Road (Route 1), Stonington (860-599-2330). Twelve air-conditioned units with fridges and TVs. $$

Lasbury's Guest House 41 Orchard Street, Stonington Borough (860-535-2681). This three-room cottage is tucked away in the secluded backyard of a private home on a quiet residential street. The smallest of the three rooms has a private bath; the larger rooms share a bath. Antique furnishings, in-room fridges and TVs; no cooking facilities, but complimentary continental breakfast. $$$

The Inn at Stonington 60 Water Street (860-535-2000). Brand-new in 2002, this twelve-room beautifully appointed inn in the heart of the borough invites guests to luxuriate comfortably in style. Web site: www.innatstonington.com. $$$$

Randall's Ordinary Route 2, North Stonington (860-599-4540). In addition to its famous open-hearth-cooked meals, the eighteenth-century inn and tavern on twenty-seven acres has three guest rooms with queen-size canopied beds, private baths, and fireplaces in the main inn; nine rooms with queen-size or double beds and private baths in the adjacent 1819 dairy barn restoration; and a unique silo suite with a fireplace and a winding staircase to a Jacuzzi. The room rate includes breakfast for two guests or a la carte breakfast for any extra guests in the same room or suite. Inquire about the dinner and lodging package for two. $$$-$$$$

Antiques and Accommodations 32 Main Street, North Stonington (860-535-1736). To-die-for antiques and gracious decor in the 1860 main house with four lavish guest rooms, one with a fireplace, all with private baths. An equally charming 1820 House in the Garden has an upper suite with two bedrooms and two baths plus a library and fireplace in a common room; downstairs is a suite with three bedrooms, a complete kitchen, a living room, a private bath, and a fireplace. Furnished throughout with antiques and queen-size canopied beds, this beautiful country inn offers a four-course candlelit breakfast to all guests. The innkeeper's collection of antique breakfast silver is outstanding and their gardens are exquisite. First and foremost a couple's romantic getaway, this B&B is also warmly welcoming to families if you think children over the age of eight can feel comfortable with and respectful of the furnishings. $$$$

Arbor House at Kruger's Old Maine Farm 75 Chester Maine Road, North Stonington (860-535-4221). Have your kids join their kids at this country-style B&B with ice-skating and cross-country skiing in winter and catch-and-release fishing on the pond in summer, plus lots of fun chores to pitch in on as the folks here care for their pigs, chickens, cats, ducks, and sheep. Pluck fresh eggs all year-round and fresh apples right off the trees in the orchard in autumn. Tour the hard-cider winery and sample Mystic Soda to quench your thirst. At night, cozy up in the second-floor guest rooms or the third-floor, two-bedroom suite with adjoining sitting room and private bath. Other options also make this cheerful place perfect for families. Full breakfast. $$$-$$$$

High Acres B&B 222 Northwest Corner Road, Stonington (860-887-4355). Way out in the country is this 1743 farmhouse with an 1840s addition. Farmland rolls in all around this homestead; horse pastures, equestrian trails, and stables are right on the property. The five guest rooms have private baths, queen- and king-size beds, and down comforters. Full breakfast. $$$$

Highland Orchards Resort Park 118 Pendleton Hill Road (Route 49), North Stonington (860-599-5101 or 800-624-0829). Family camping resort located on eighty-five acres of a former colonial farm. Offers 270 wooded and open RV and tent sites; swimming pool, fishing pond, miniature golf, playground, basketball, shuffleboard, game room, rest rooms, free showers, laundry room, dump station, hookups, firewood, ice, groceries, camp supplies. Open year-round. Nightly and weekly rates; reservations recommended. $

Public Boat Launch

Barn Island Wildlife Management Area Ramp off Palmer Neck Road for Long Island Sound access; take Route 1 to Greenhaven Road, go south on Greenhaven to Palmer Neck, 1.5 miles to end. Parking for sixty-five cars. Seasonal fee. Very popular on weekends.

For Further Information

Stonington Community Center (860-535-2476). This organization operates the public DuBois Beach, a community senior center, and four tennis courts also open to the visiting public.

Stonington Historical Society (860-535-1131). Sponsors occasional walking tours and special events.

State Welcome Center I-95 southbound, entering Connecticut at North Stonington from Rhode Island. Open daily year-round; rest rooms; staff in summer. Maps, state tourism guides, brochures.

General Index

Special Indexes

Beaches

Anchor Beach (Milford), 84
Calf Pasture Beach (Norwalk), 42
Clinton Town Beach, 159–60
DuBois Beach (Stonington), 255
East Beach (Groton), 224
East Haven Town Beach, 118
East Wharf Beach (Madison), 149
Esker Point Beach (Noank), 234
Esposito Beach (Clinton), 161
Greenwich, 2
Gulf Beach (Milford), 84
Hammonasset State Park
    (Madison), 150–51
Harvey's Beach
    (Old Saybrook), 176–77
Jacobs Beach (Guilford), 138
Jennings Beach (Fairfield), 57
Lake Quonnipaug, 139–40
Long Beach (Stratford), 78
Main Beach (Groton), 224
Middle Beach (Westbrook), 165
Ocean Beach Park
    (New London), 217–18
Peartree Point Beach (Darien), 25
Penfield Beach (Fairfield), 57
Seaside Park (Bridgeport), 69
Shady Beach (Norwalk), 42
Short Beach (Branford), 128–30
Short Beach (Stratford), 75–76
Silver Sands (Milford), 84
Sound View Beach
    (Old Lyme), 188–89
South Beach (Groton), 224
Southport Beach (Fairfield), 57
Surf Club (Madison), 149
Rocky Neck State Park, 193–95
Walnut Beach (Milford), 84
Webster Point Beach (Madison), 149
Weed Beach (Darien), 25
West Wharf Beach
    (Madison), 149
Westbrook town beach, 164–65
White Sands Beach (Old Lyme), 187

Seafood Shacks and Restaurants

Abbott's Lobster in the Rough, 236
Allen's East, 80
Aqua Restaurant, 161
Beach Street Waterfront Grille, 93
Beachhead Restaurant, 119
Beacon, 19
Bill's Seafood Restaurant, 168–69
Captain's Cove Seaport
    Restaurant, 69–71
Captain's Galley, 93
Captain Scott's Lobster Dock
    Restaurant, 221
Chick's Drive-In, 93
Clam Castle, 153
Constantine's, 200
Costello's Clam Company, 236–37
Dad's Restaurant, 200–201
Fisherman, 230
Flanders Fish Market and
    Restaurant, 200
Flood Tide, 246
Fred's Shanty, 221
Go Fish, 247
Harbor Lights, 38
Jeffrey's, 89
Jimmie's of Savin Rock, 93
Johnny Ad's, 179
Knapp's Landing, 79
Lenny's Indian Head Inn, 126, 130
Lenny and Joe's Fish Tale, 152
Lighthouse Inn's Mansion
    Restaurant, 220
Mooring, The, 245
Noah's, 259–60
Old Lyme Inn, 189–90
Place, The, 144
Plouf! Le Bistro de la Mer, 80
Restaurant at Rowayton Seafood, 38
Sam's Dockside, 130
Sandpiper Restaurant, 119
Saybrook Fish House, 178
Scribner's, 88

Museums

About the Author

A lifelong resident of the Connecticut shore, with the exception of a three-year sabbatical on the California coast, Doe Boyle works as a freelance writer and editor in a shoreline house that has been cooled by the breezes from Long Island Sound for more than 250 years. Beach peas and salt-spray roses rugosa bloom in her gardens; four daughters have blossomed beside them. Author of Globe Pequot's *Fun with the Family in Connecticut* and eleven children's picture books published by Soundprints in association with the National Wildlife Federation and the Smithsonian Institution, Boyle is also a master teaching artist of the Connecticut Commission on the Arts. When not busy sampling boat rides and clam chowders, Boyle is often engaged in classes with Connecticut's young writers.